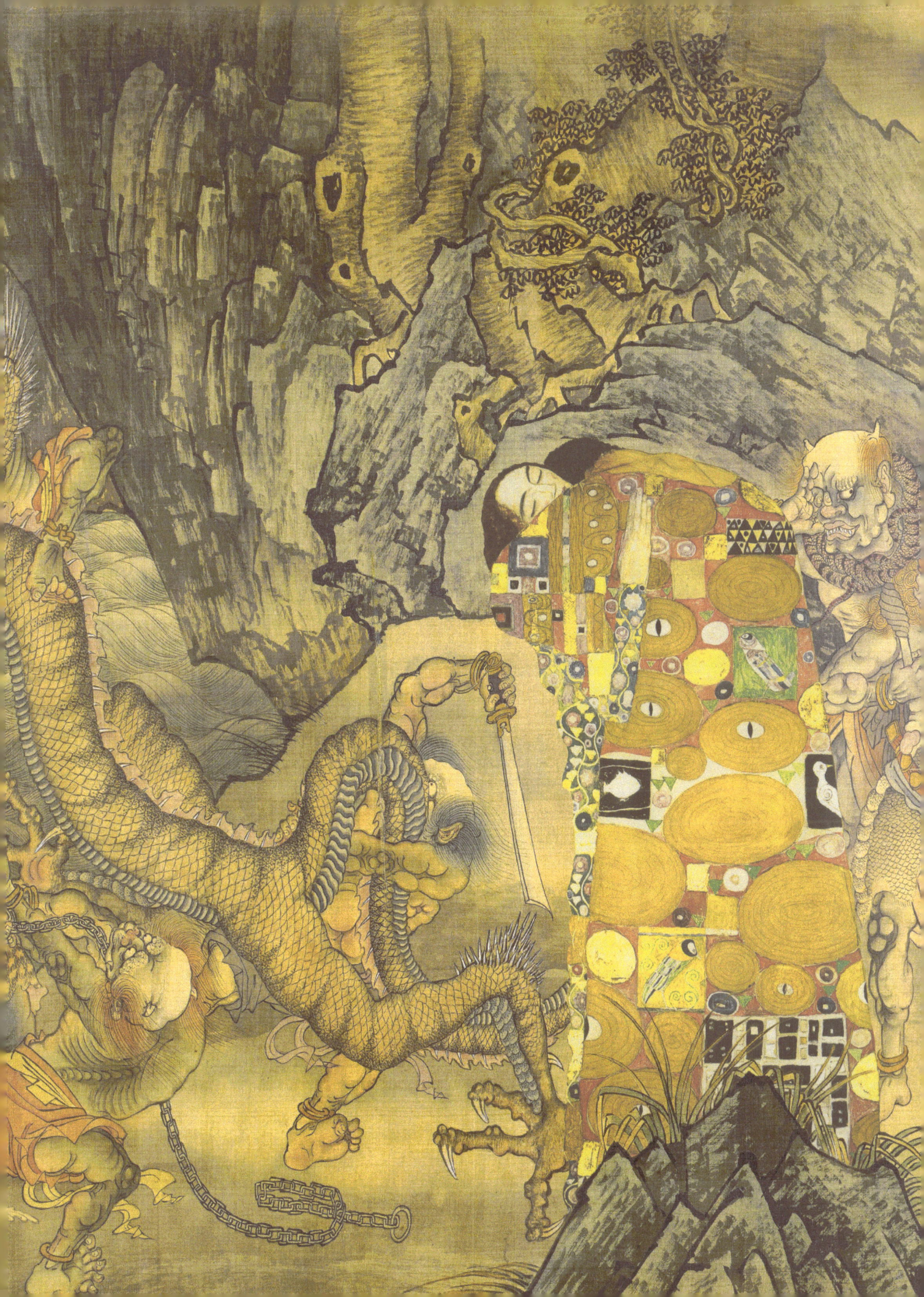

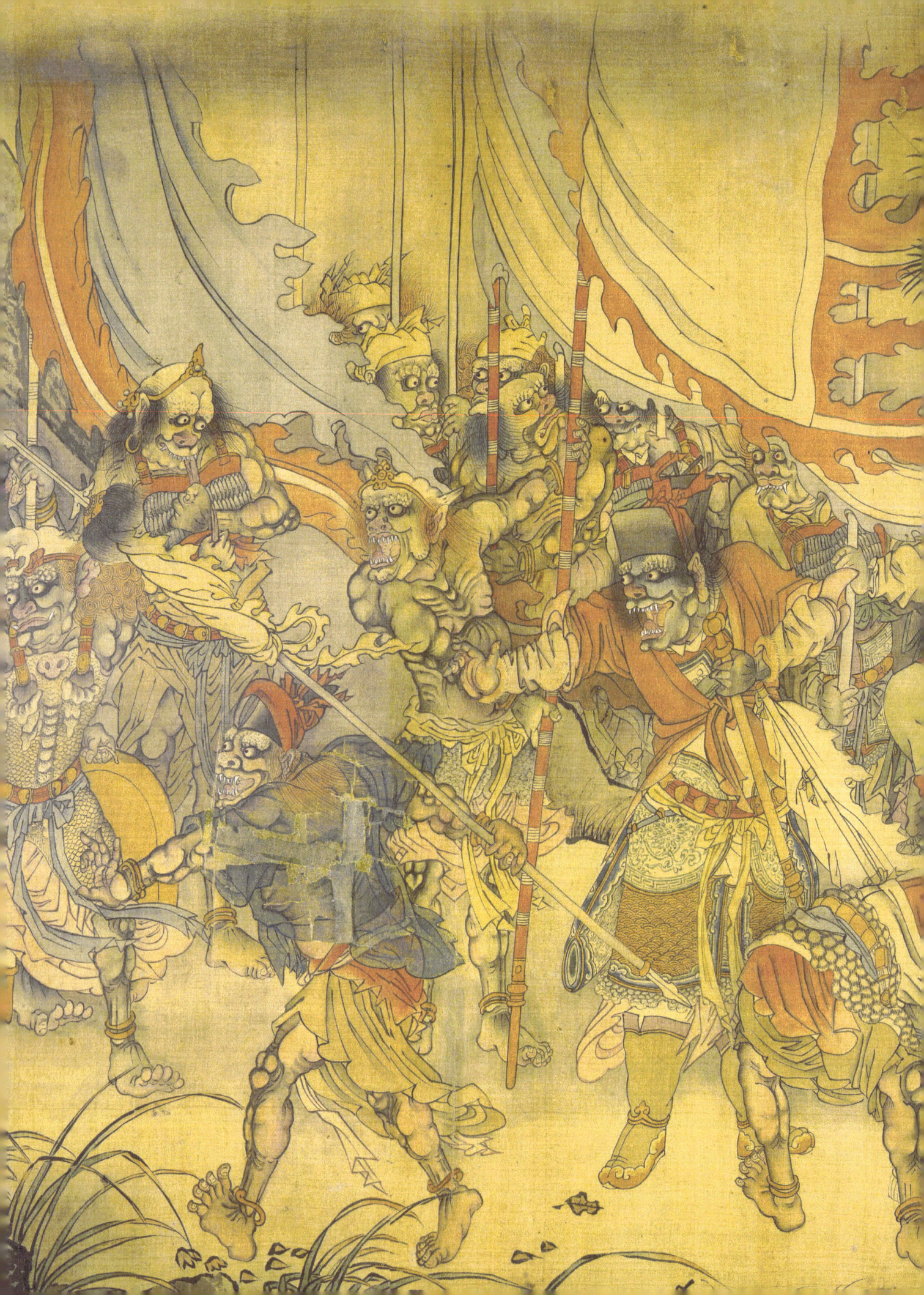

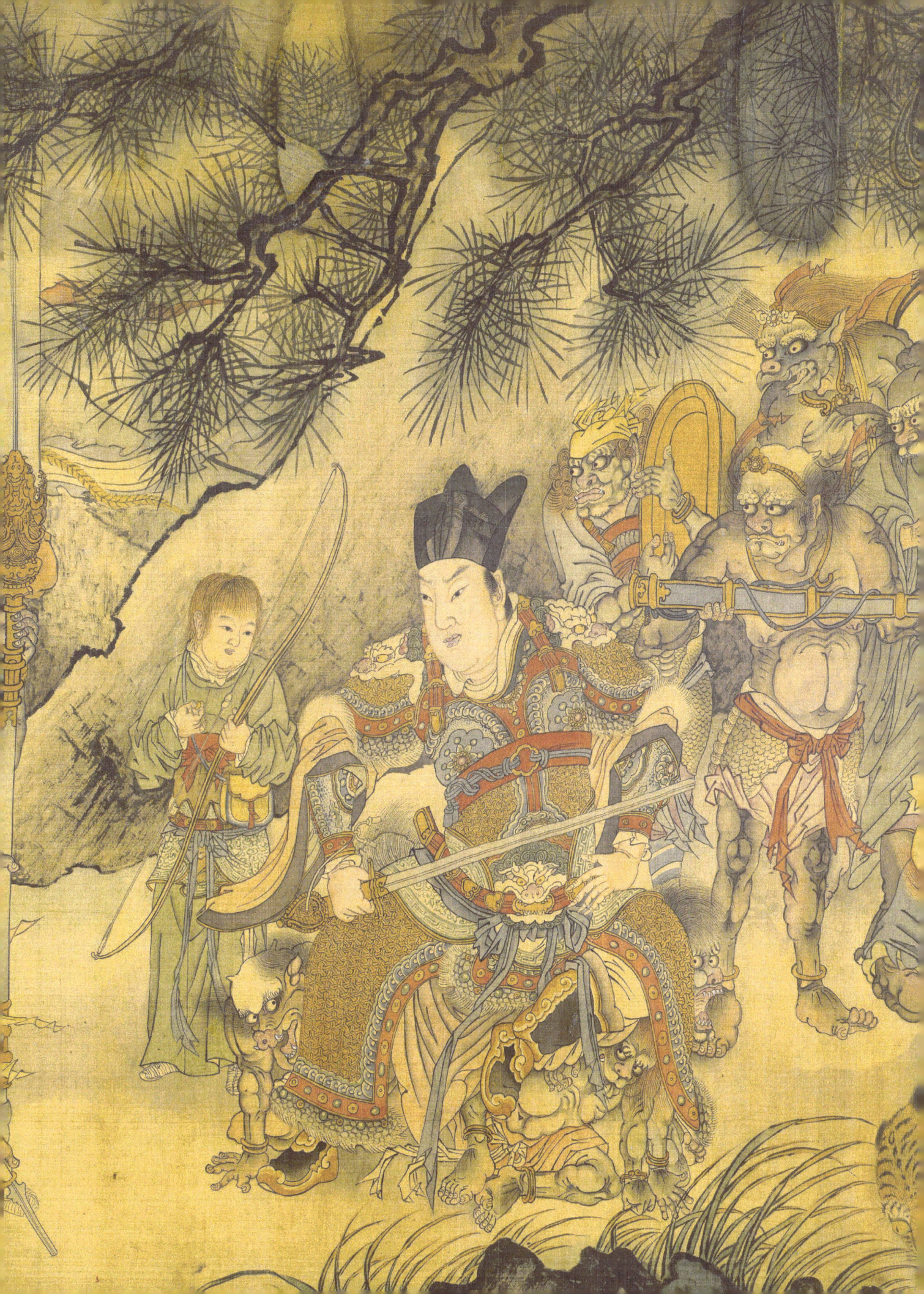

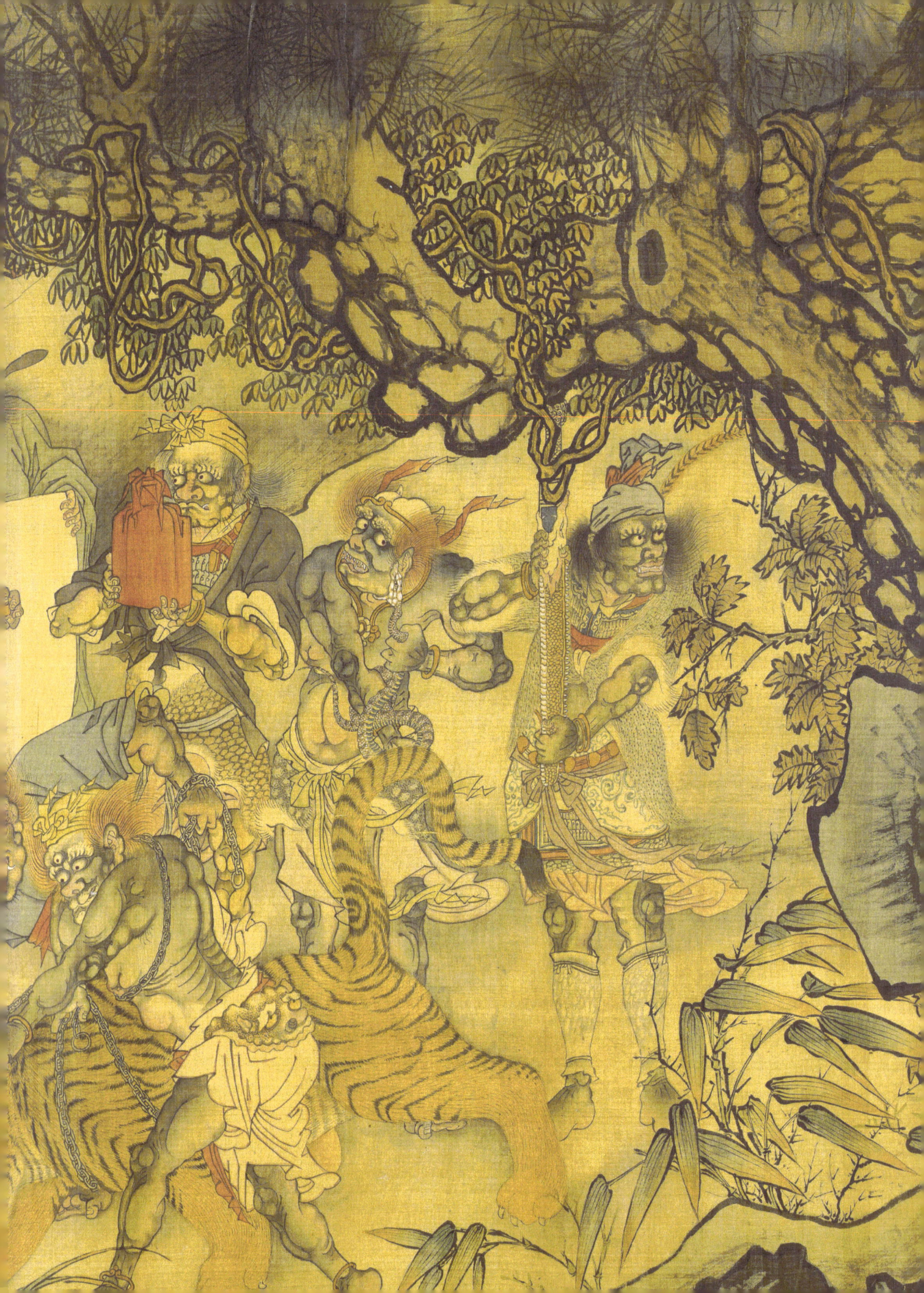

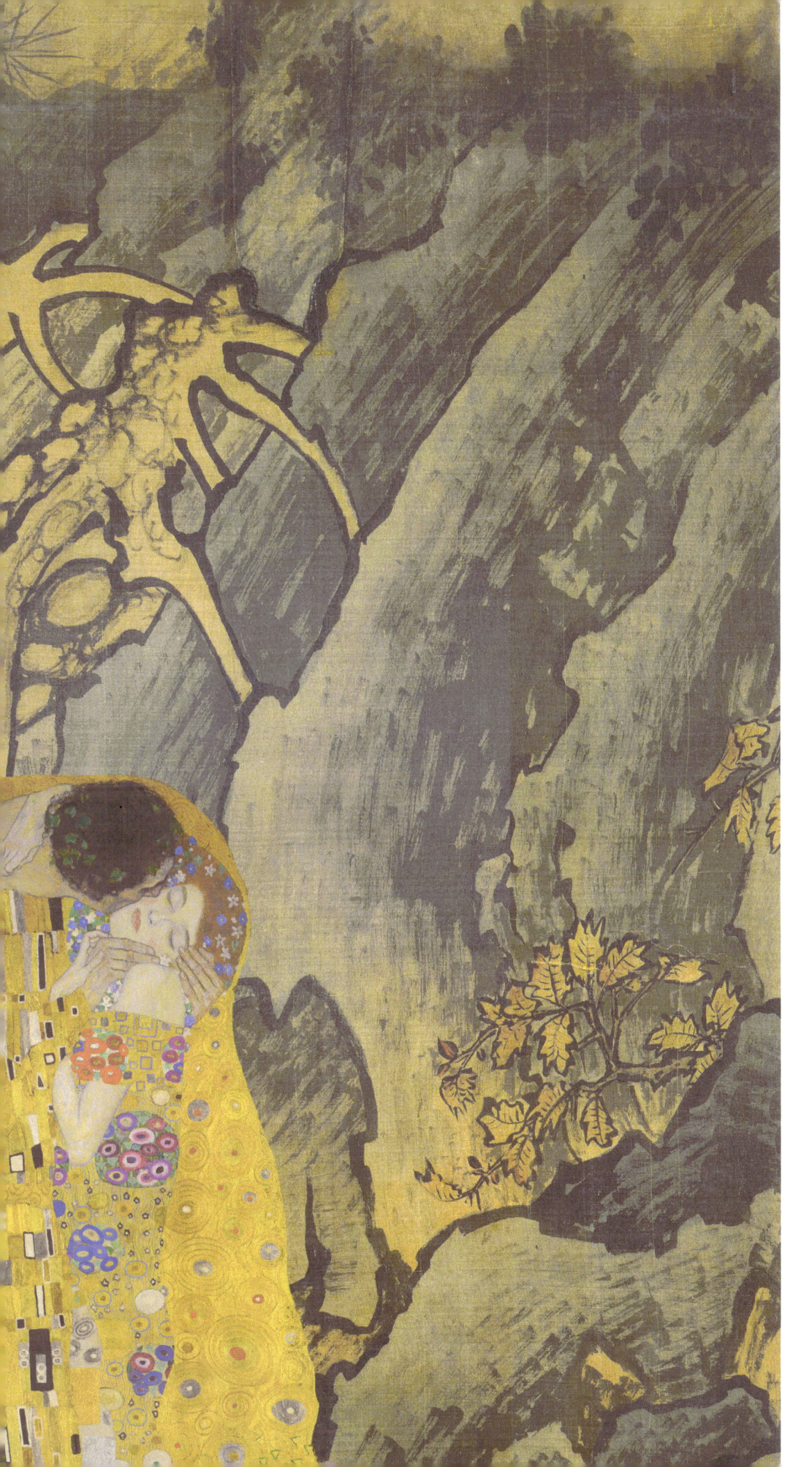

Mark Harris: East 100

Artist: Mark Harris
Editor-in-Chief: Mark Harris
Editors: Kehui Li, Elaine V. Kuang

Artist: Mark Harris
Editor-in-Chief: Mark Harris
Editors: Kehui Li, Elaine V. Kuang
Cover design/Book design: Mark Harris

LOSGET Copyright © 2021-2022 by Mark Harris
All rights reserved.
Published in the United States by Losget Press, Los Angeles.
Originally published in paperback in the United States by Losget Press, in 2022.
Library of Congress Cataloging-in-Publication Data
Names: Harris, Mark, author.
Title: Mark Harris: East 100/ Mark Harris.
Description: First edition. | Los Angeles: Losget Press, 2022.
Identifiers: LCCN: 2022904733/ ISBN: 978-1-951364-11-3
Cover design/Book design by Mark Harris
www.imarkharris.com
E-mail: contact@losget.com
First printing. 2022.

INTRODUCTION

EAST 100 is a collection of one hundred artworks by artist Mark Harris in Los Angeles at the end of 2021. The project composes harmonious combinations of world-famous western paintings and art from ancient China.

With this bold fusion of East and West, Mark Harris presents us with artworks that are fascinating to the eye and enchanting to the heart.

Mark Harris

*Union of differences can be the source of beauty;
Division of opinions need not be the cause of war.*

--Mark Harris, March 2022.

CONTENTS

East #1 3
East #2 4
East #3 5
East #3 (detail).. 6
East #4 7
East #5 8
East #6 9
East #7 10
East #8 11
East #9 12
East #9 (detail). 13
East #10 14
East #11 15
East #12 16
East #12 (detail) 17
East #13 18
East #14 19
East #15 20
East #16 21
East #16 (detail) 22
East #17 23
East #18 24
East #19 25
East #20 26
East #21 27
East #22 28
East #22 (detail) 29
East #23 30
East #24 31
East #25 32
East #26 33
East #27 34
East #28 35
East #29 36
East #30 37
East #31 38
East #32 39
East #33 40
East #34 41

East #35 42
East #35 (detail) 43
East #36 44
East #36 (detail) 45
East #37 46
East #38 47
East #39 48
East #40 49
East #41 50
East #41 (detail) 51
East #42 52
East #43 53
East #44 54
East #45 55
East #46 56
East #47 57
East #48 58
East #49 59
East #50 60
East #51 61
East #52 62
East #53 63
East #54 64
East #55 65
East #56 66
East #57 67
East #58 68
East #59 69
East #60 70
East #61 71
East #62 72
East #63 73
East #64 74
East #65 75
East #66 76
East #67 77
East #68 78
East #69 79
East #70 80

East #71 81
East #72 82
East #73 83
East #74 84
East #75 85
East #76 86
East #77 87
East #78 88
East #79 89
East #80 90
East #81 91
East #82 92
East #83 93
East #84 94
East #85 95
East #86 96
East #87 97
East #88 98
East #89 99
East #90 100
East #91 101
East #91 (detail1) 102
East #91 (detail2) 103
East #92 104
East #93 105
East #94 106
East #95 107
East #96 108
East #97 109
East #98 110
East #99 111
East #100 112
Sources 113
Mark Harris 121
Bookselling ... 122
For More 123
Publication information 126

East #1-100

Mark Harris

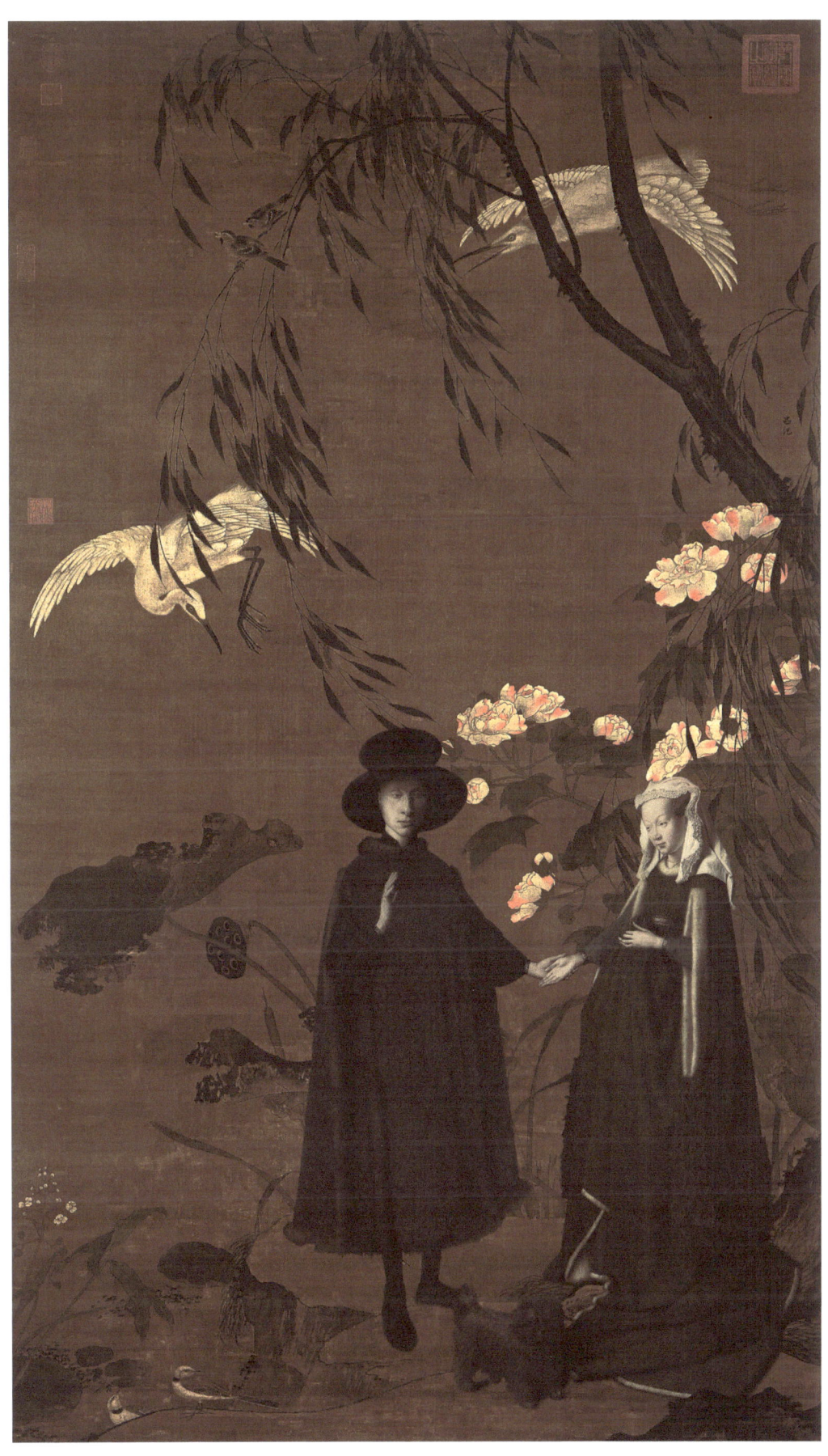

East #1

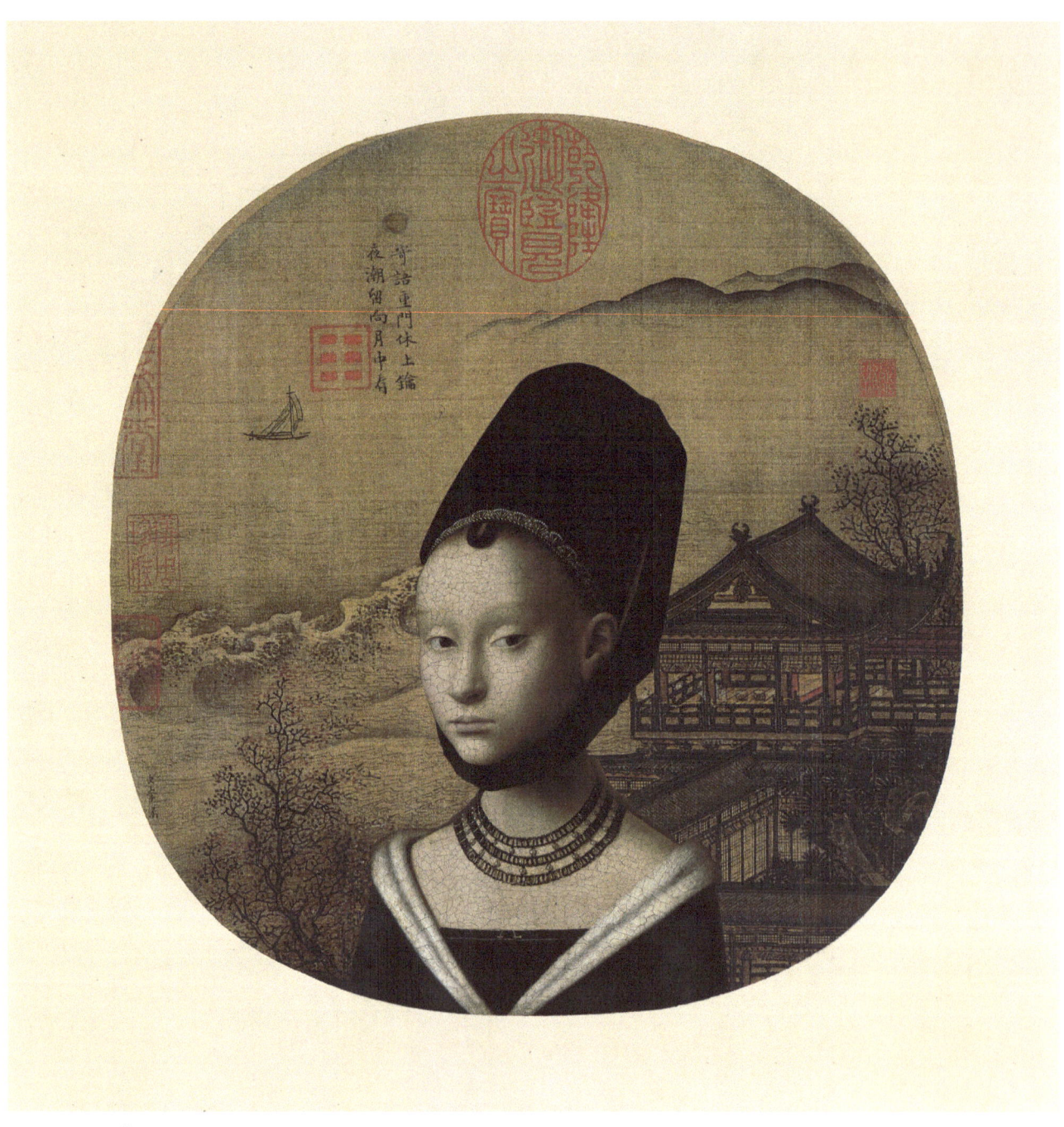

East #2

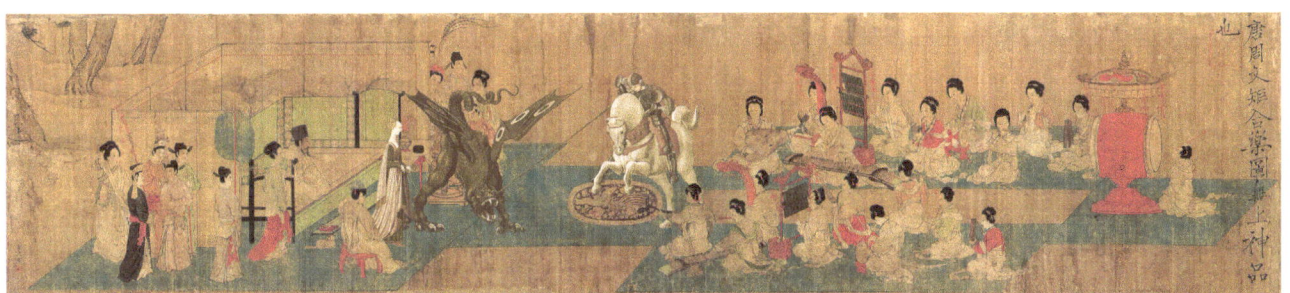

East #3

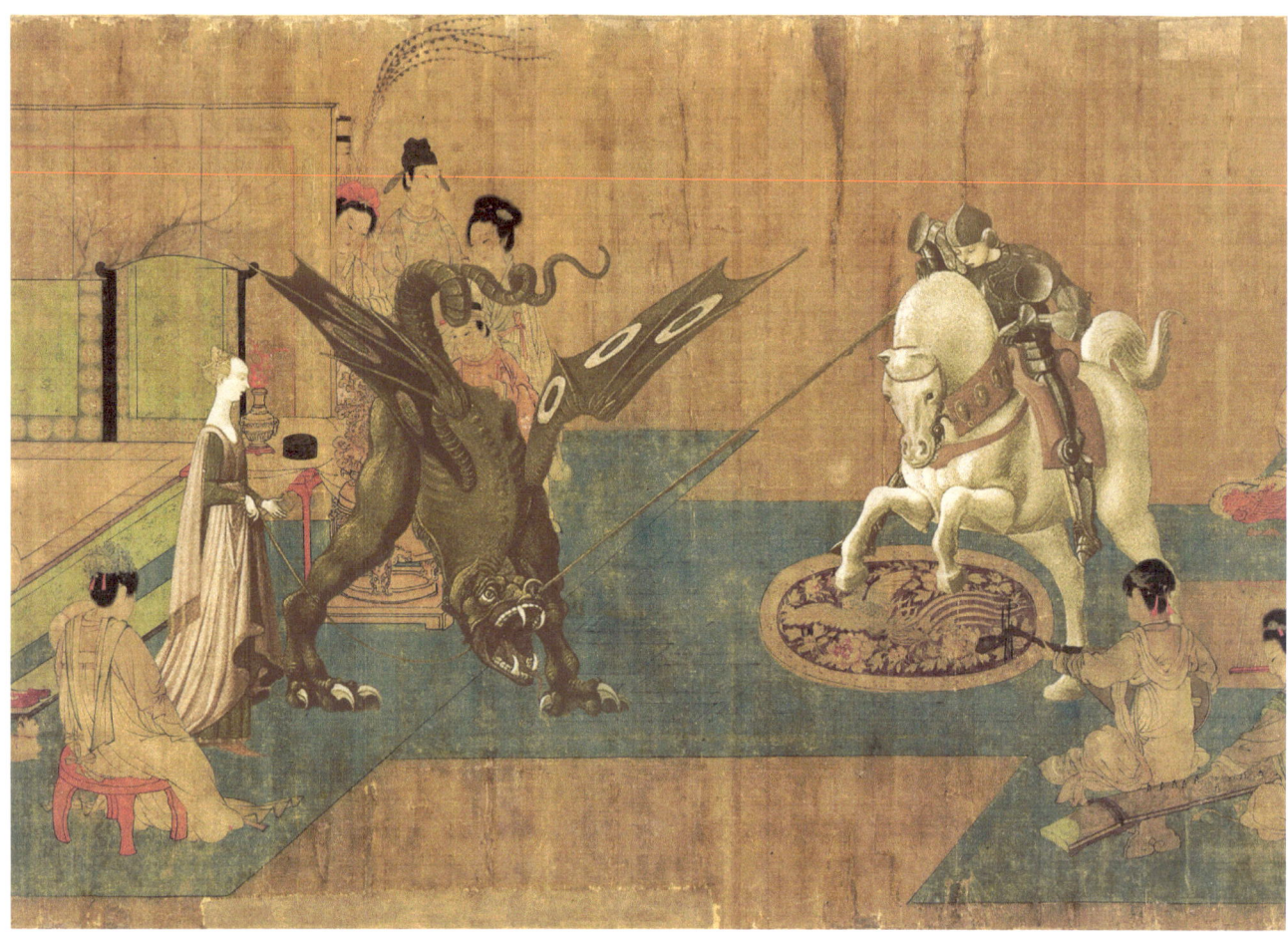

East #3 (detail)

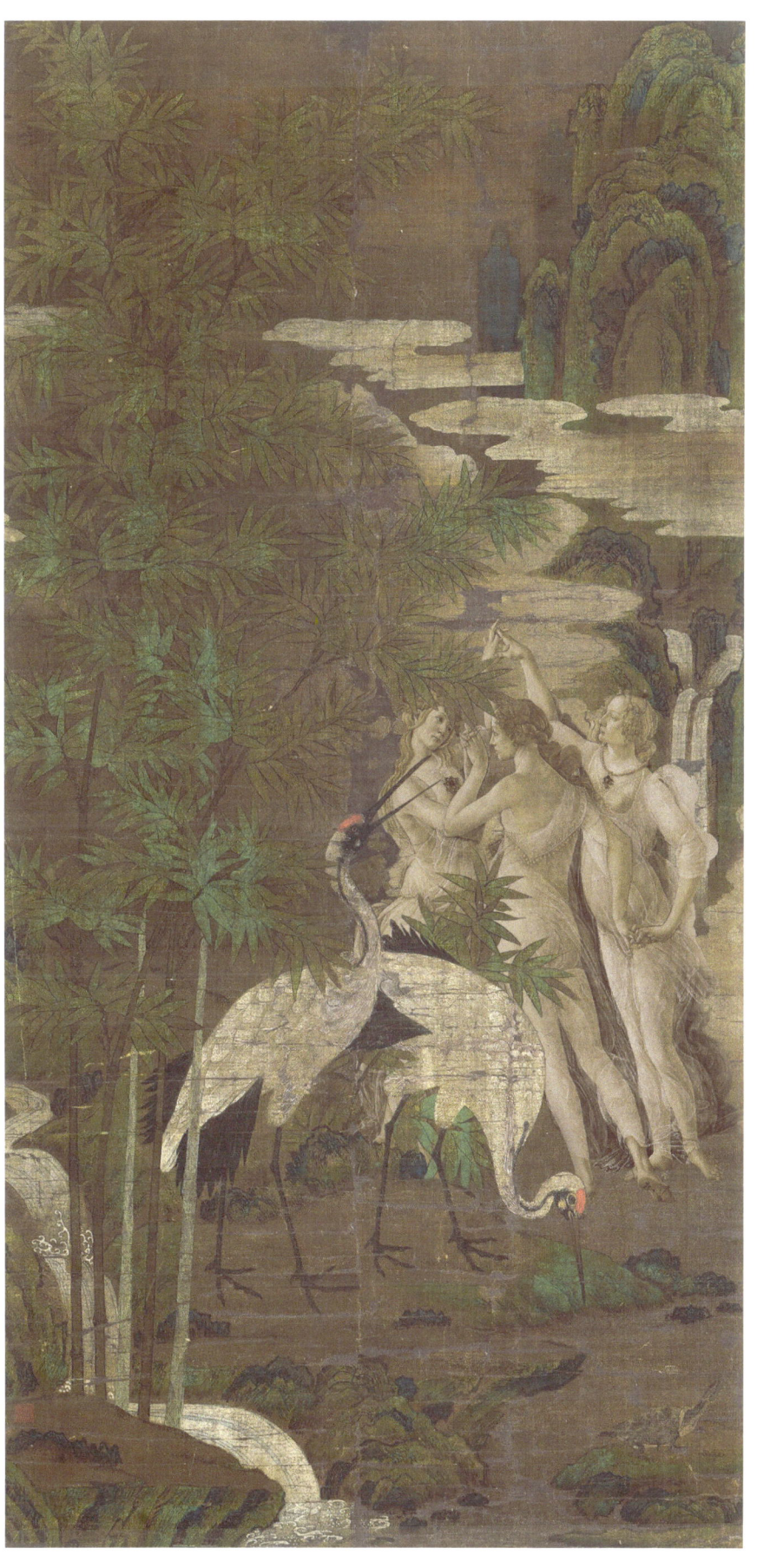

East #4

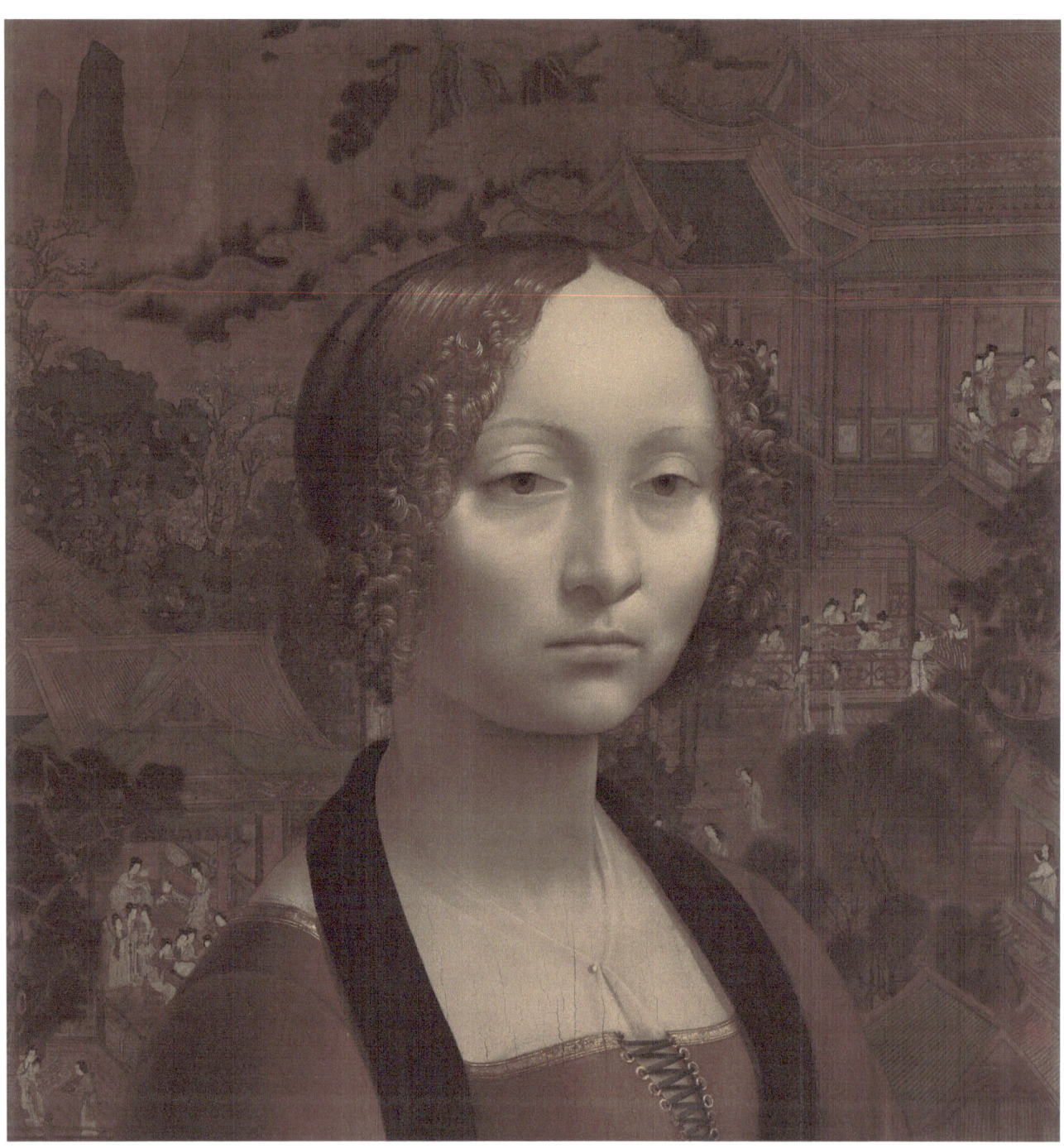

East #5

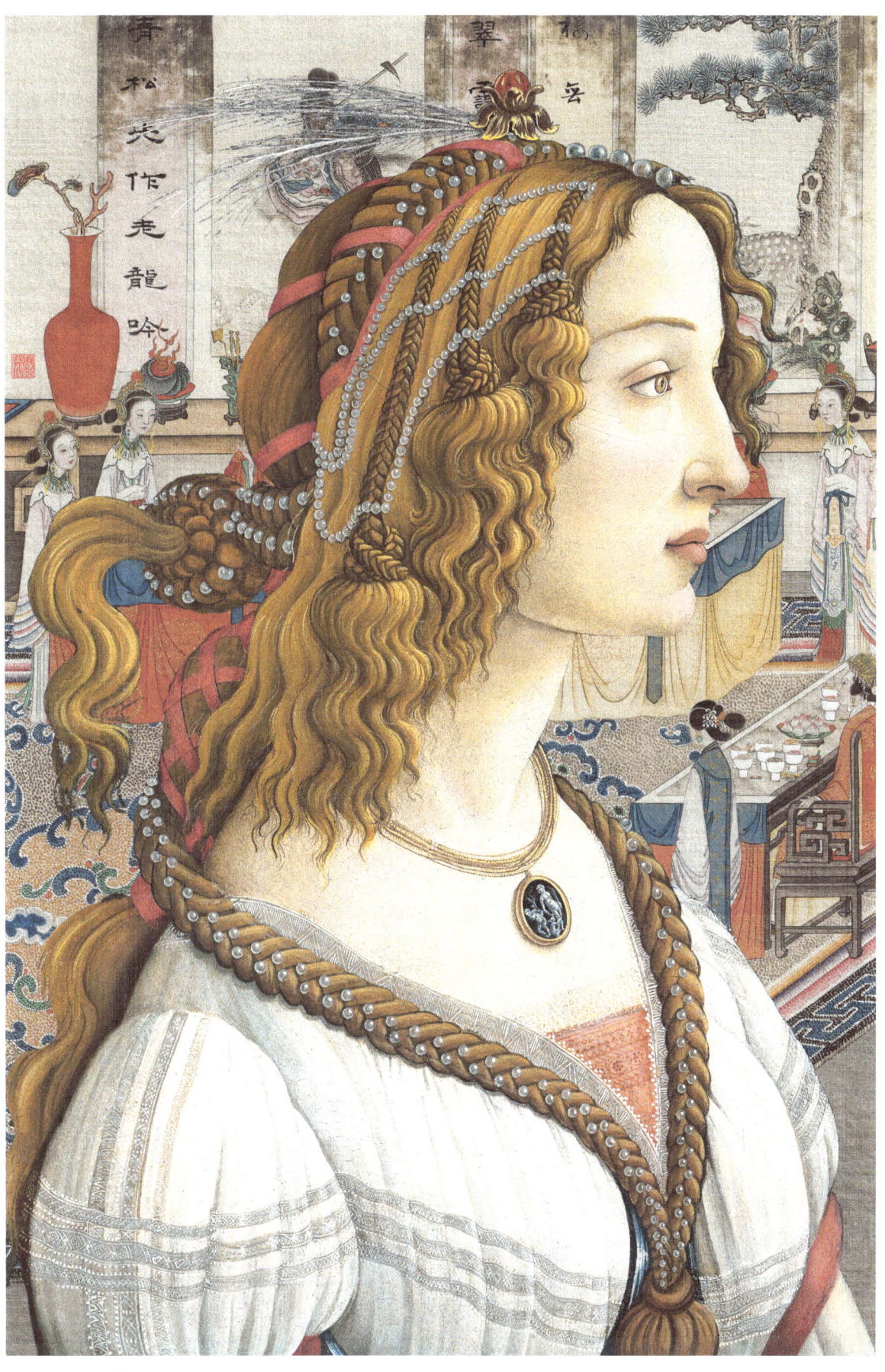

East #6

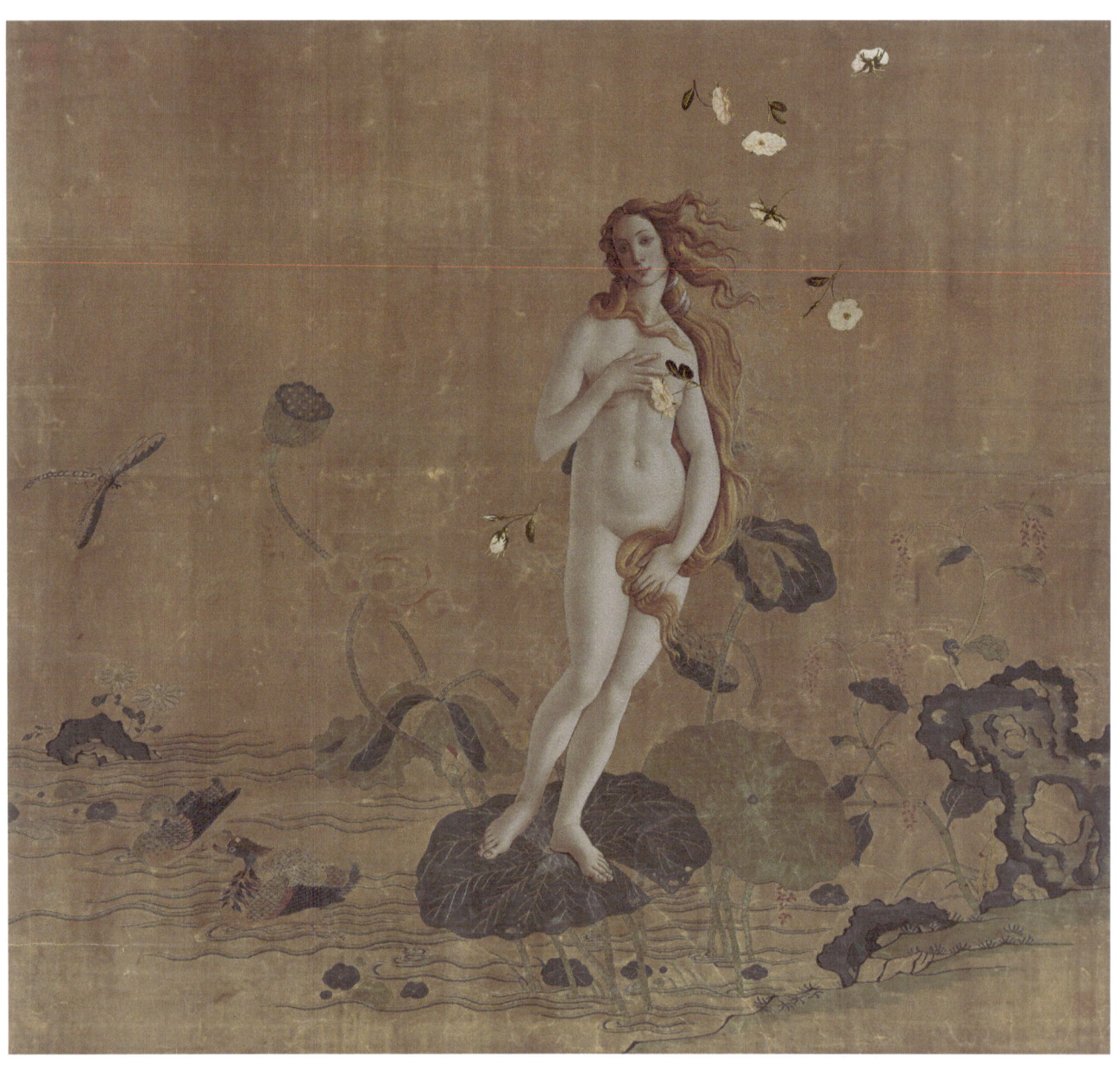

East #7

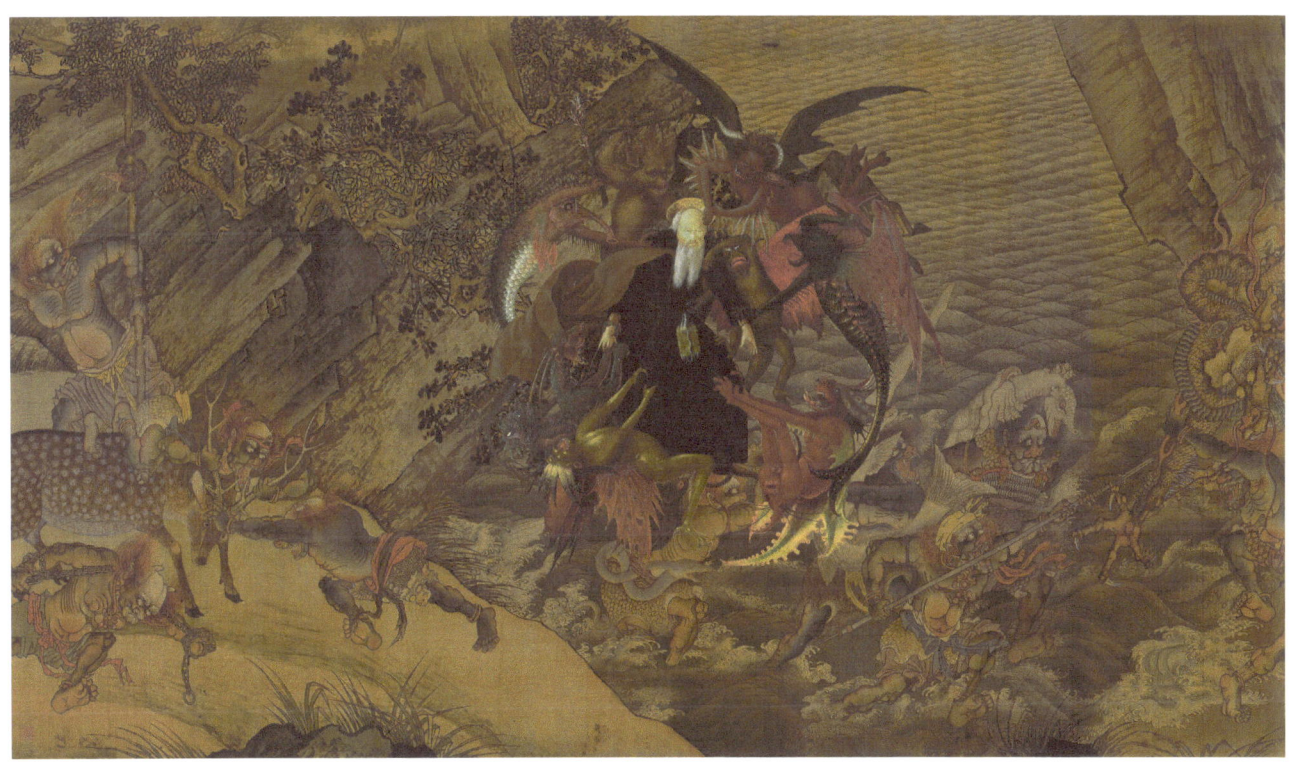

East #8

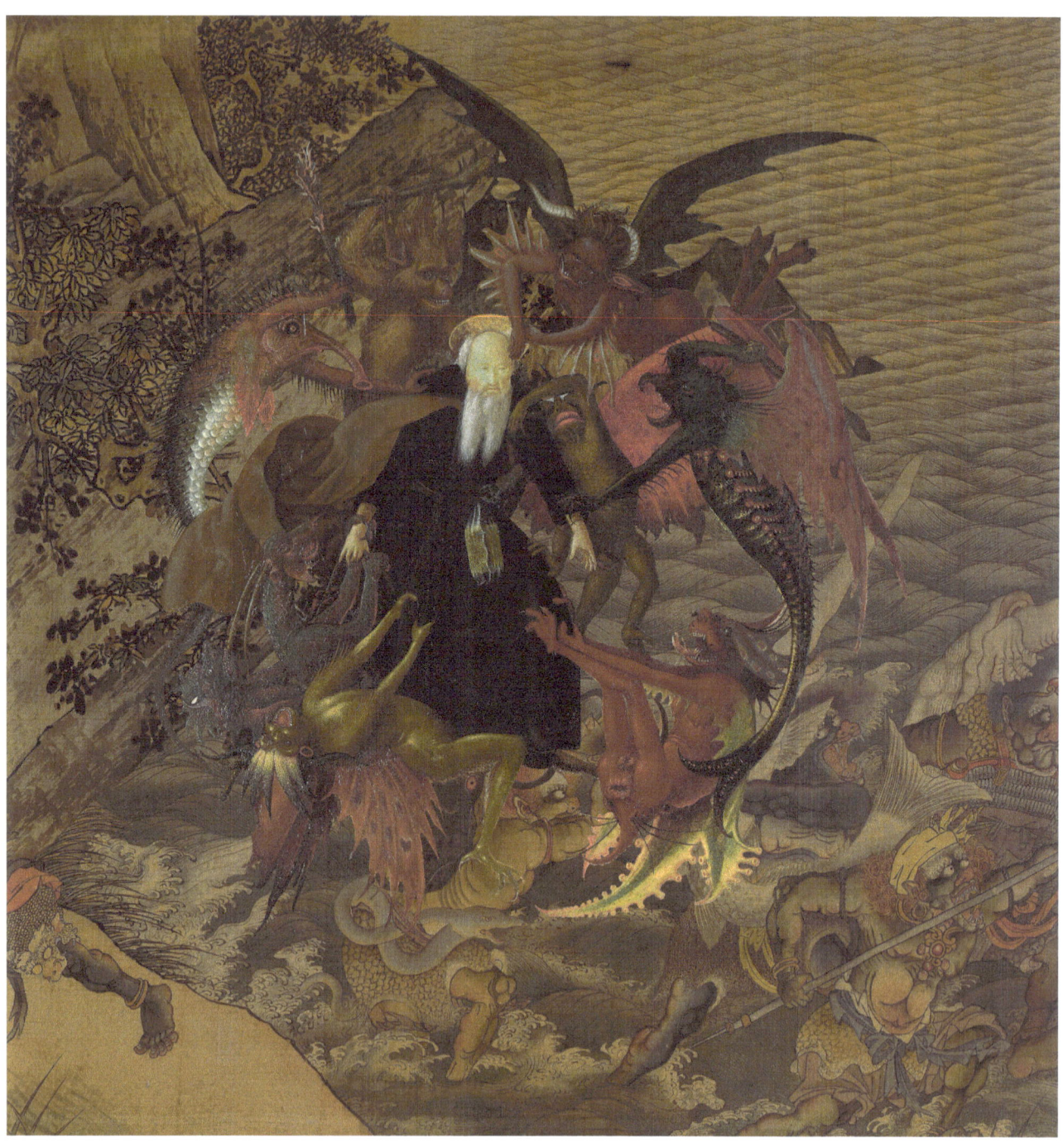

East #8 (detail)

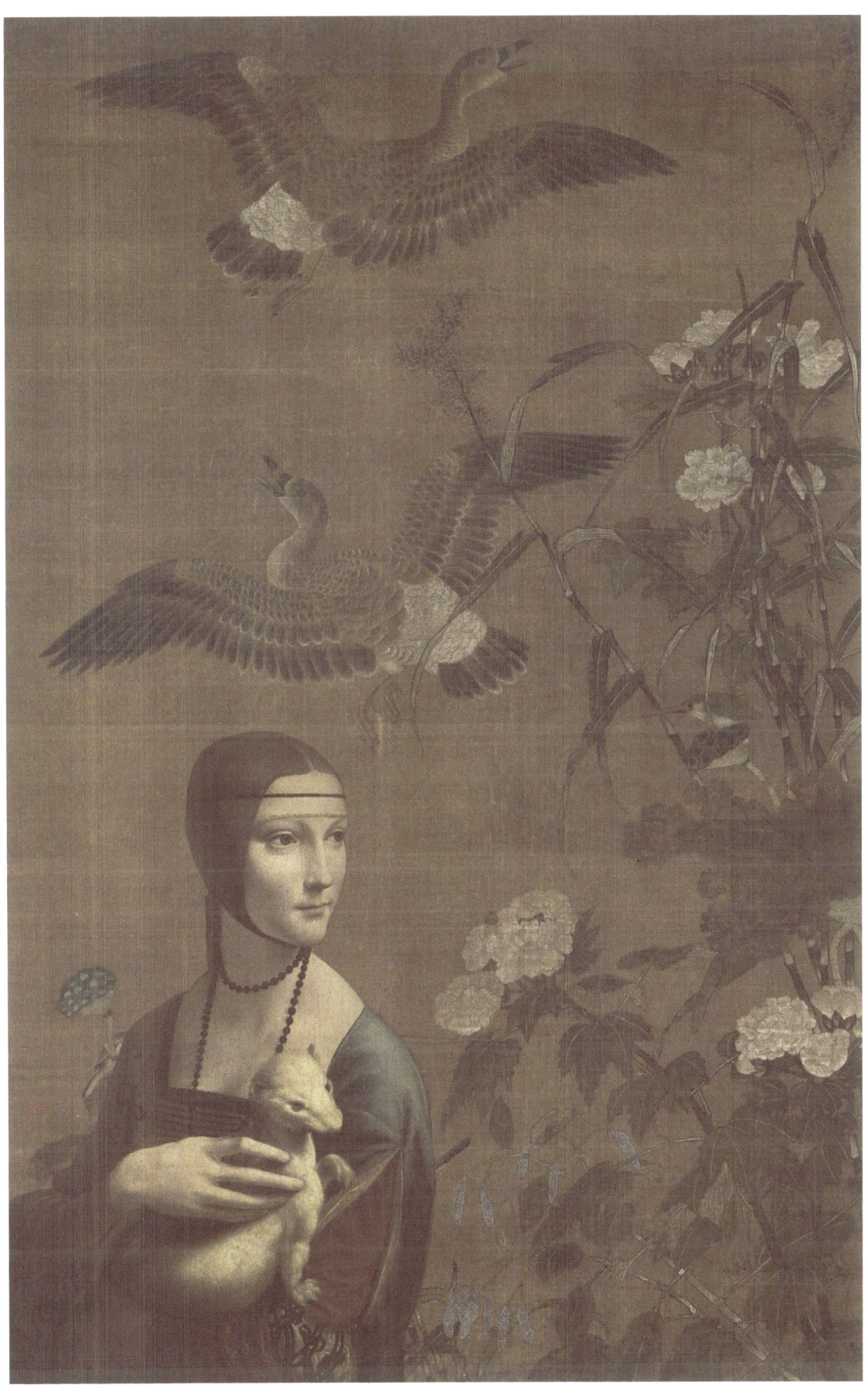

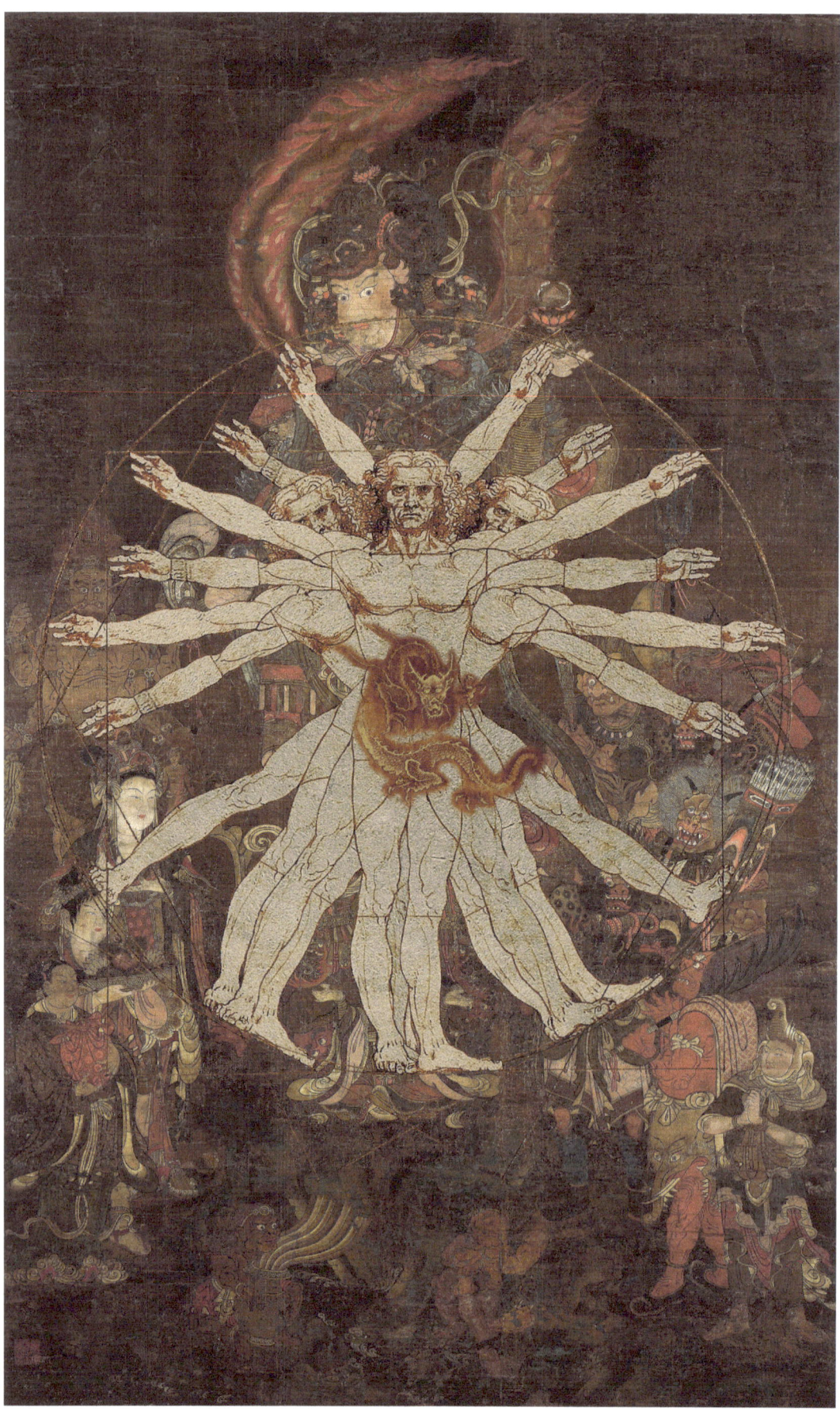

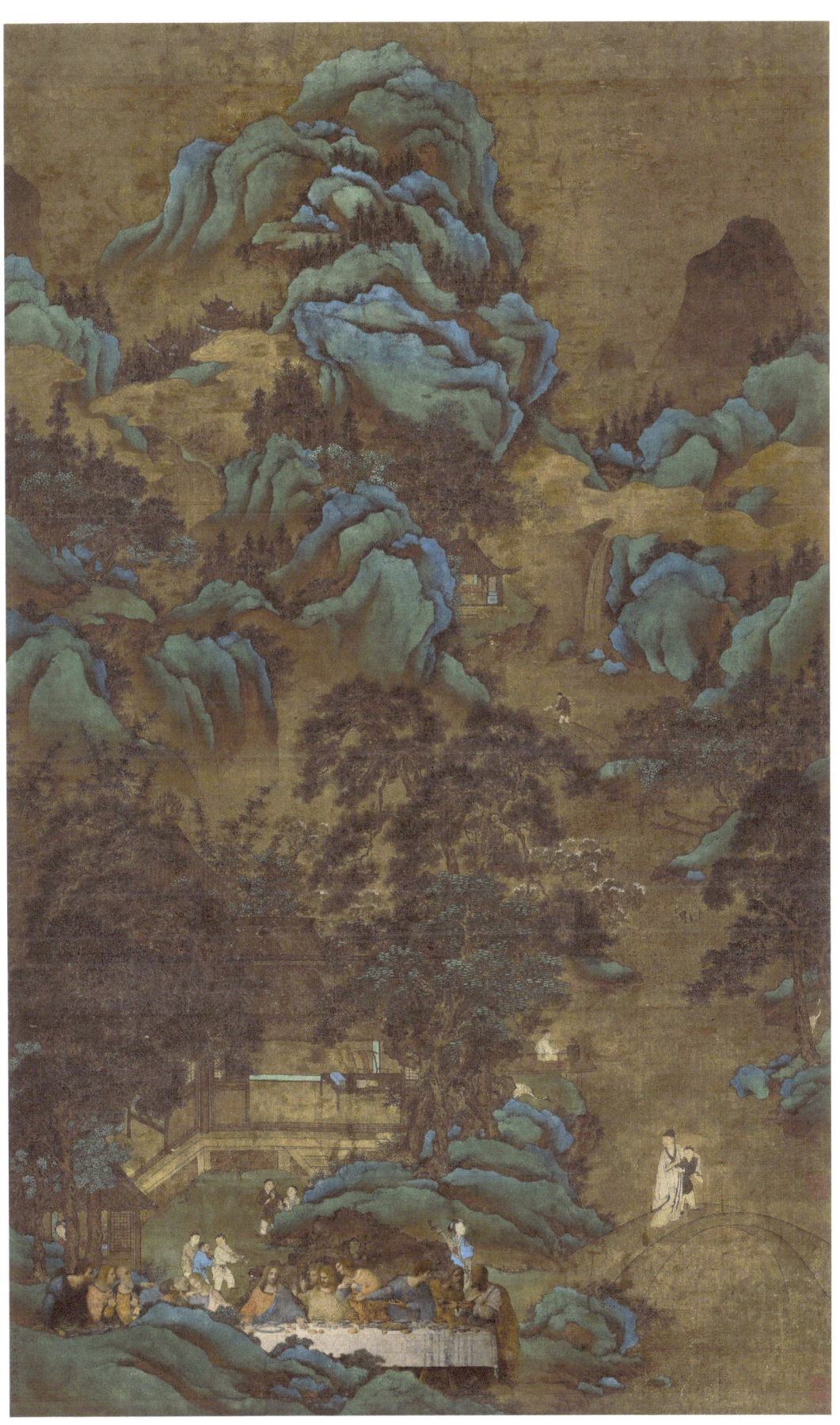

East #11

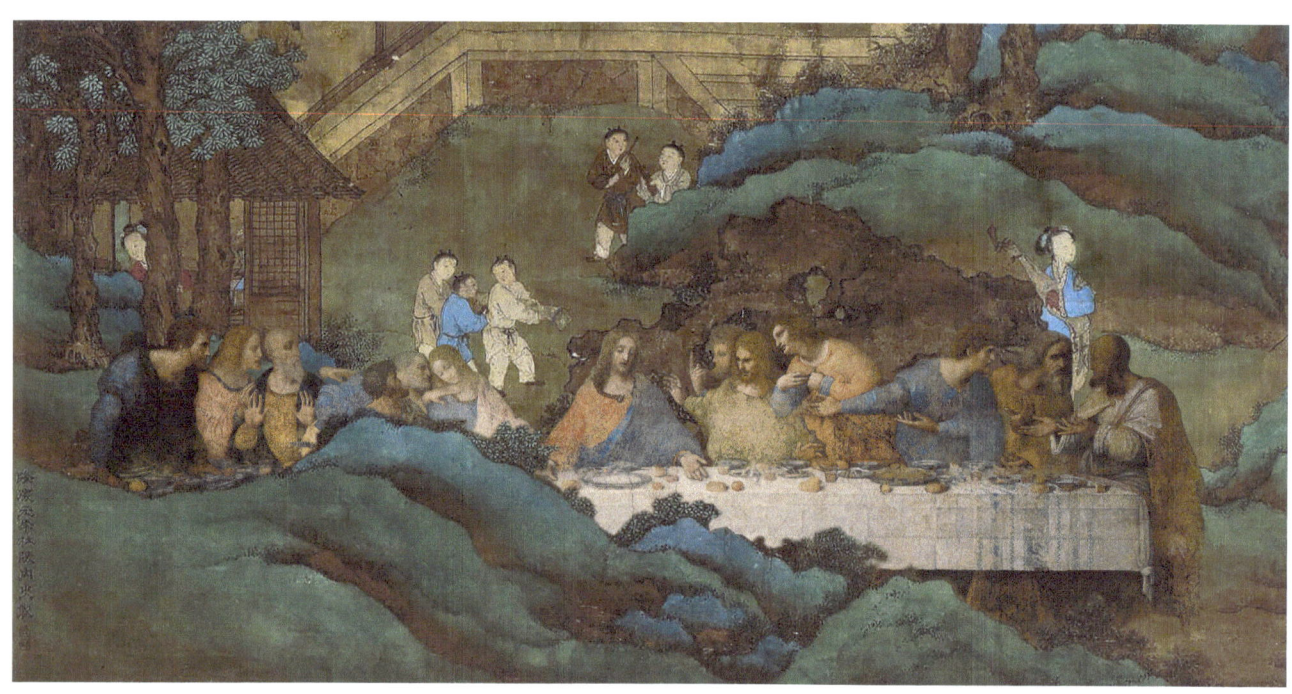

East #11 (detail)

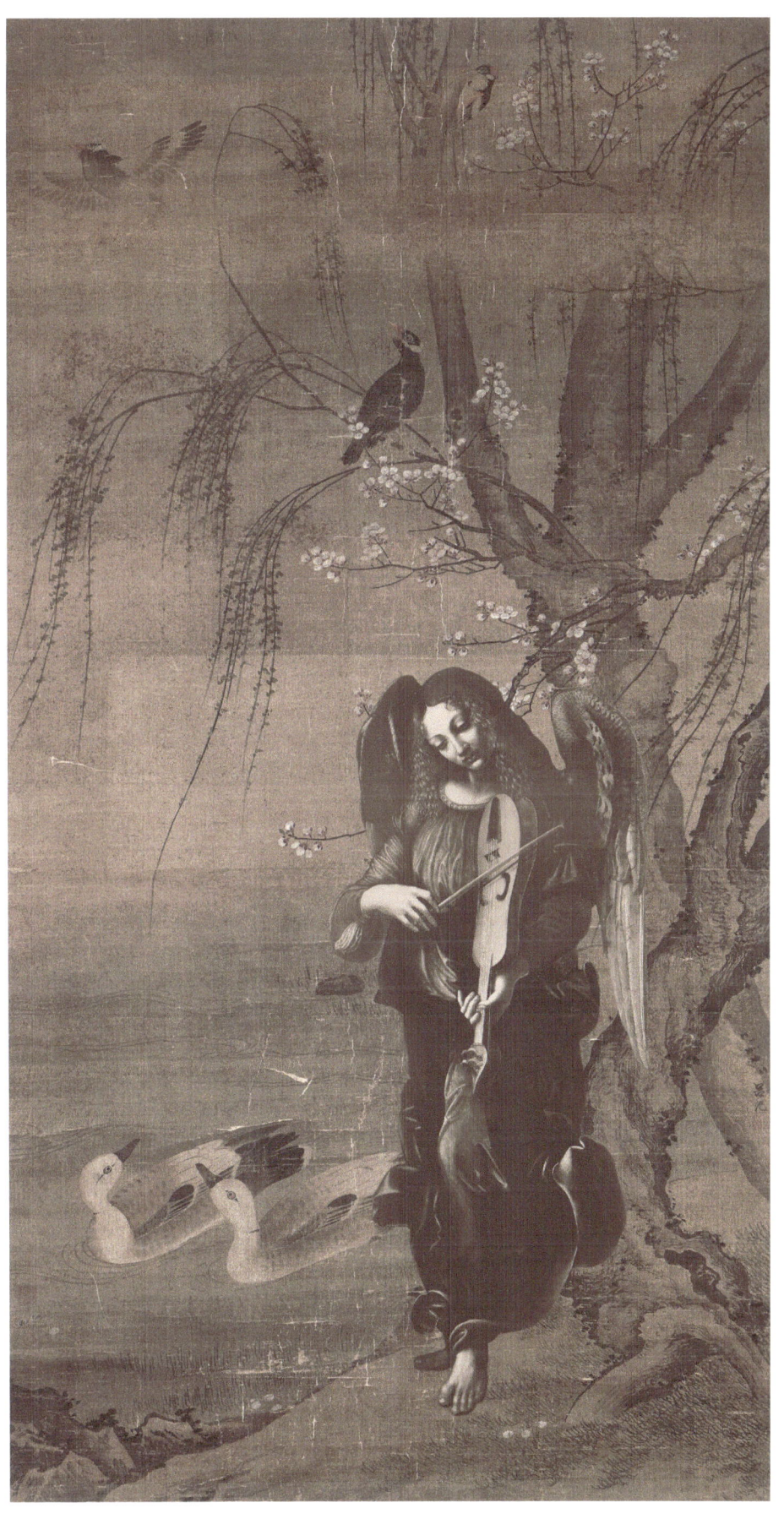

East #12

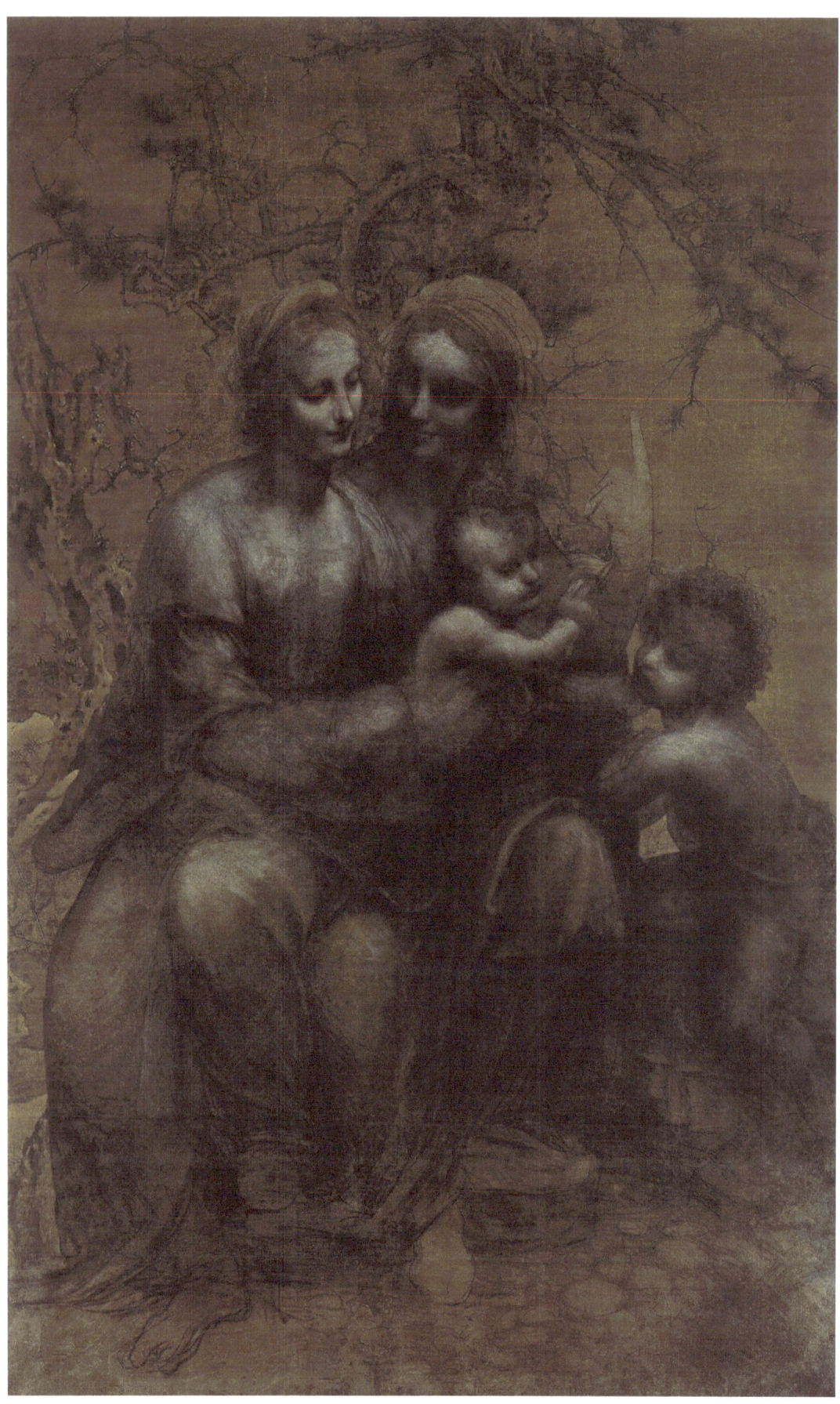

East #14

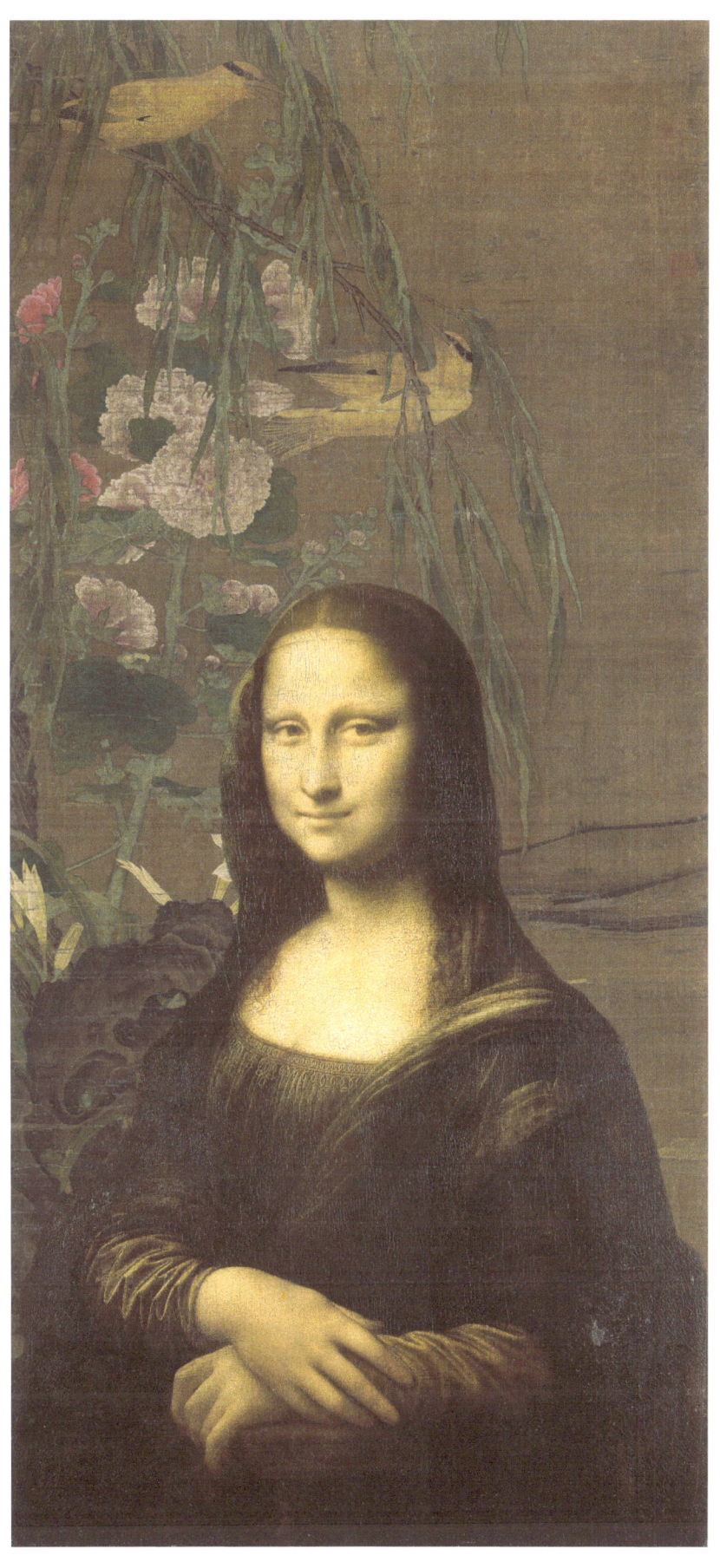

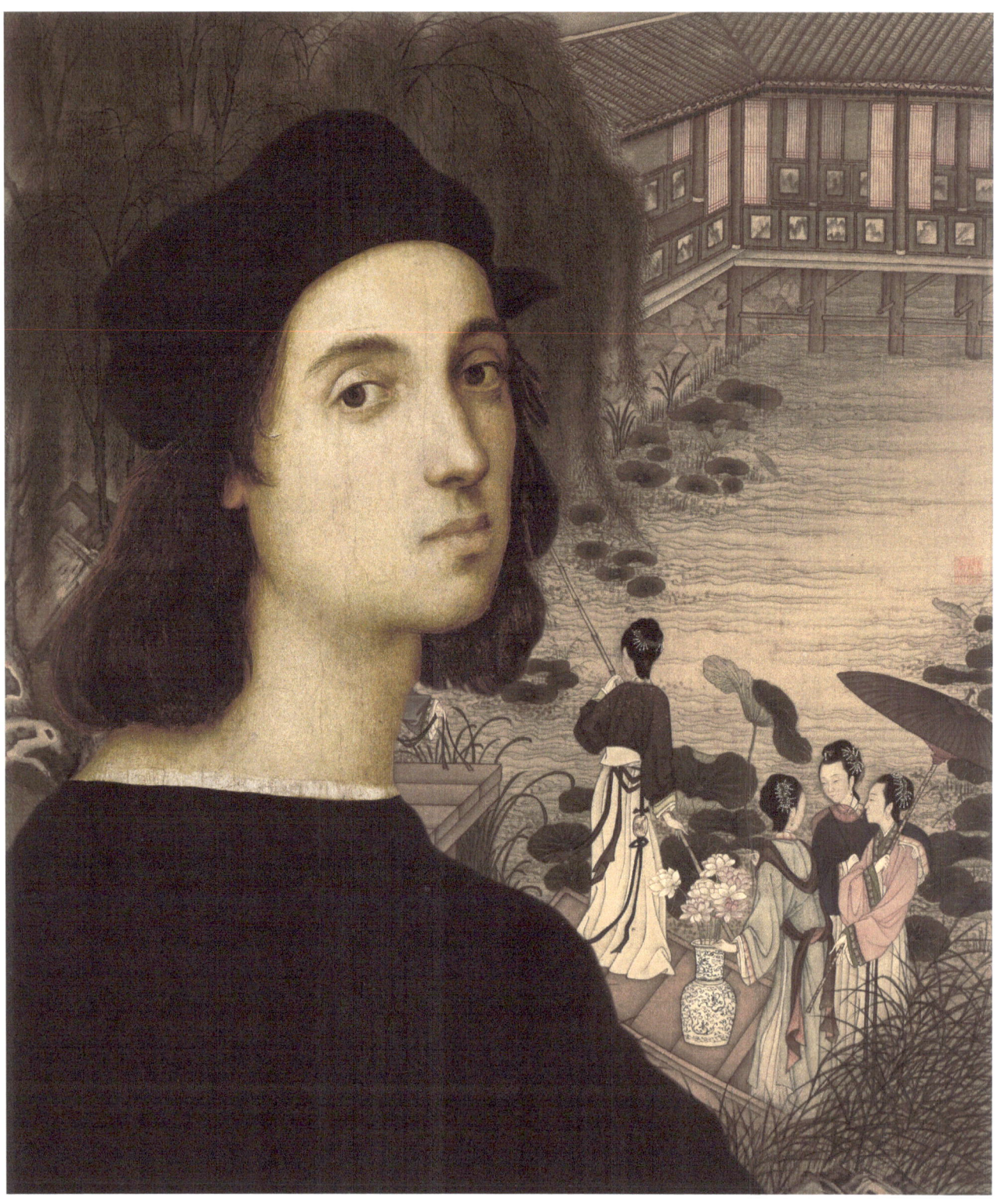

East #15

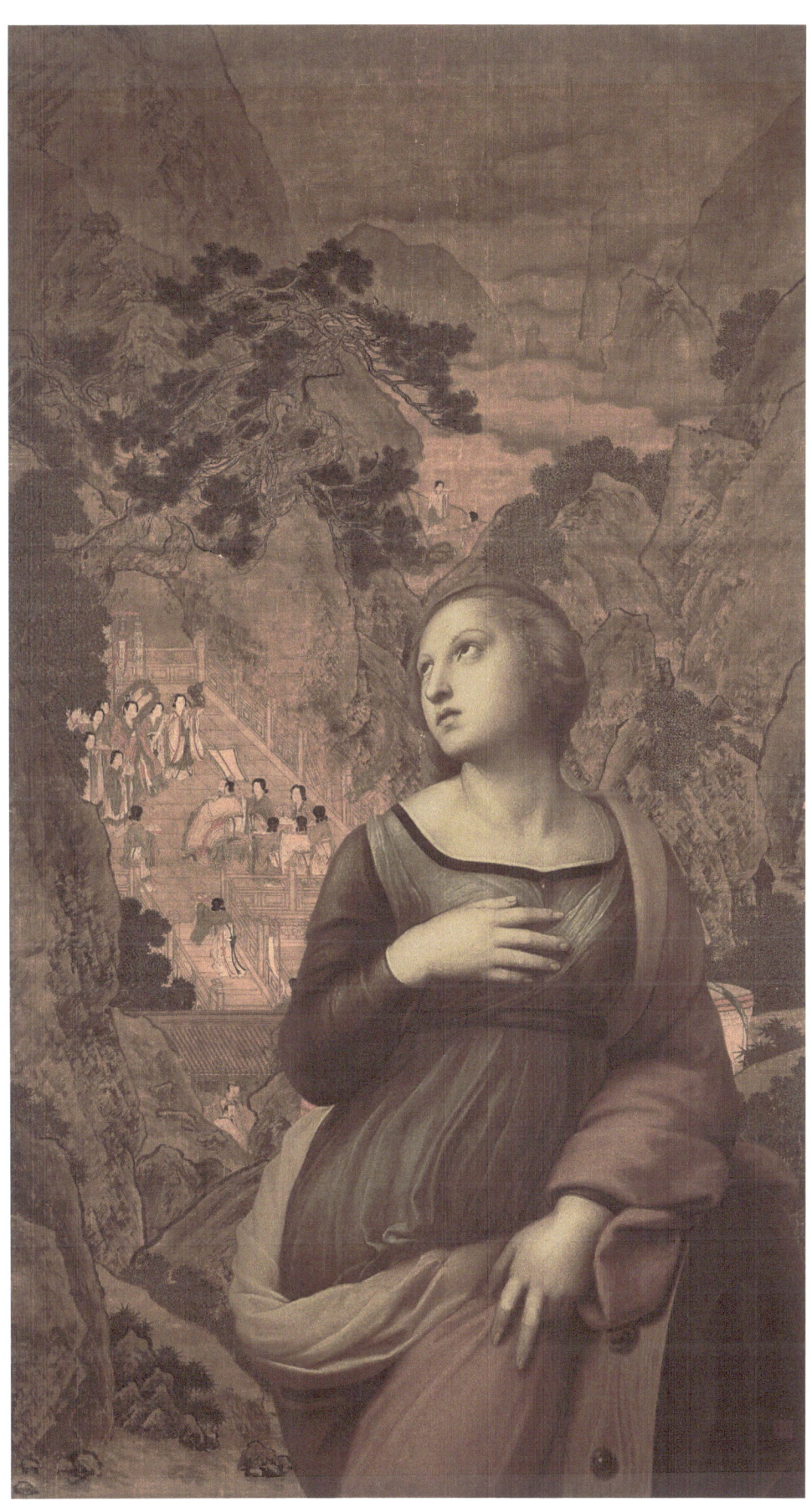

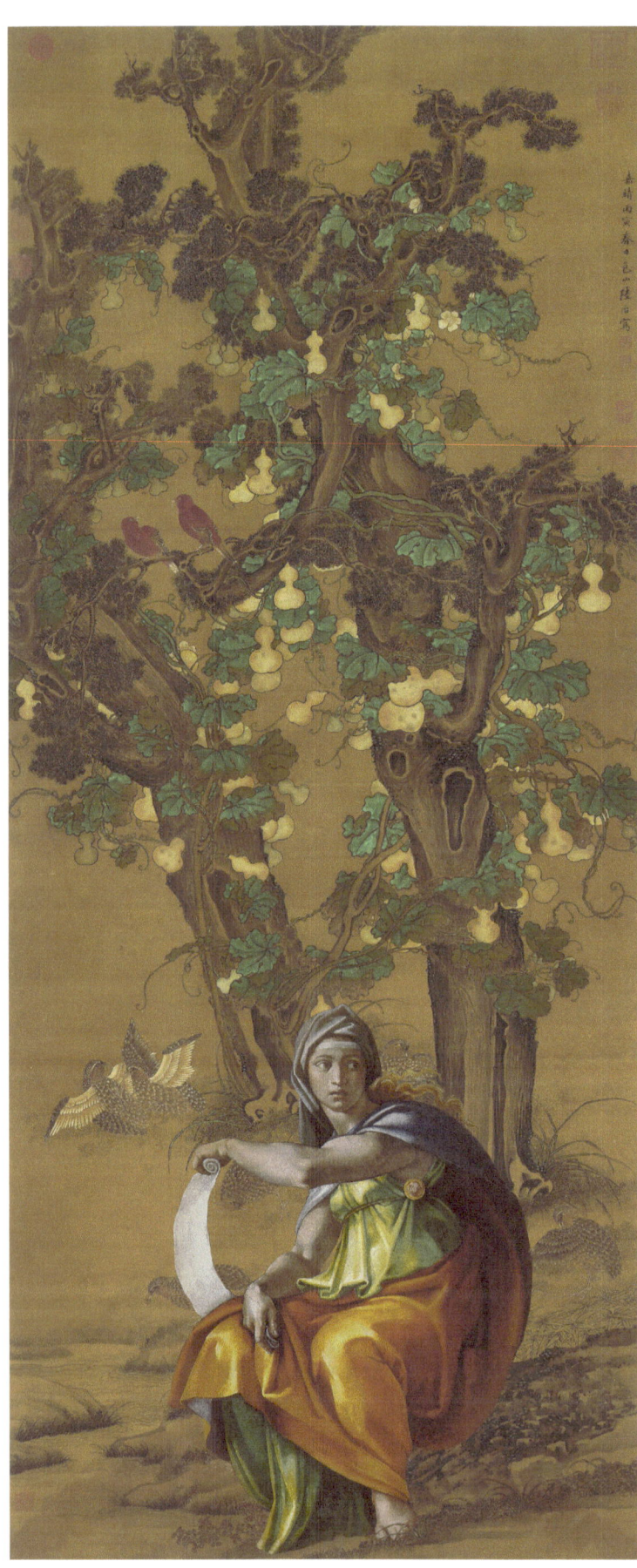

East #17

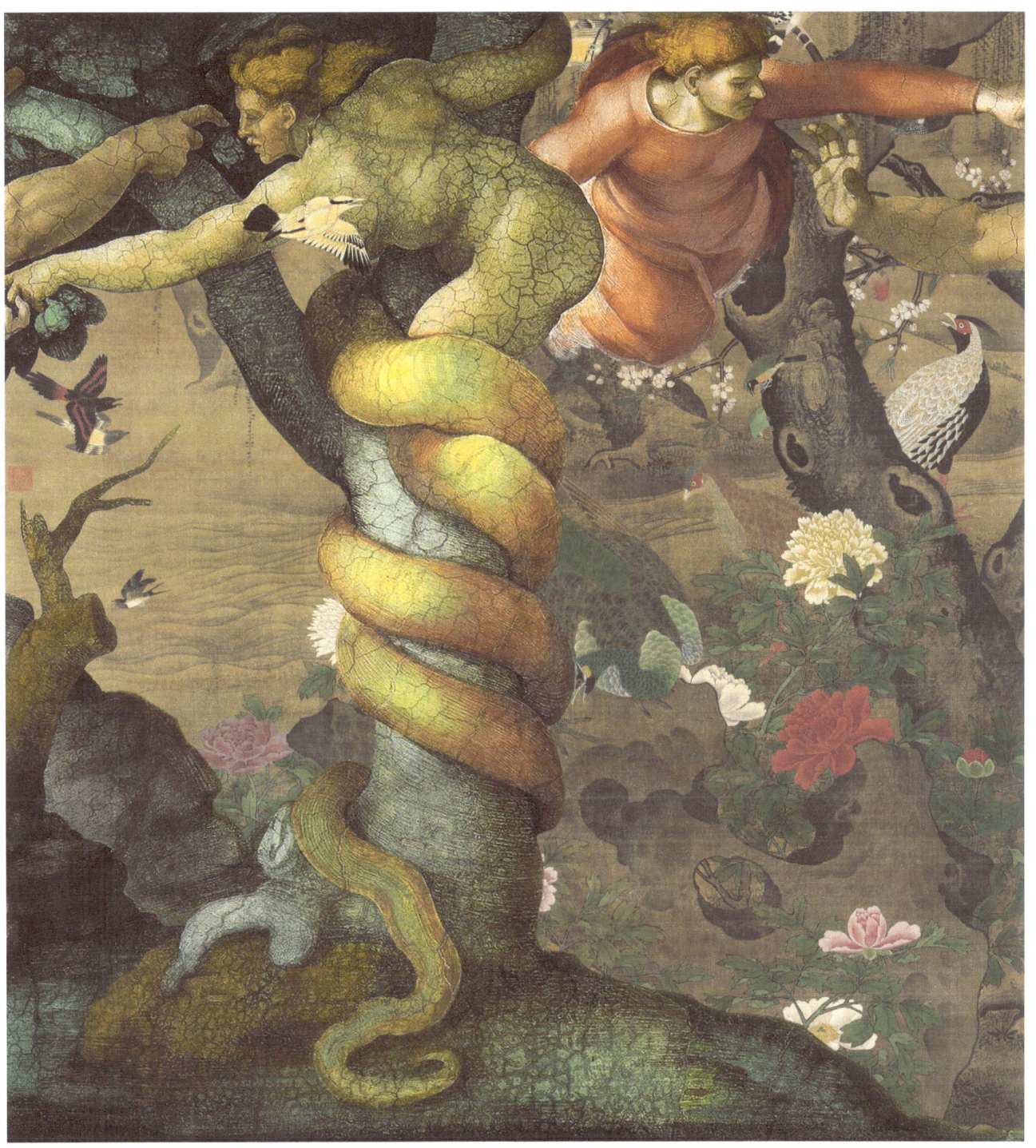

East #18

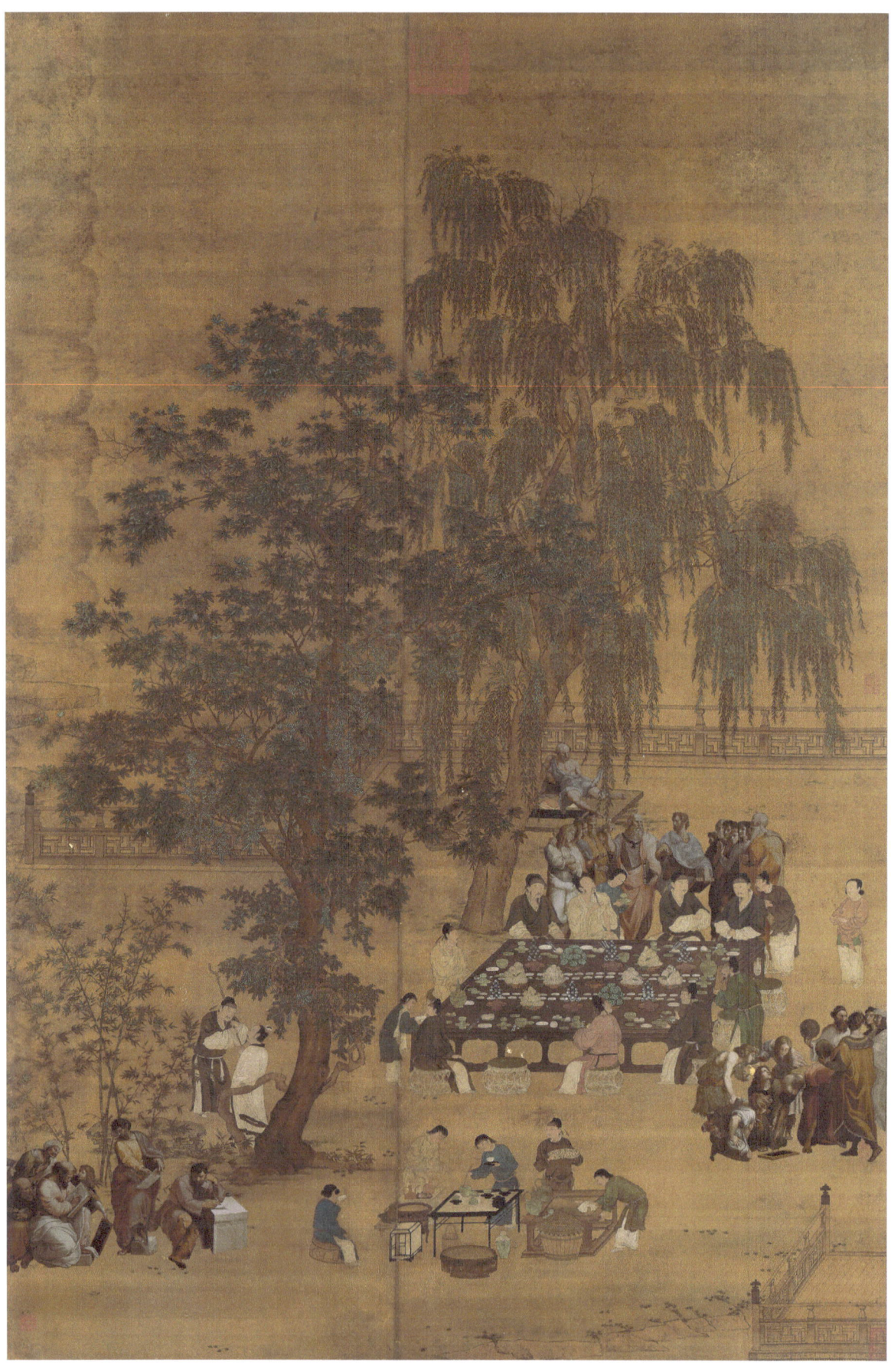

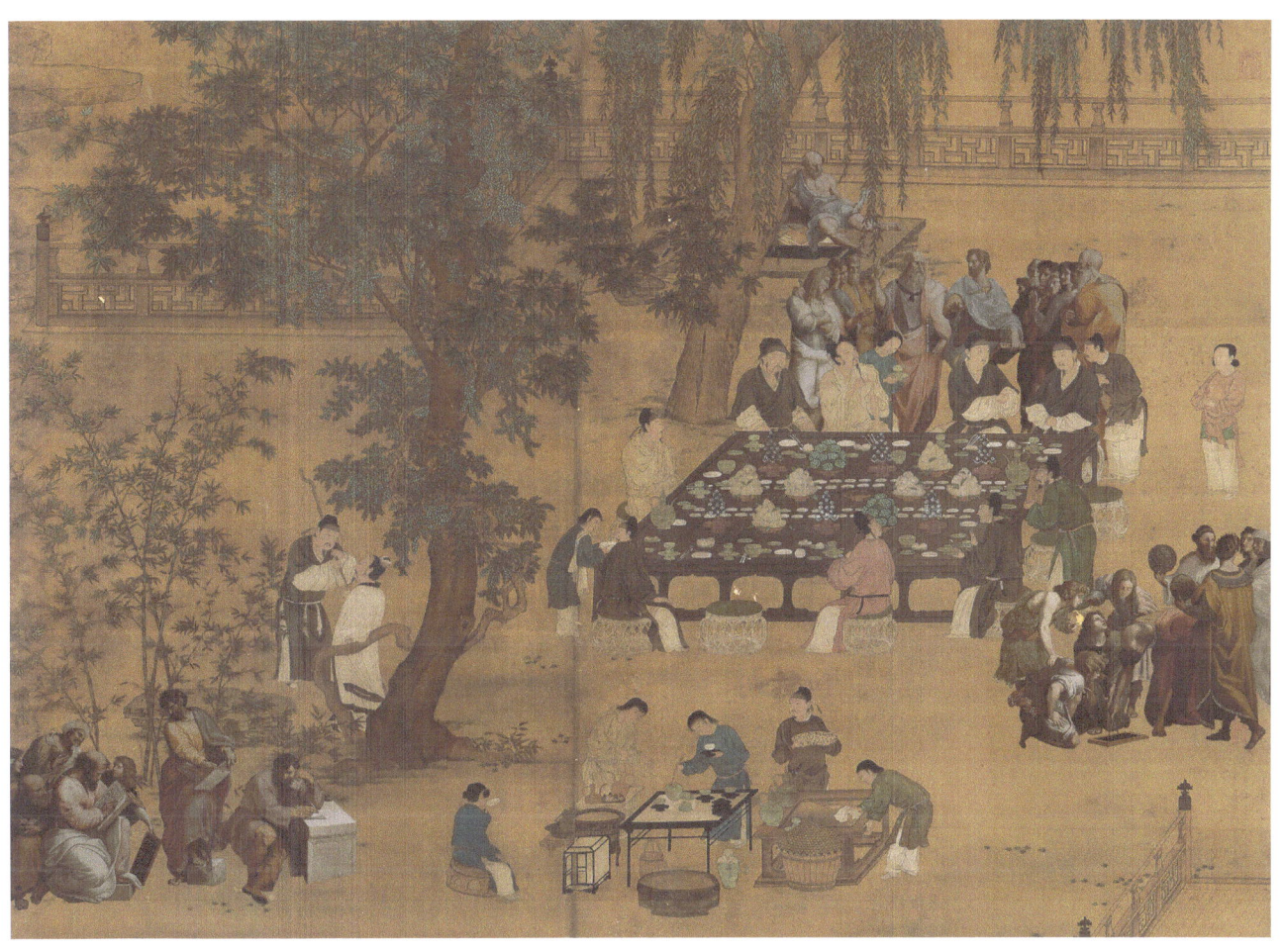

East #19 (detail)

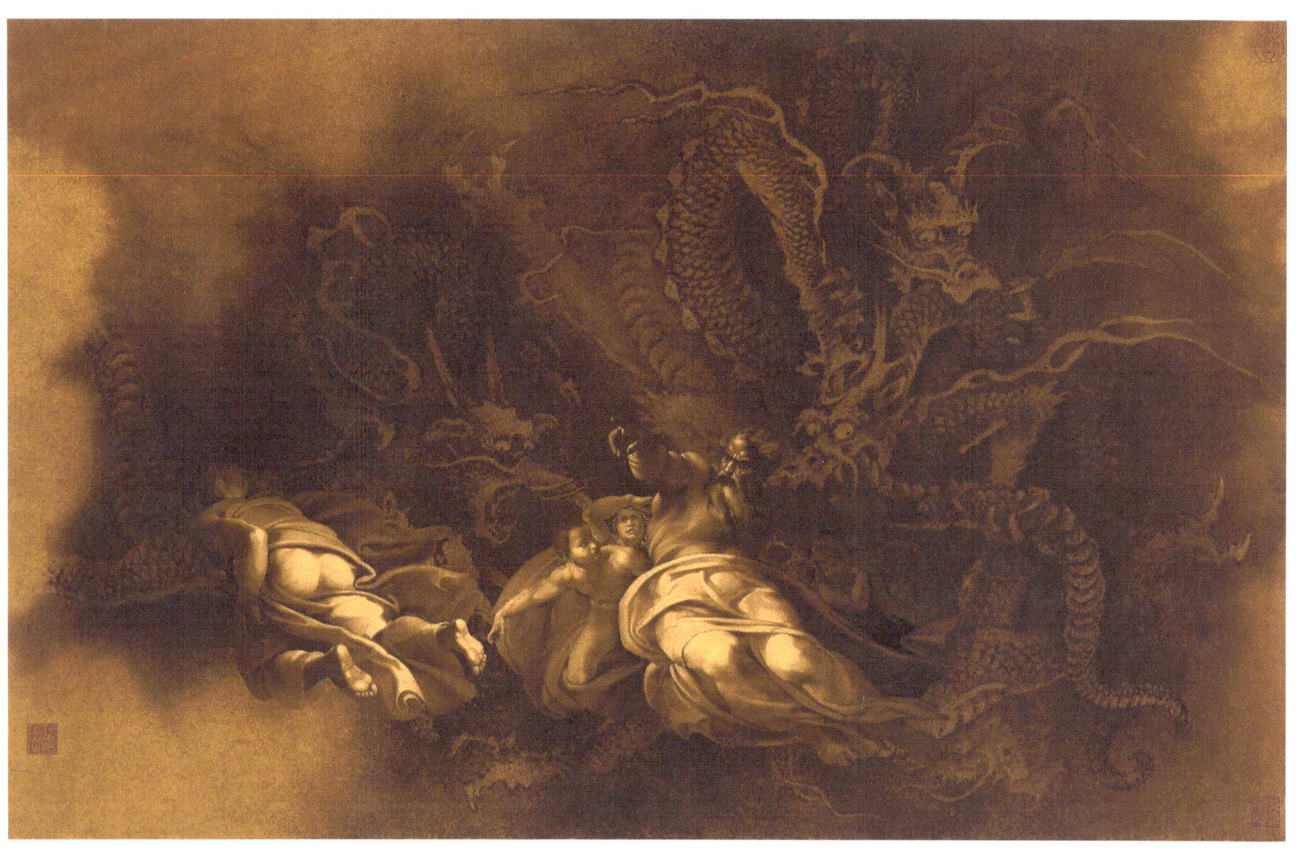

East #20

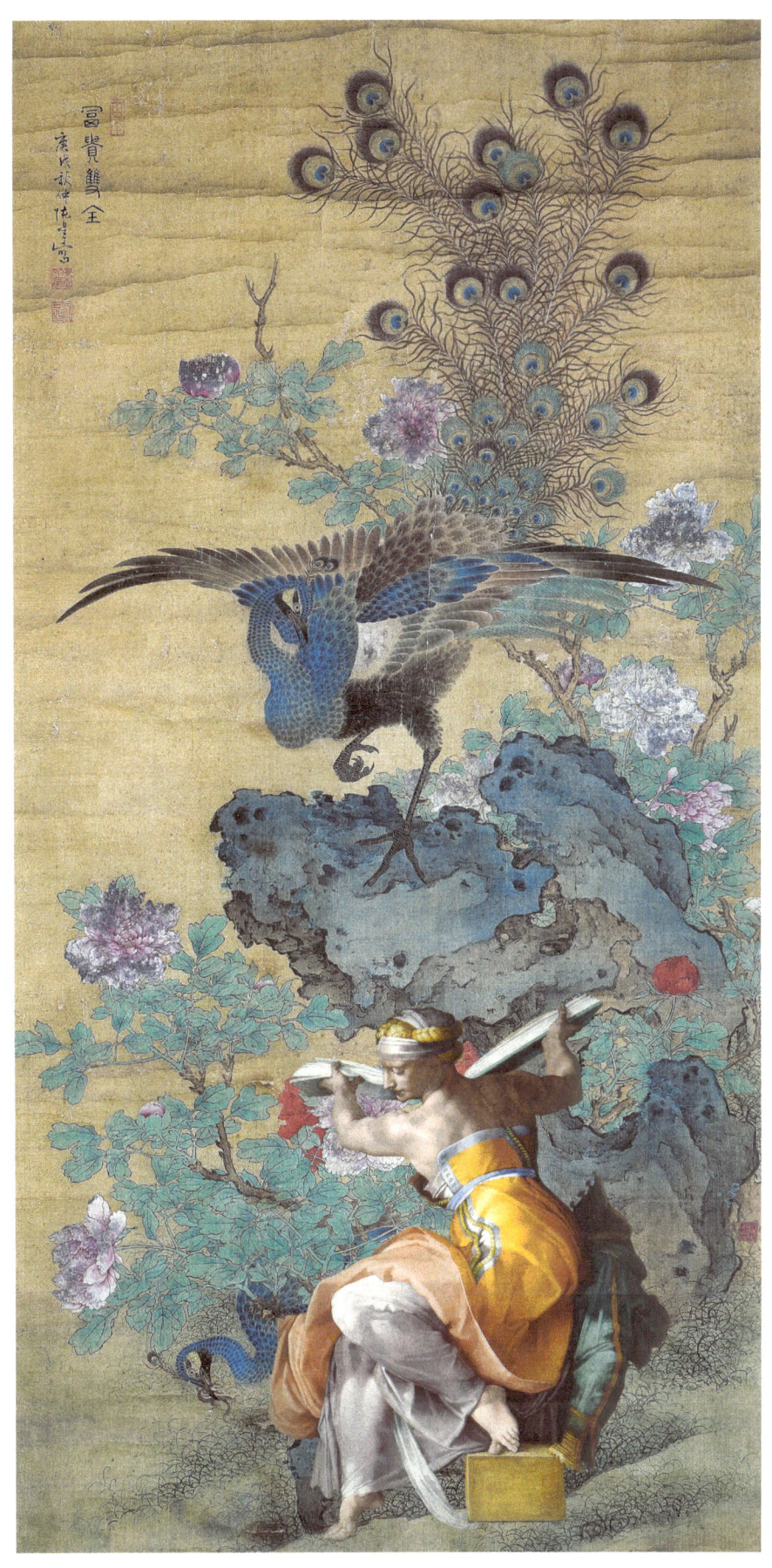

East #21

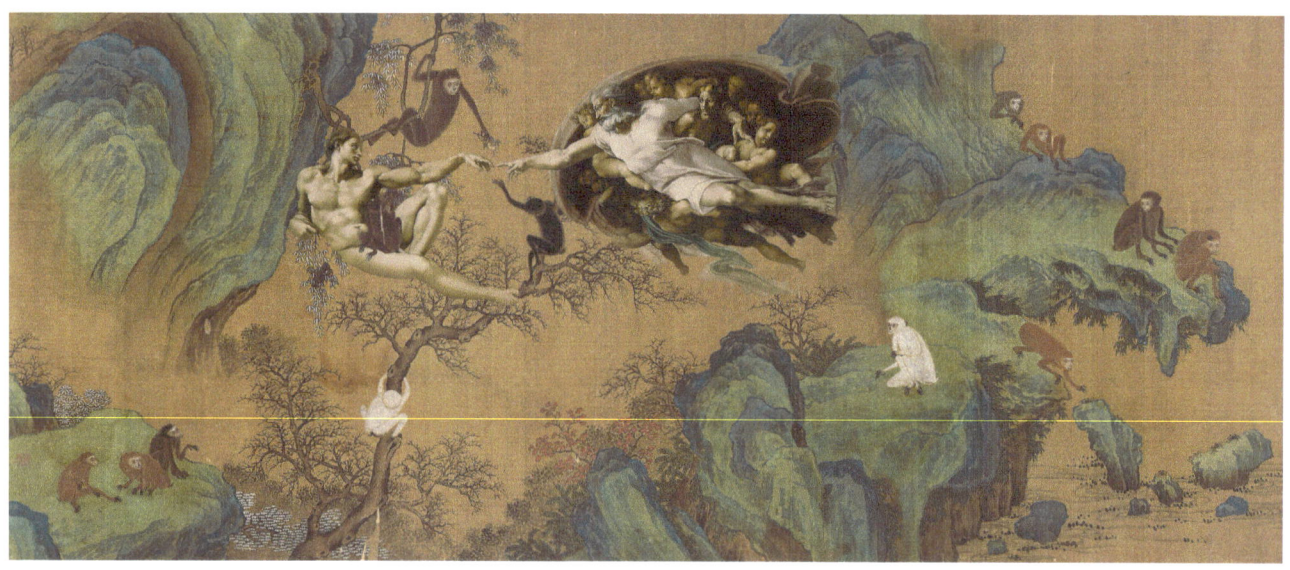

East #22

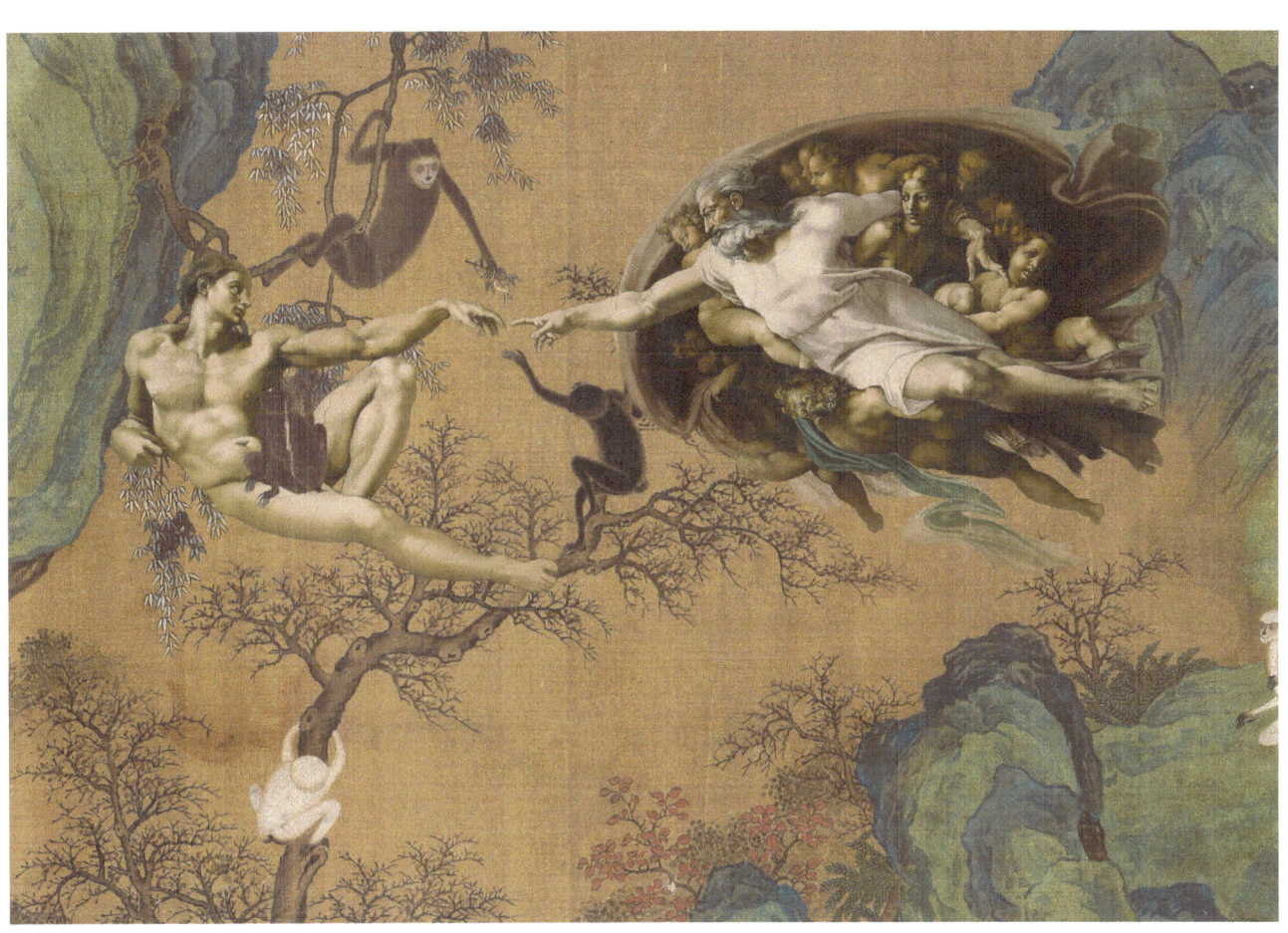

East #22 (detail)

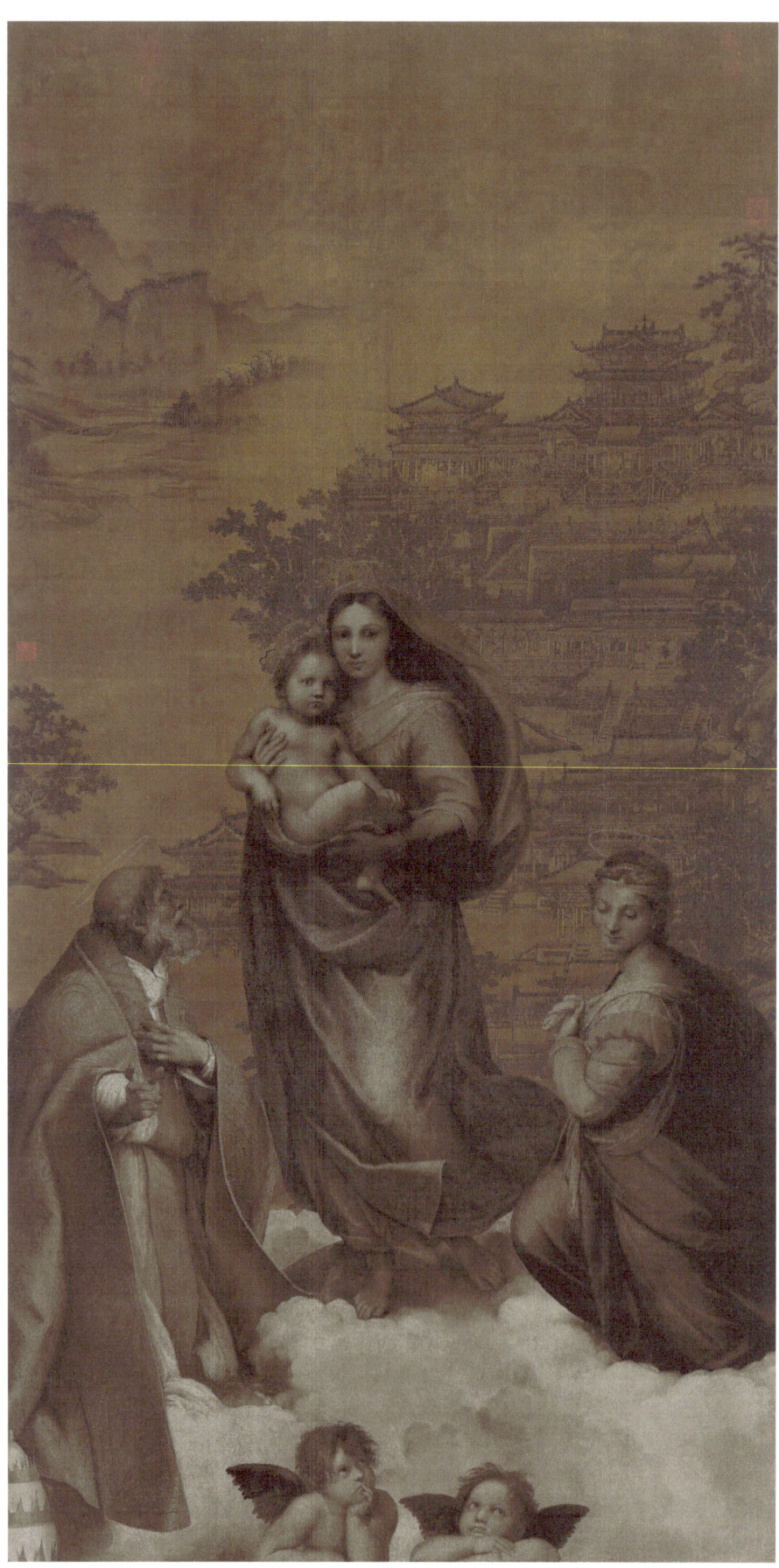

East #23

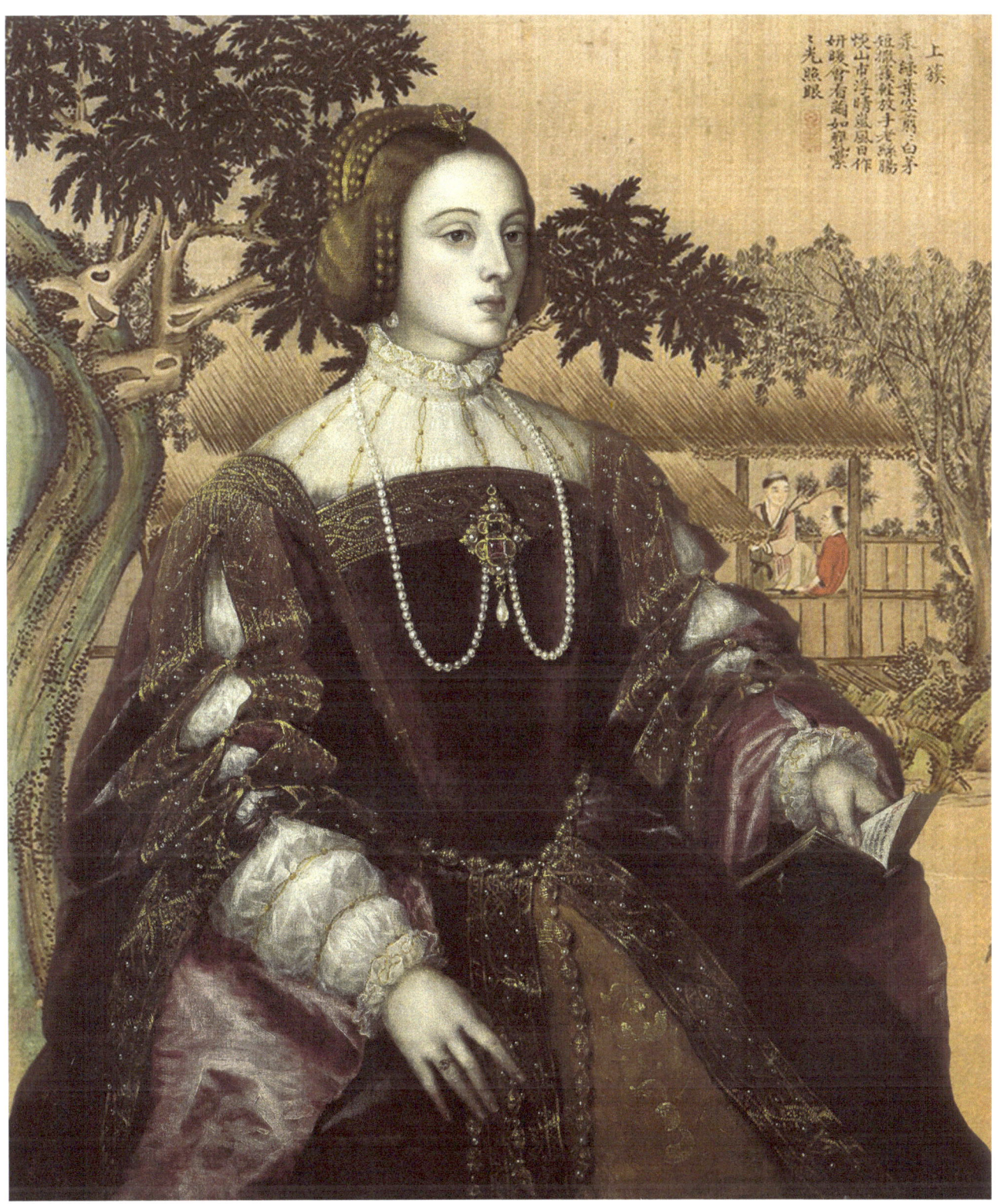

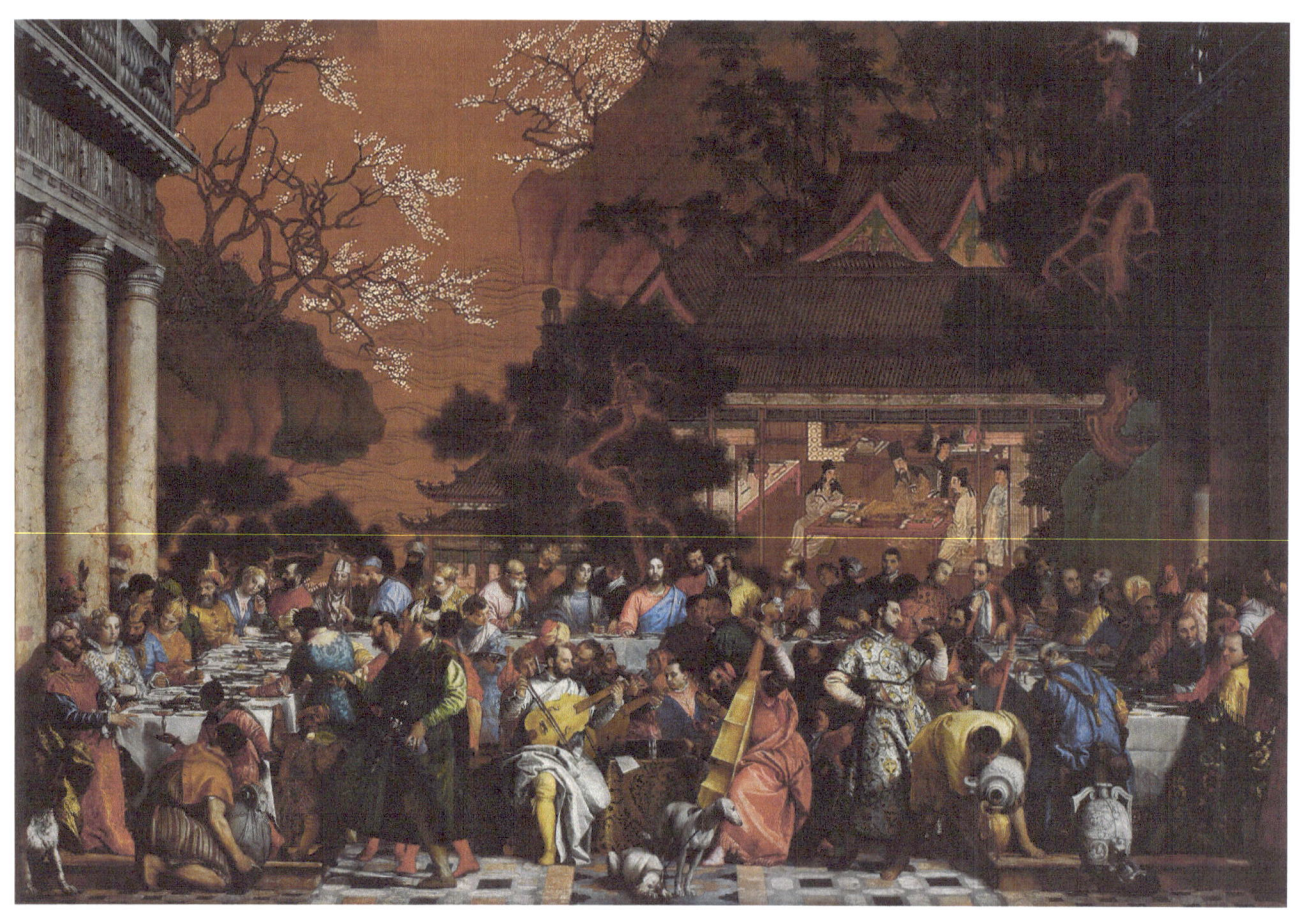

East #25

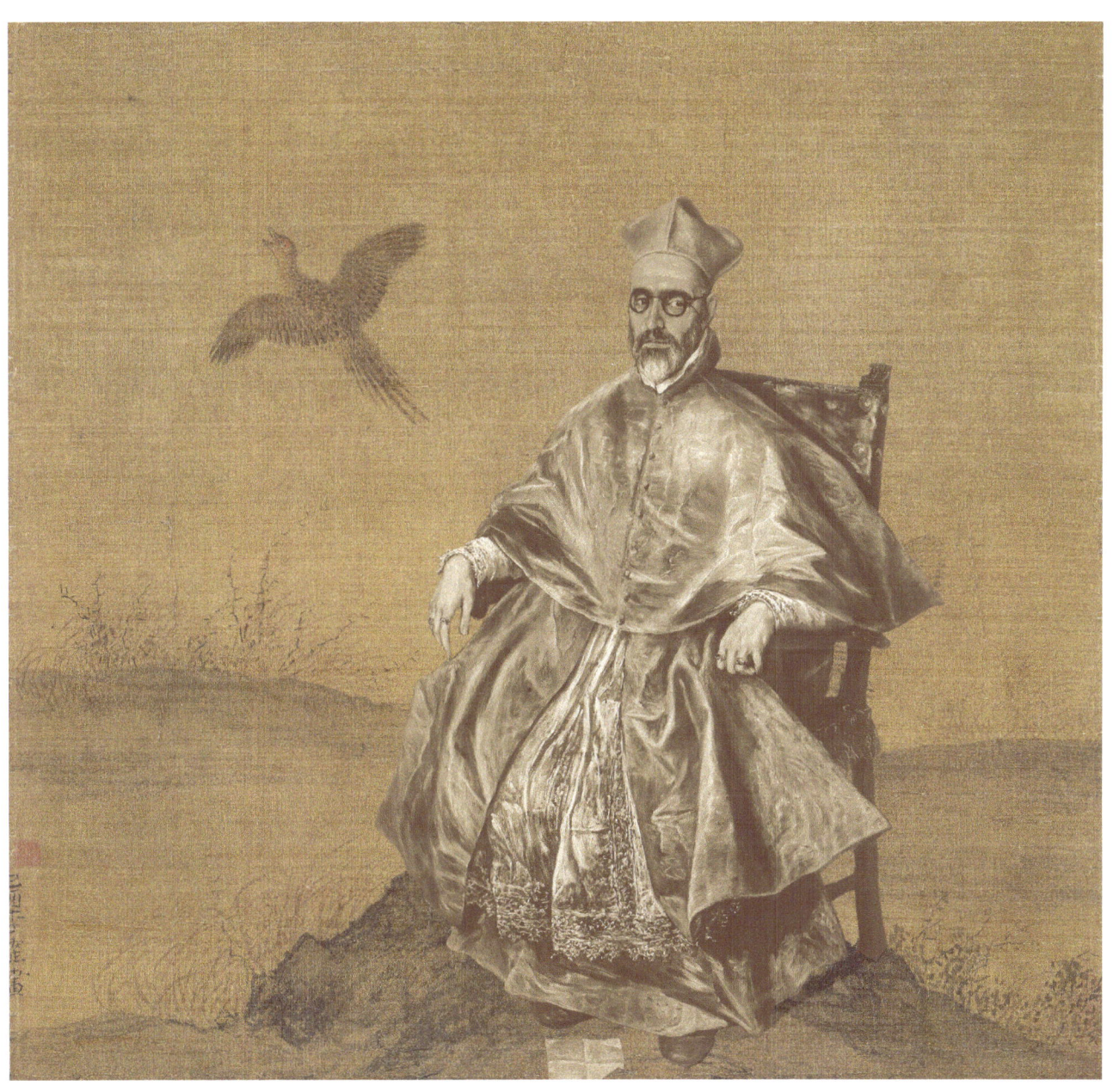

East #26

Mark Harris

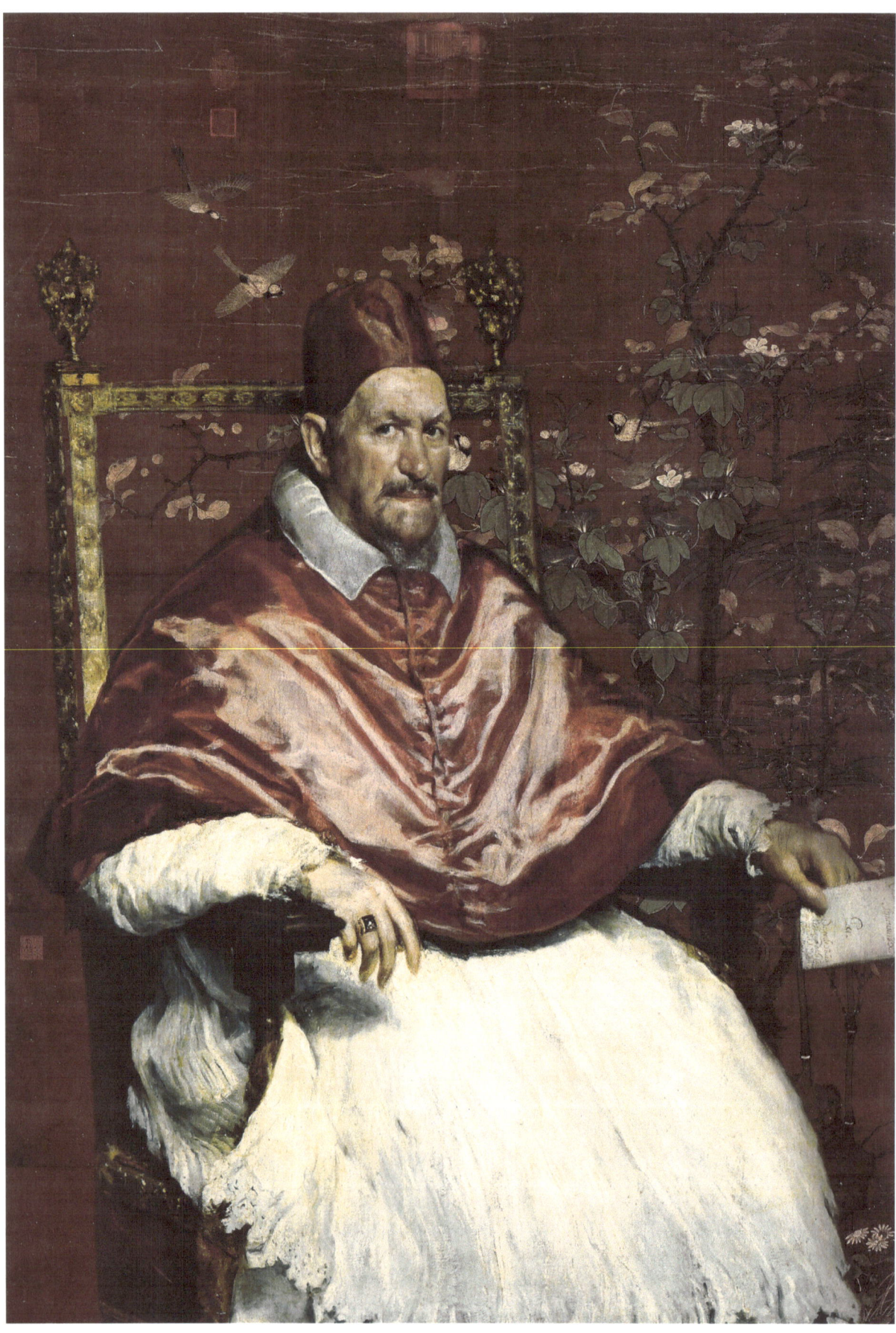

East #27

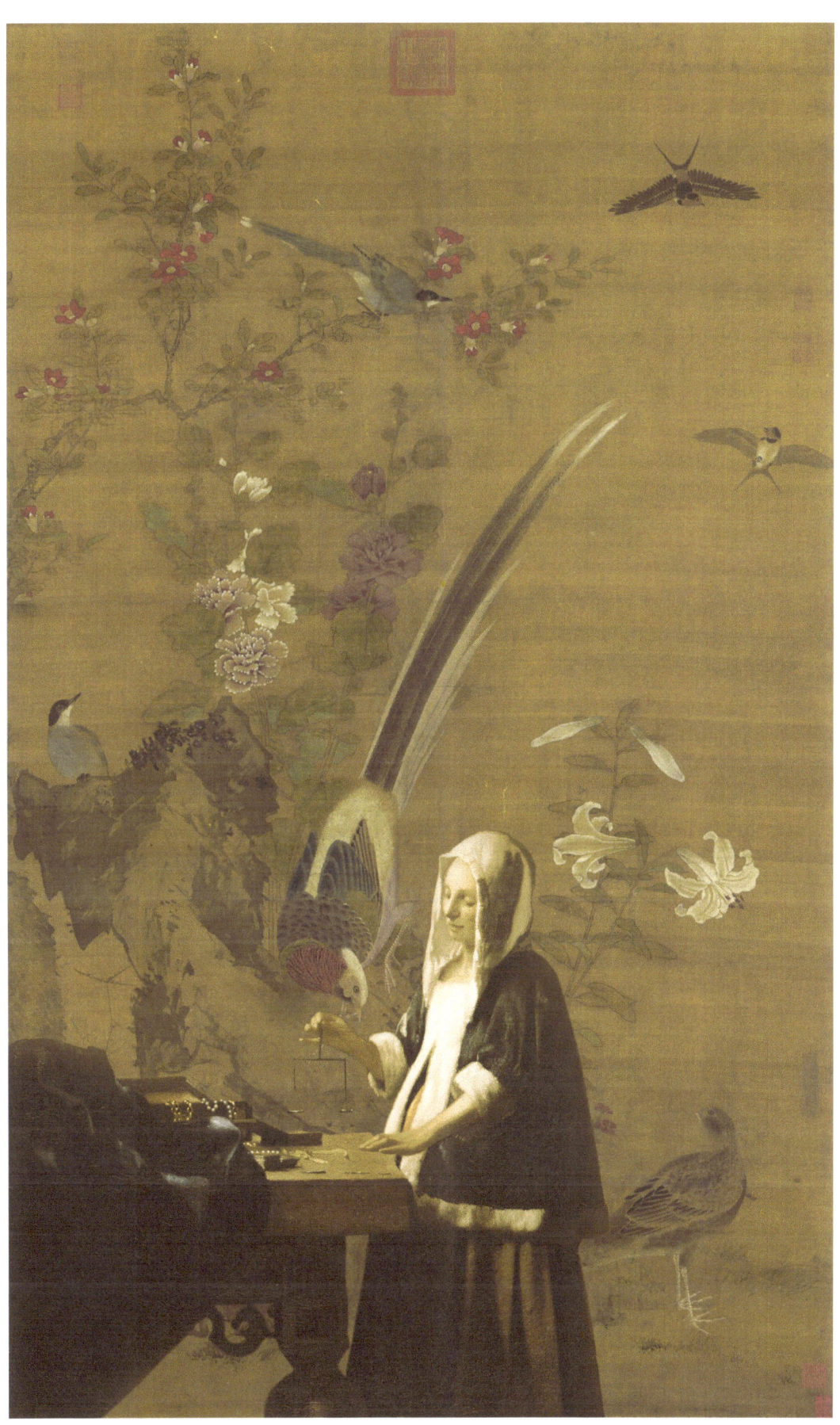

East #28

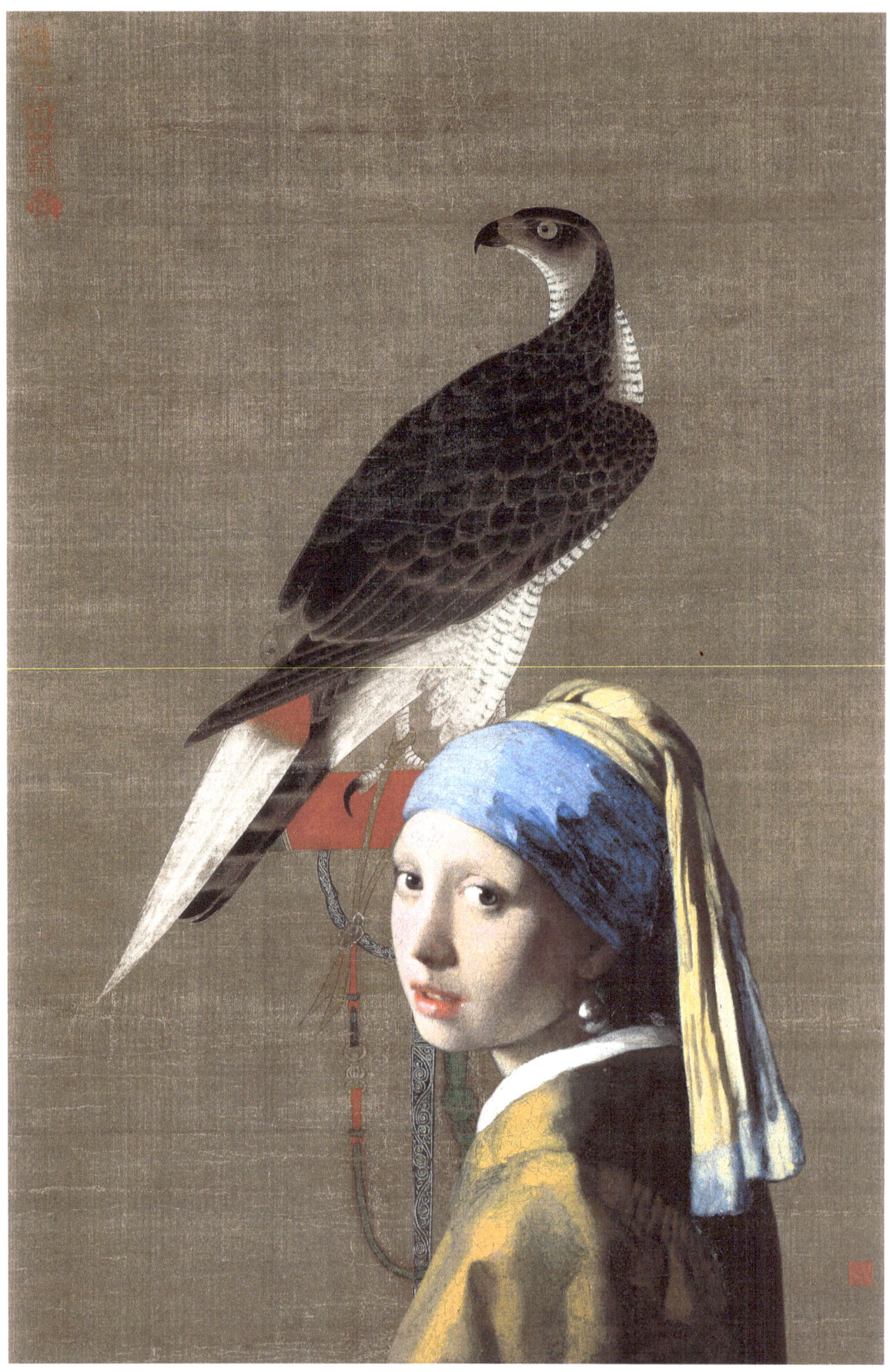

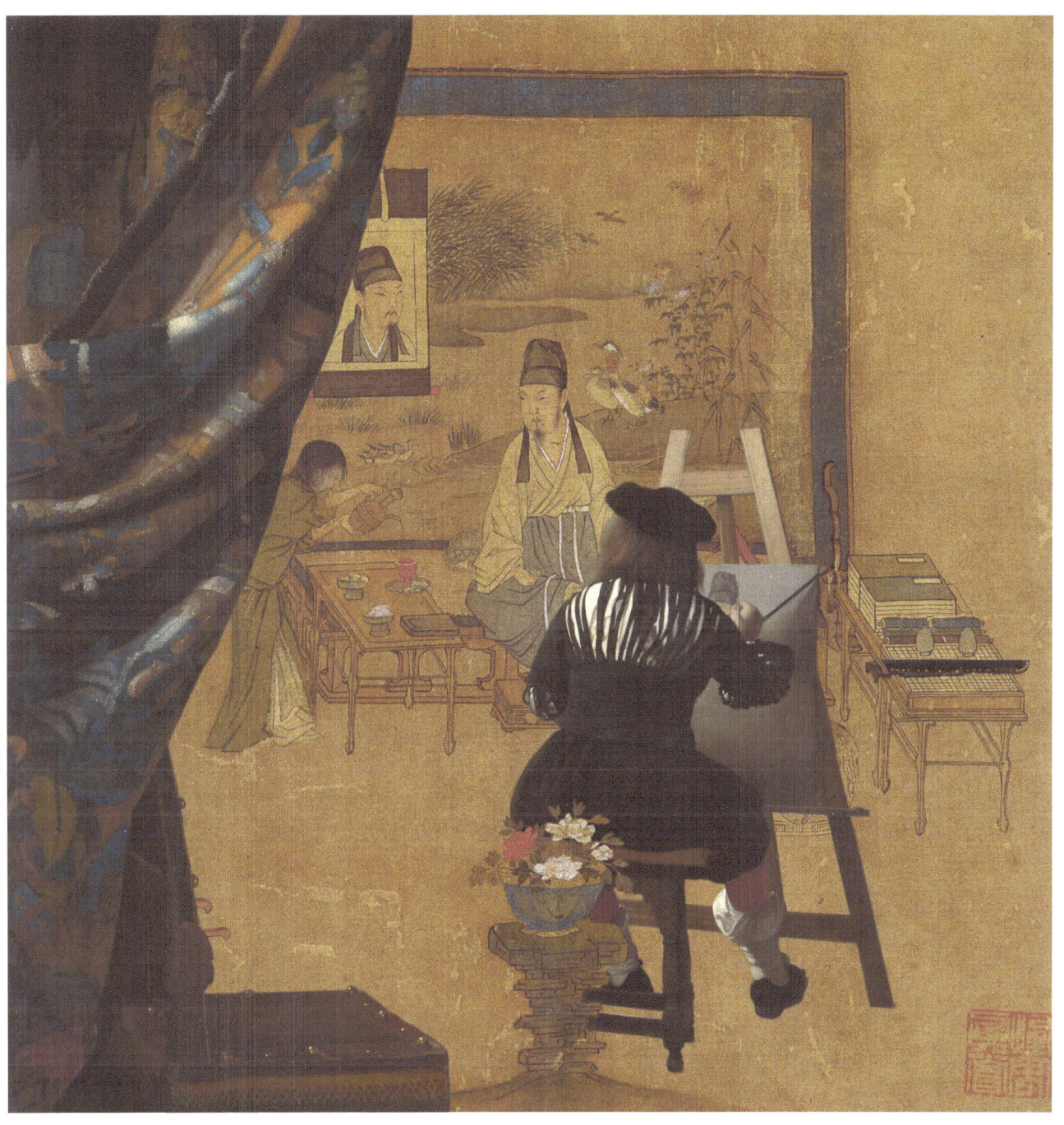

East #30

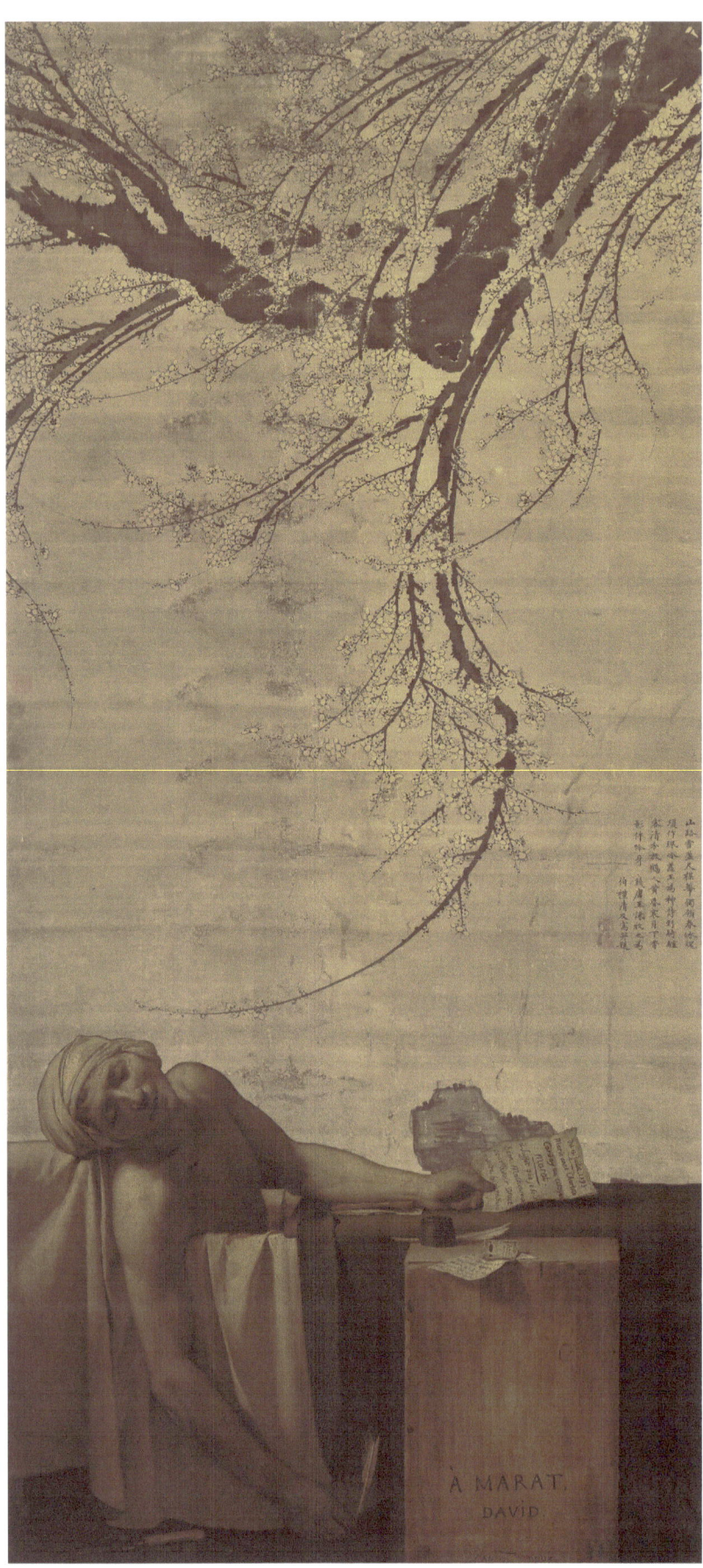

East #31

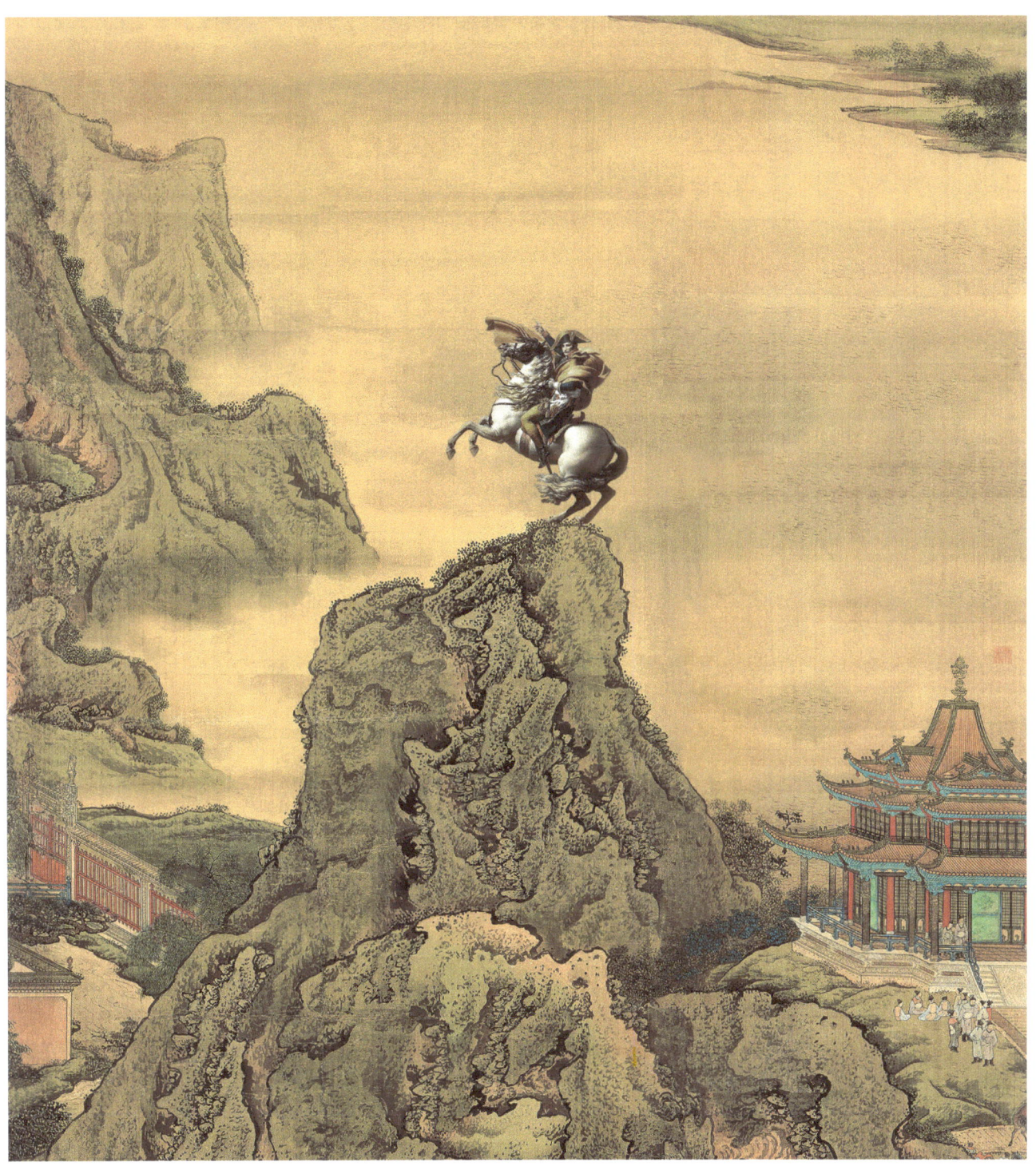

East #32

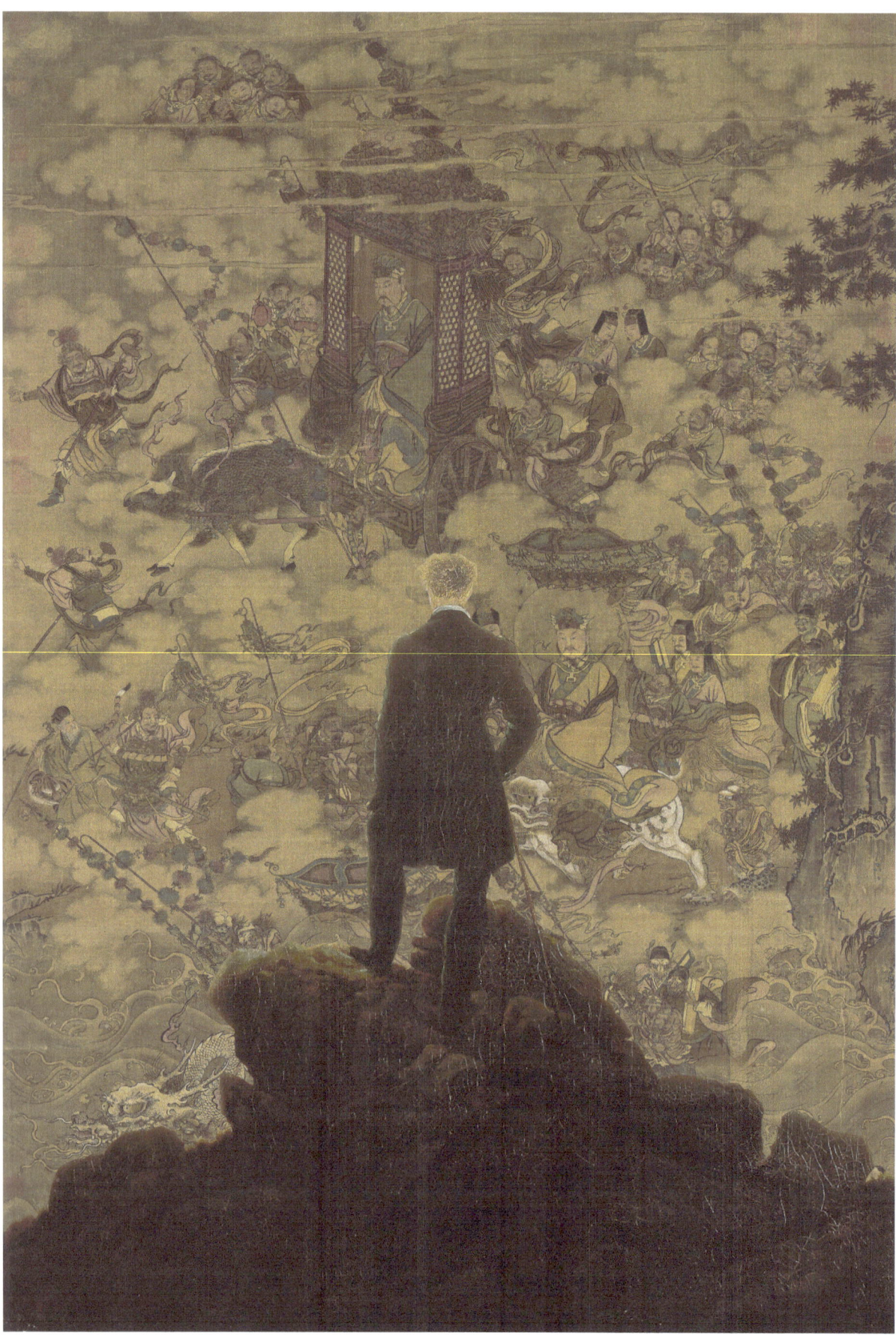

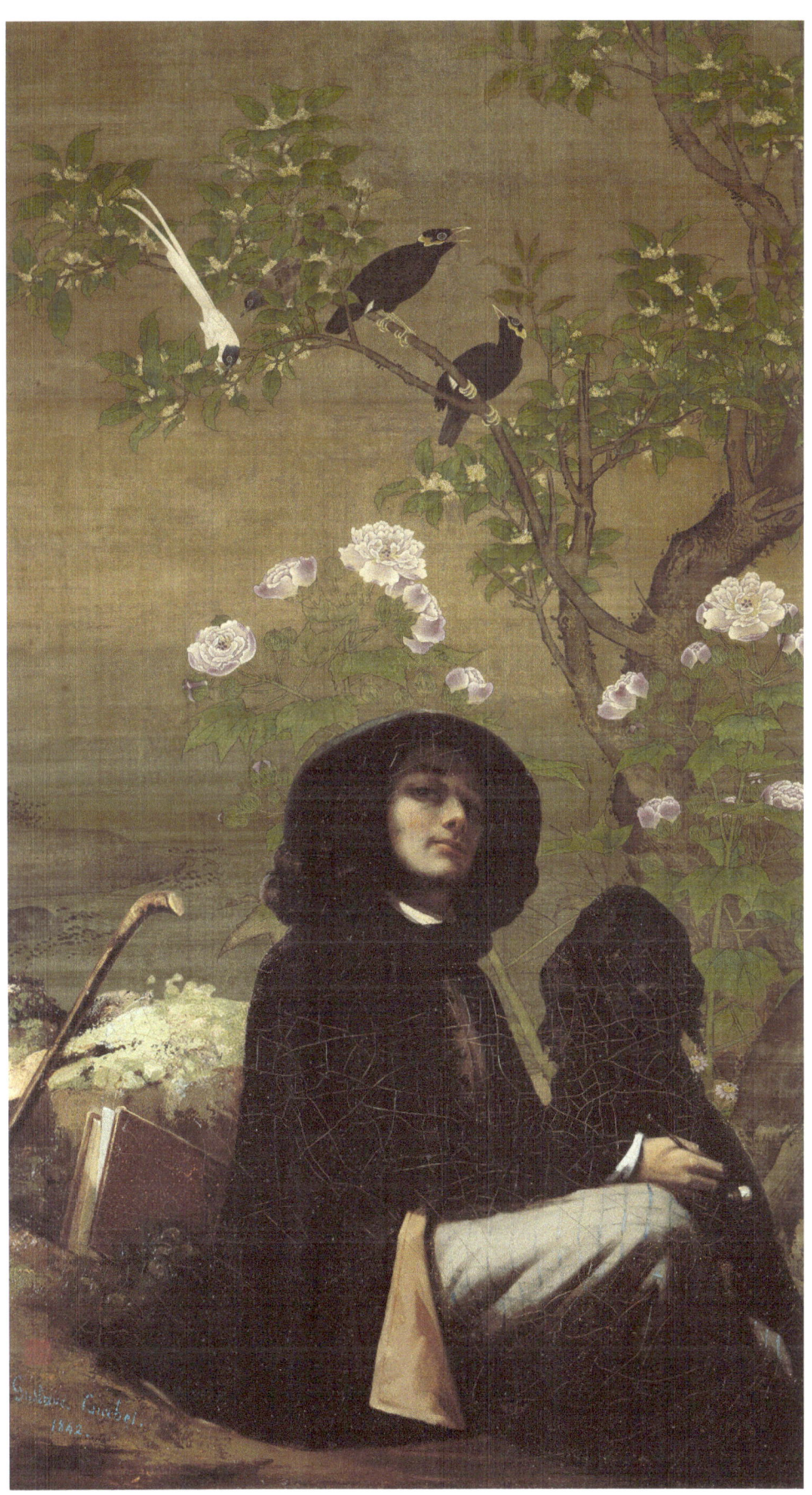

East #34

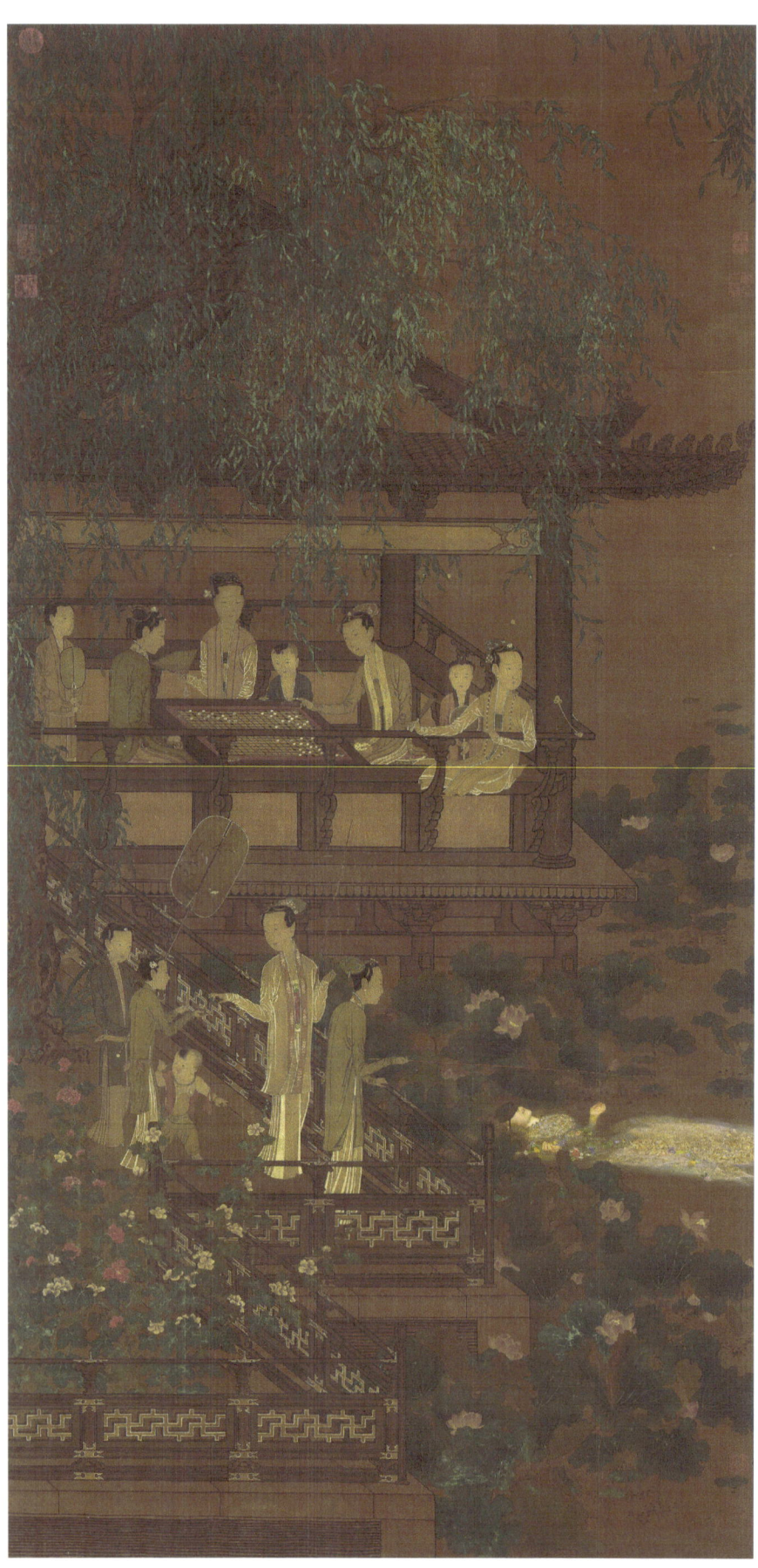

East #35

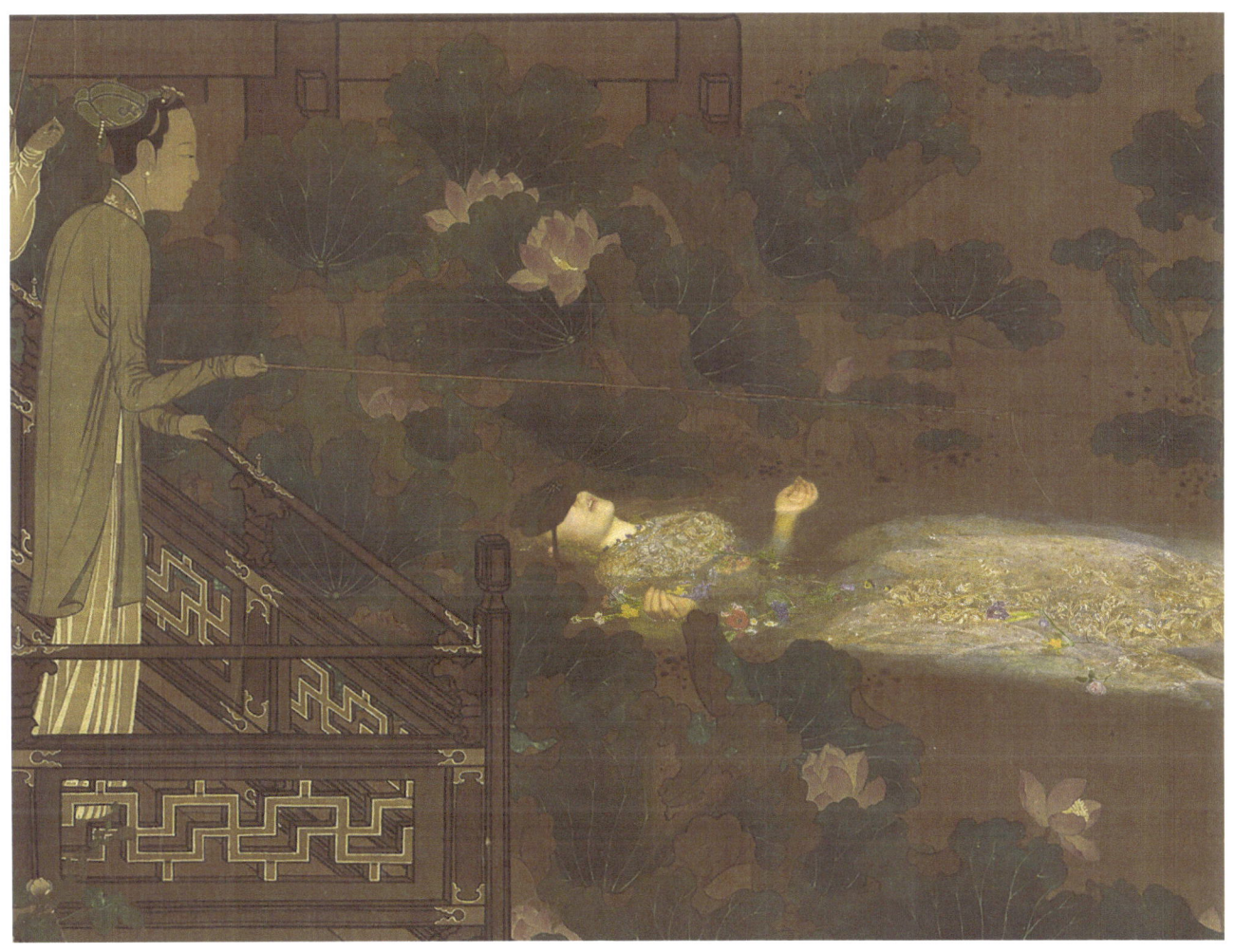

East #35 (detail)

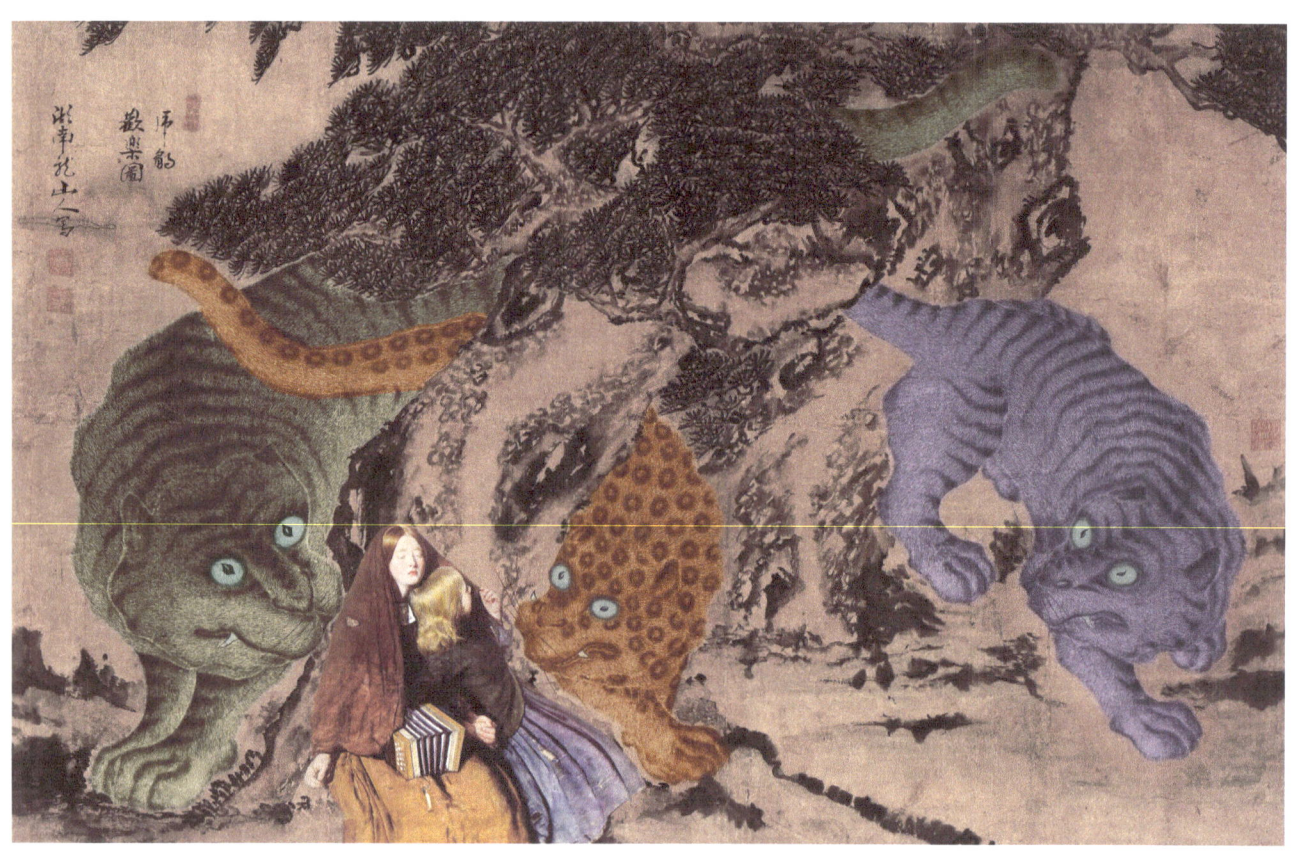

East #36

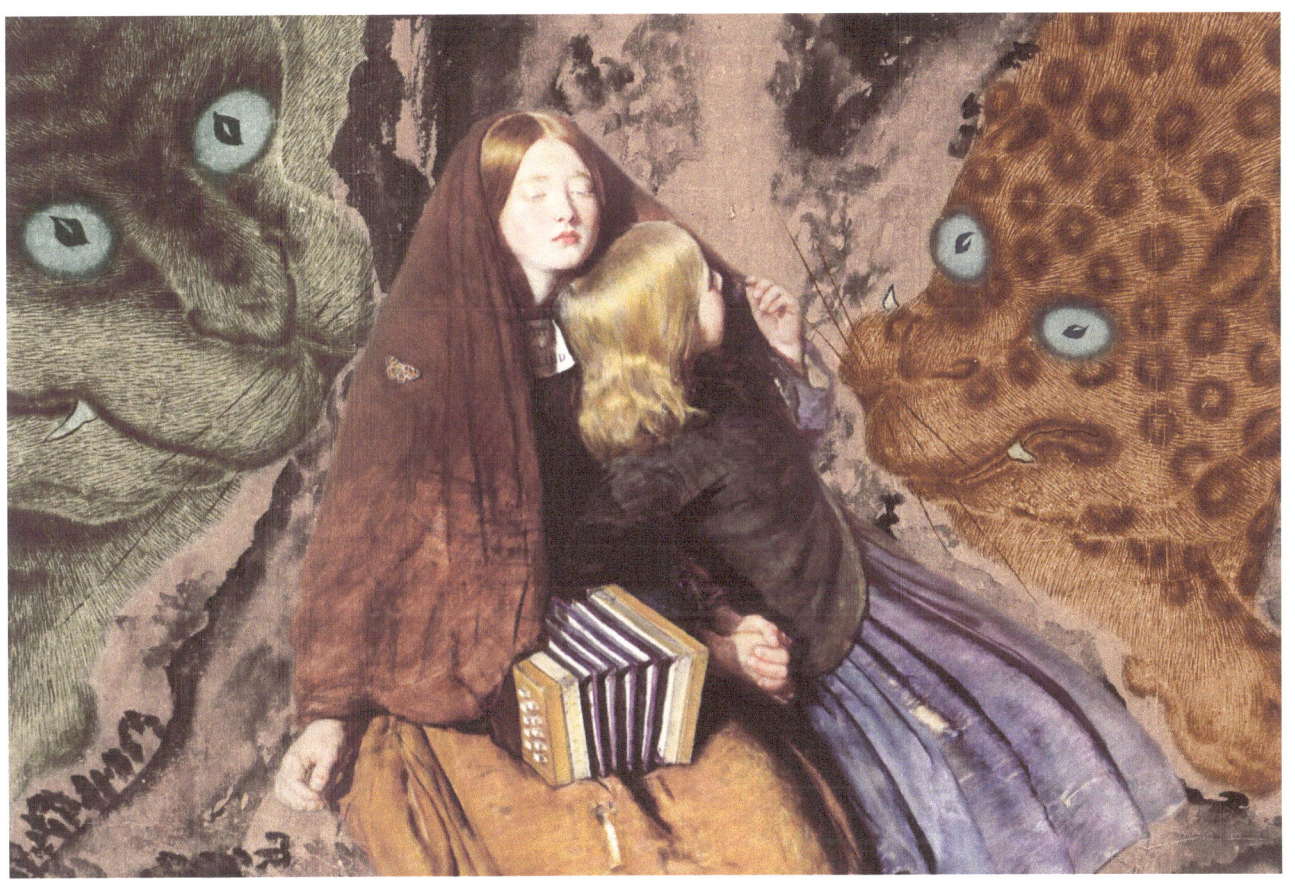

East #36 (detail)

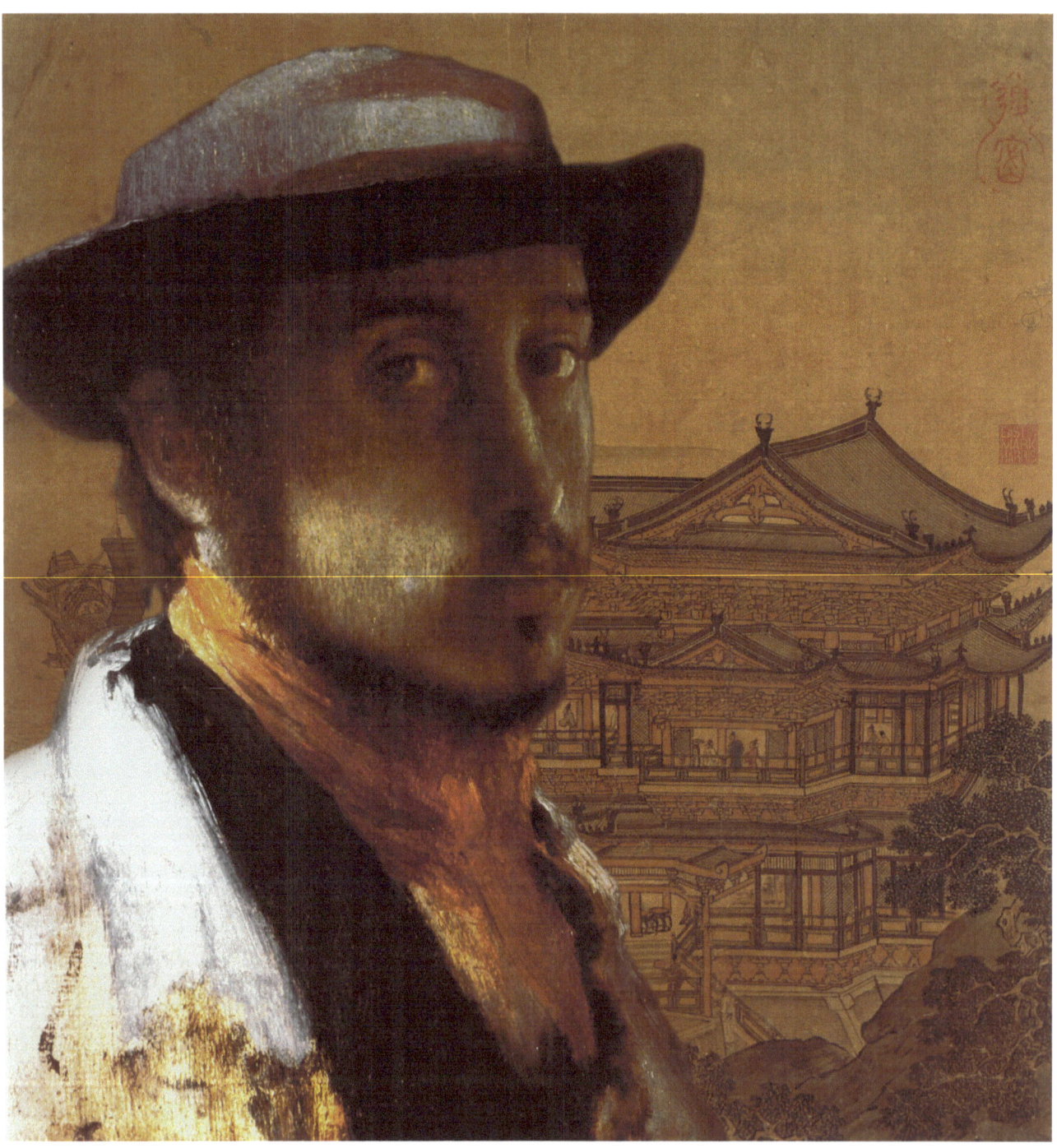

East #37

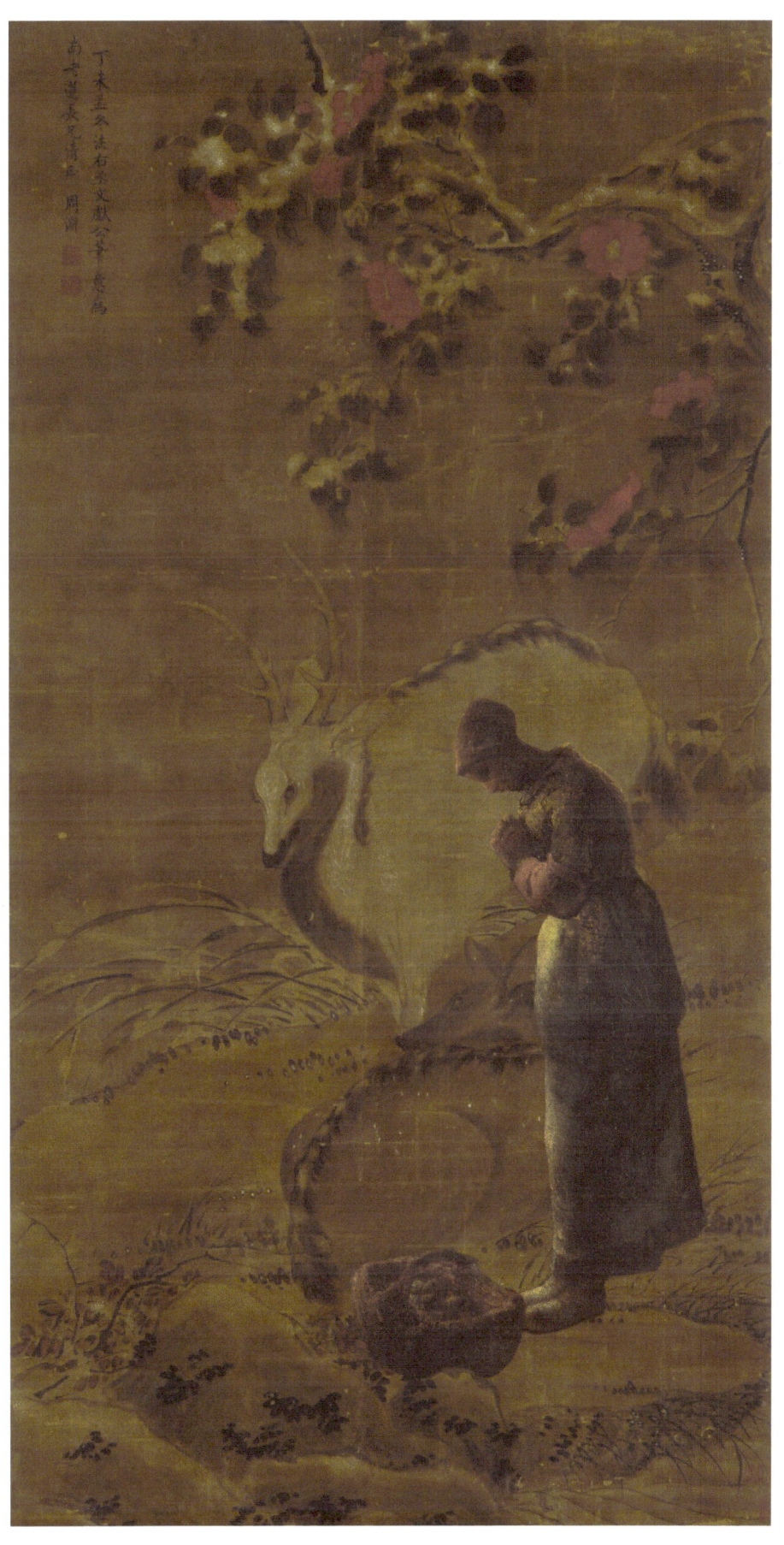

East #38

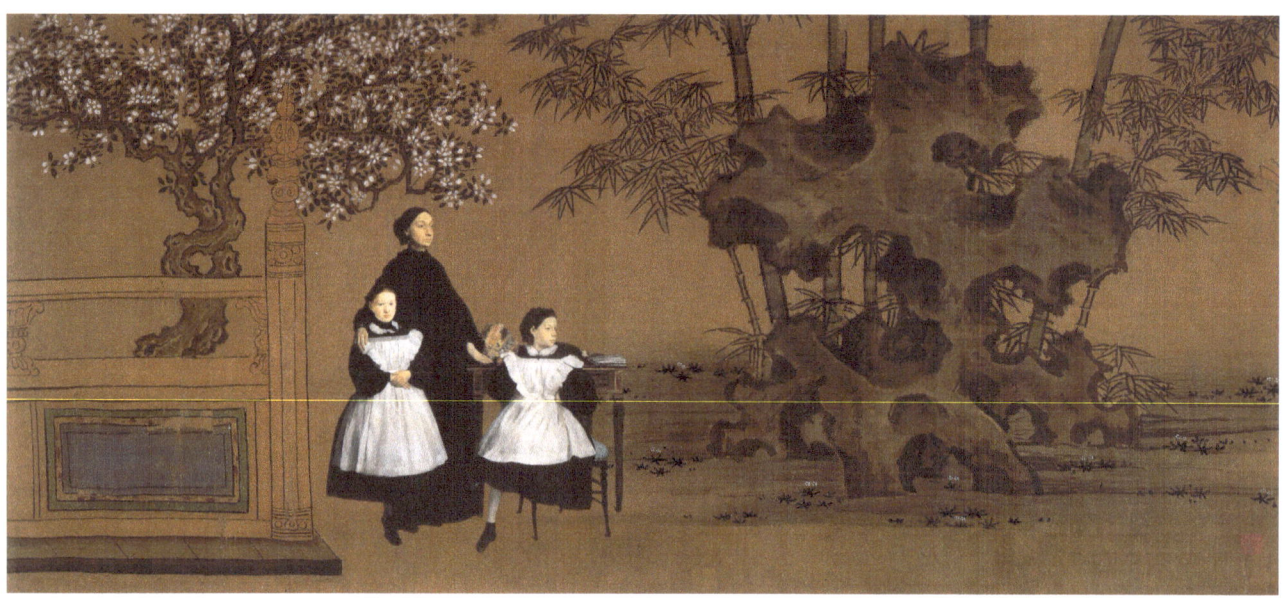

East #39

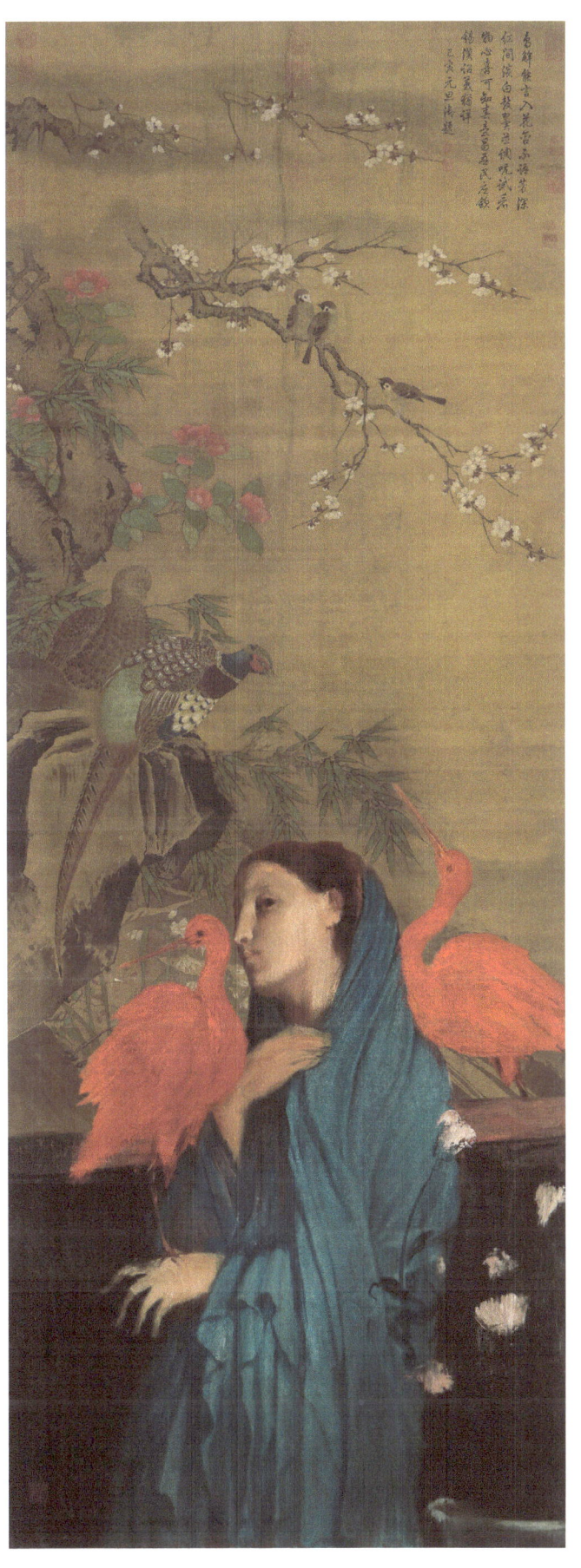

East #40

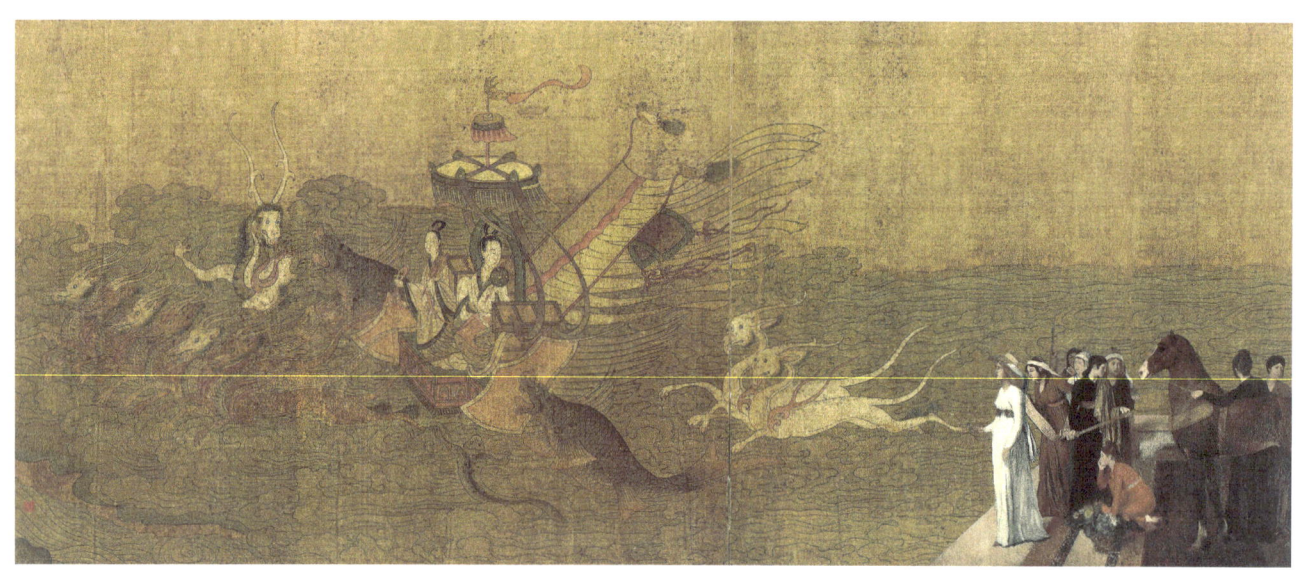

East #41

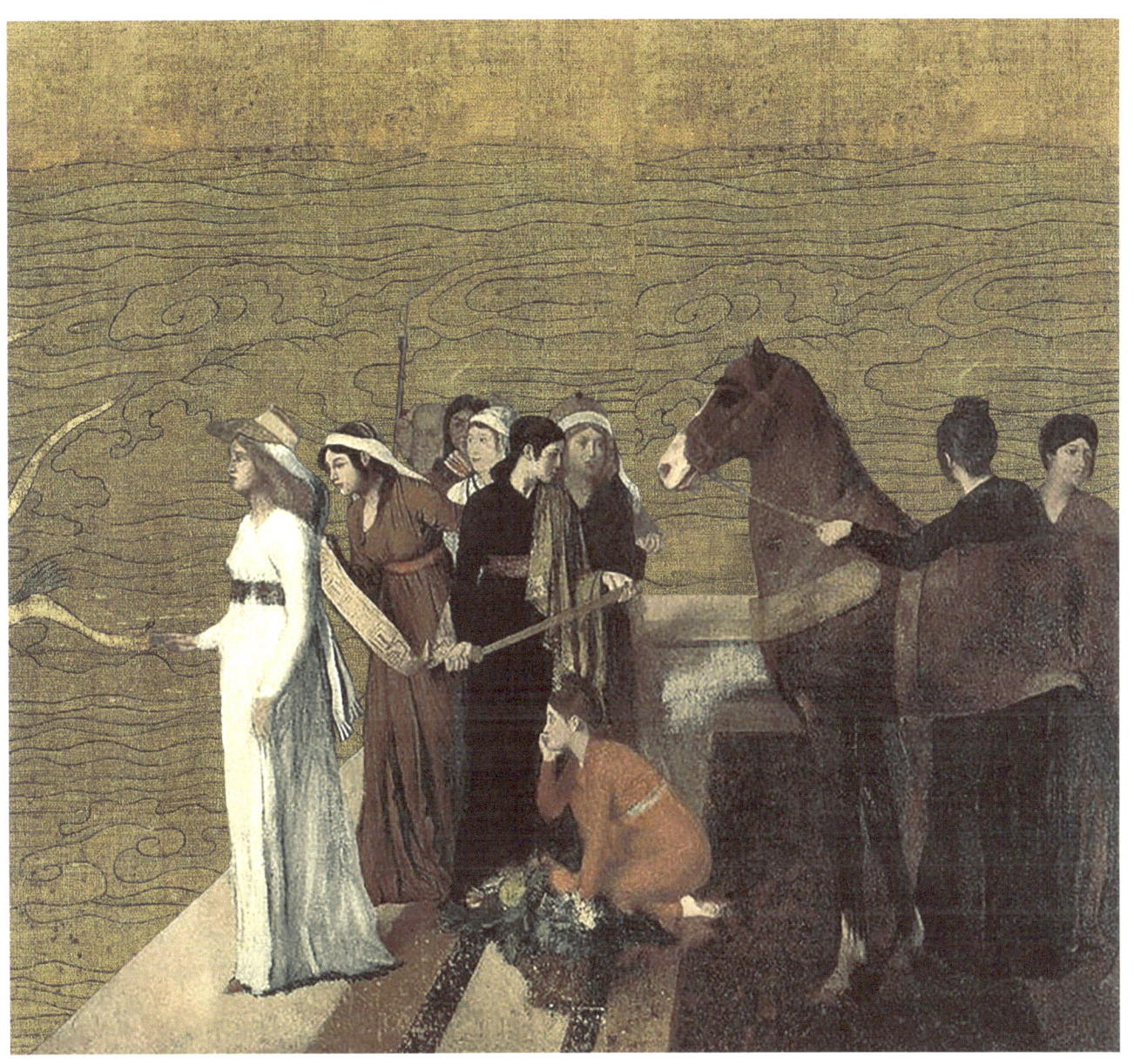

East #41 (detail)

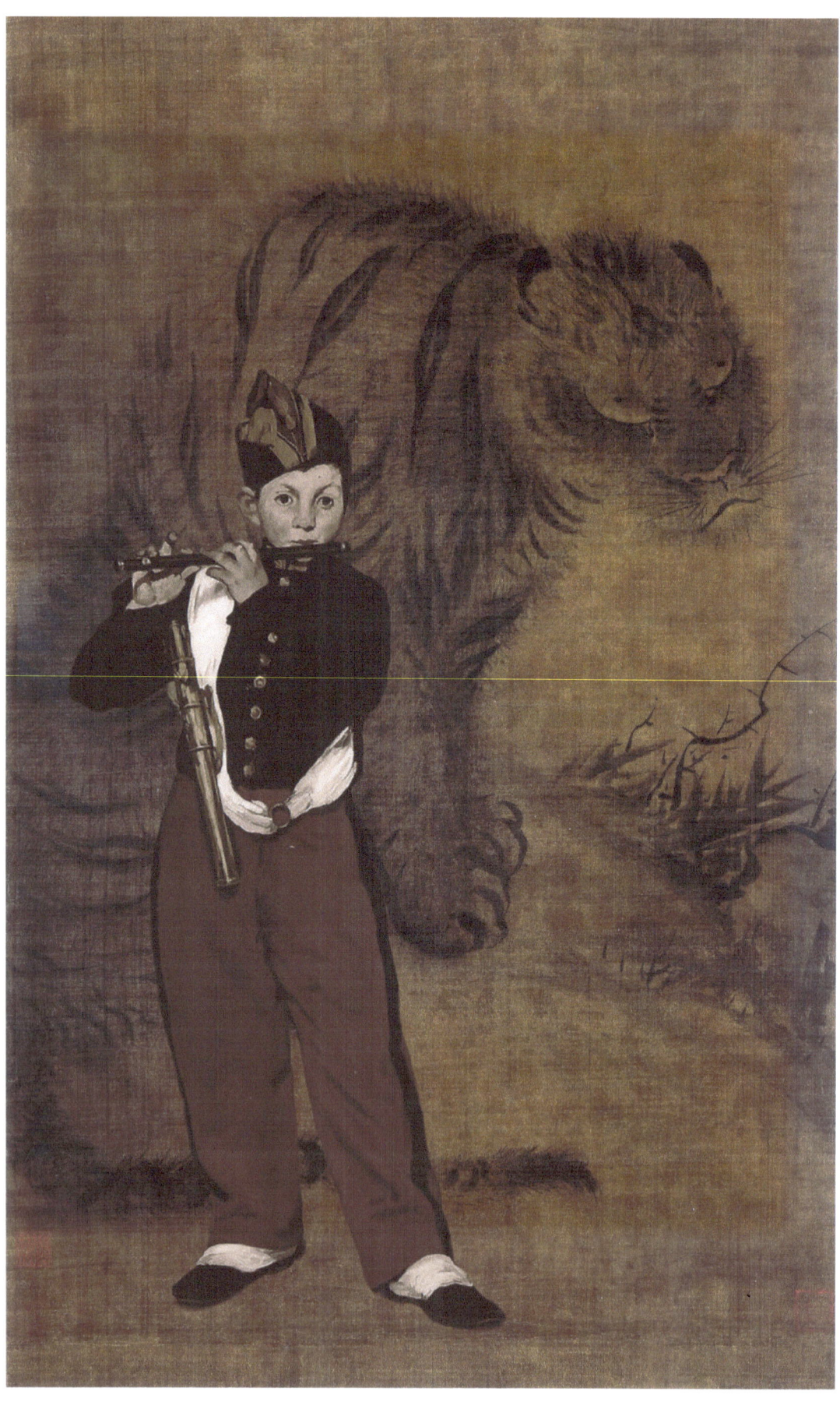

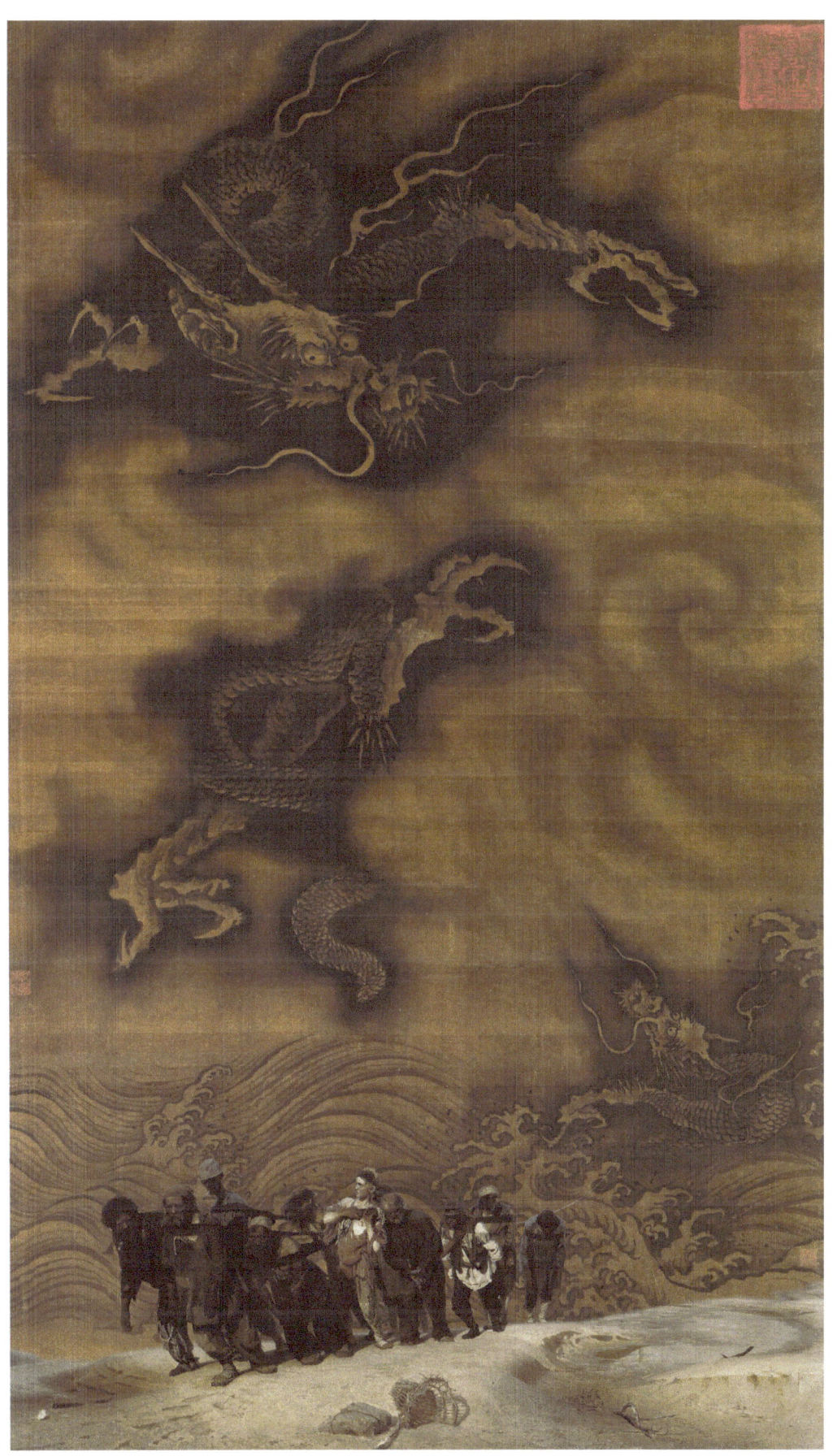

East #43

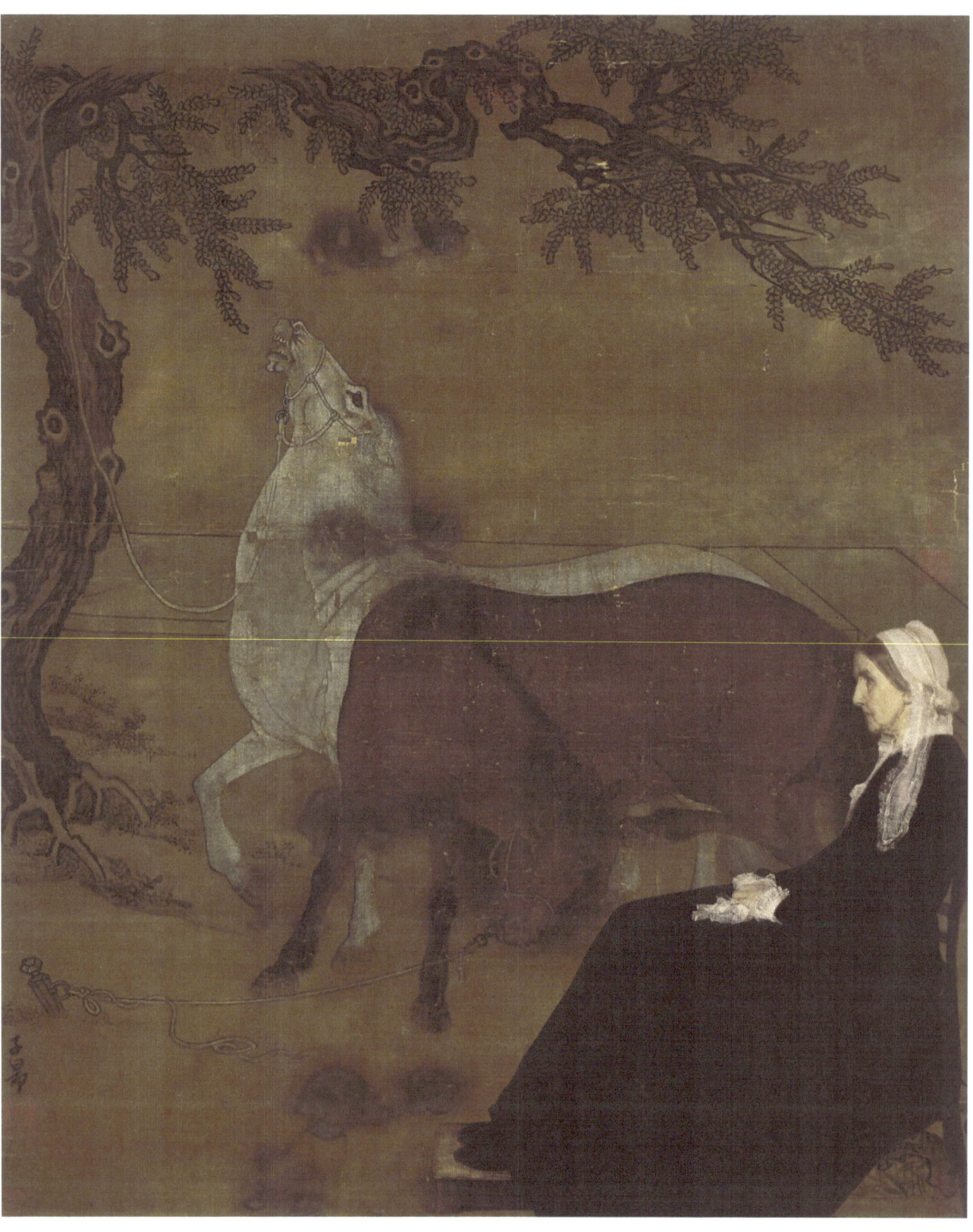

East #44

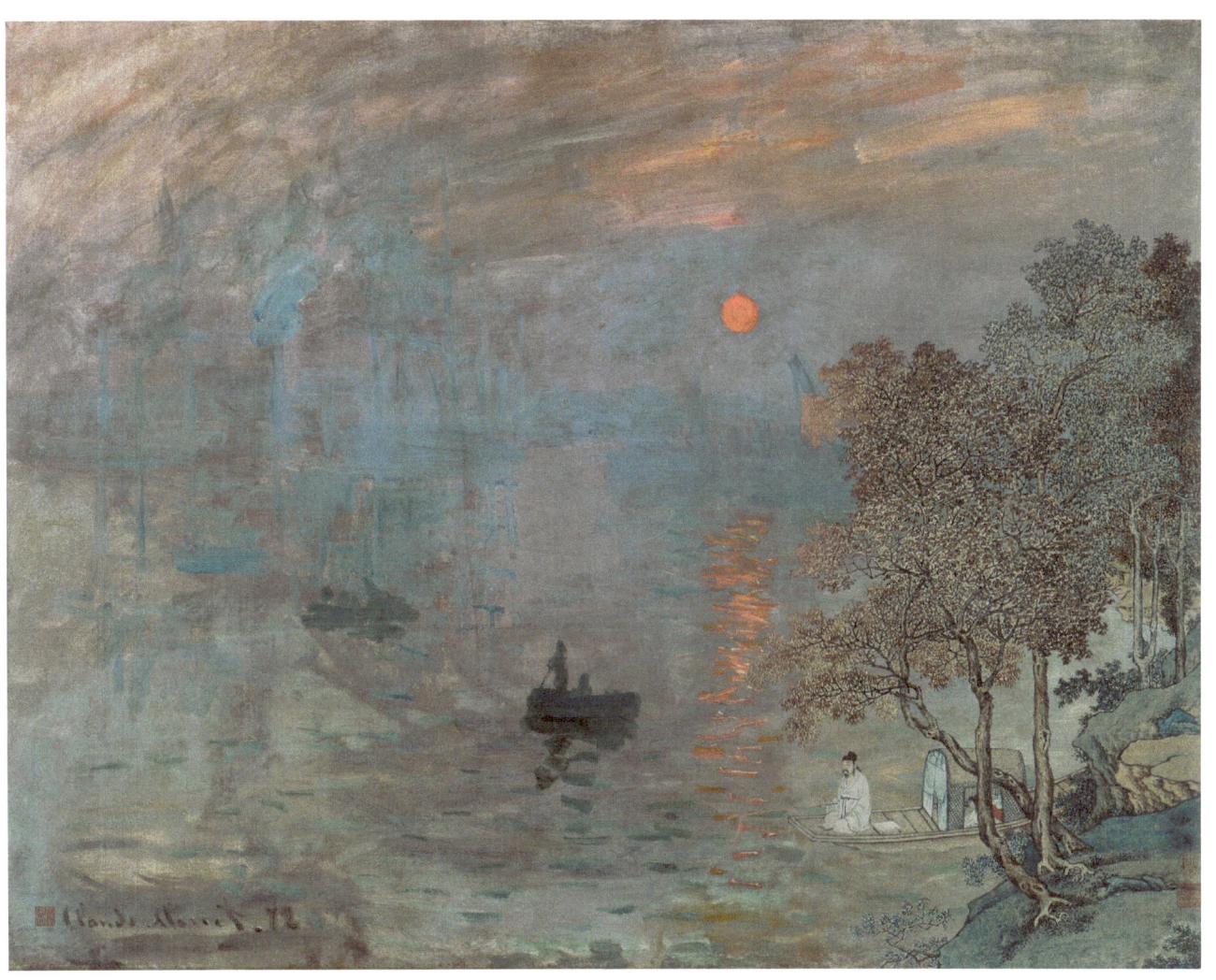

East #45

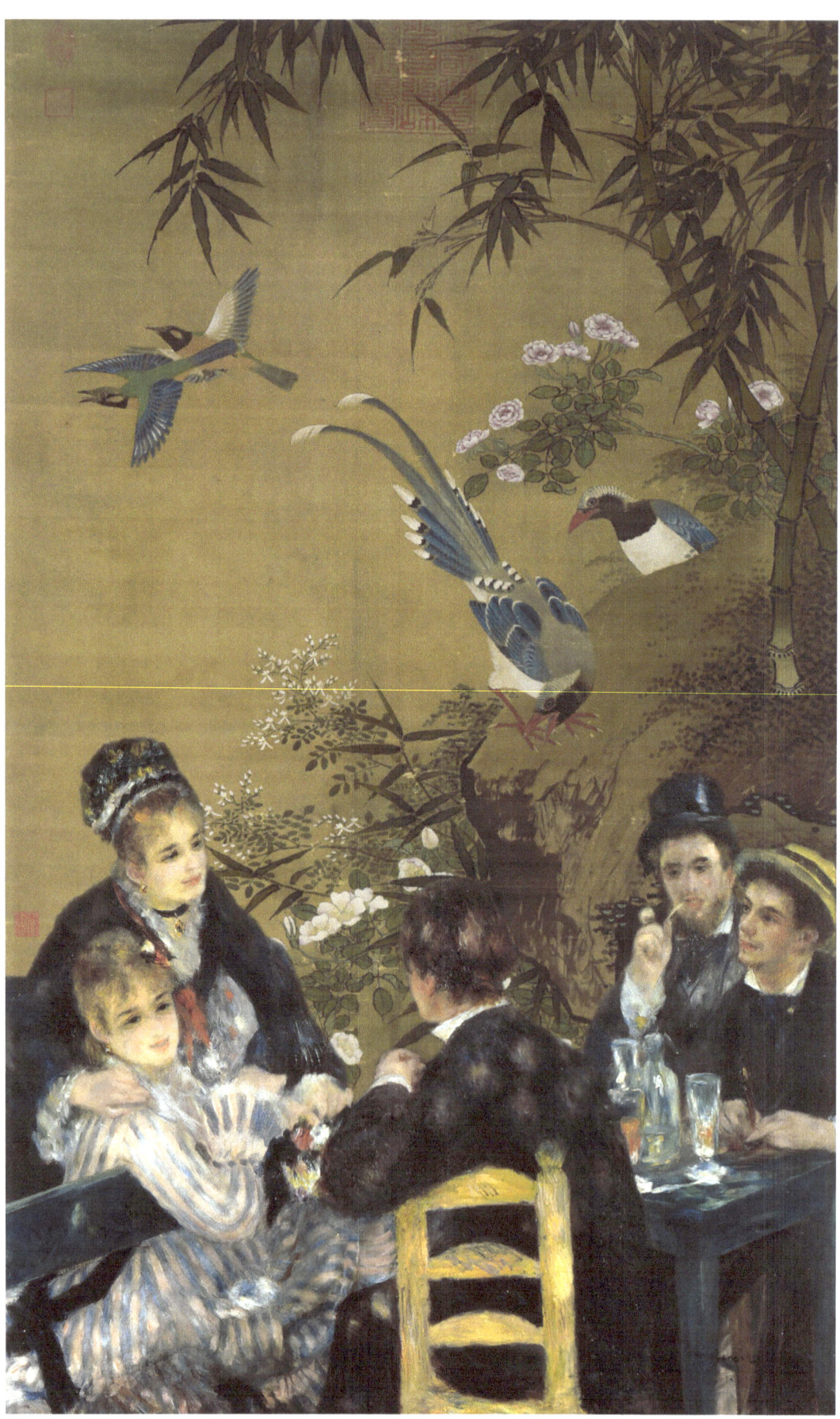

East #46

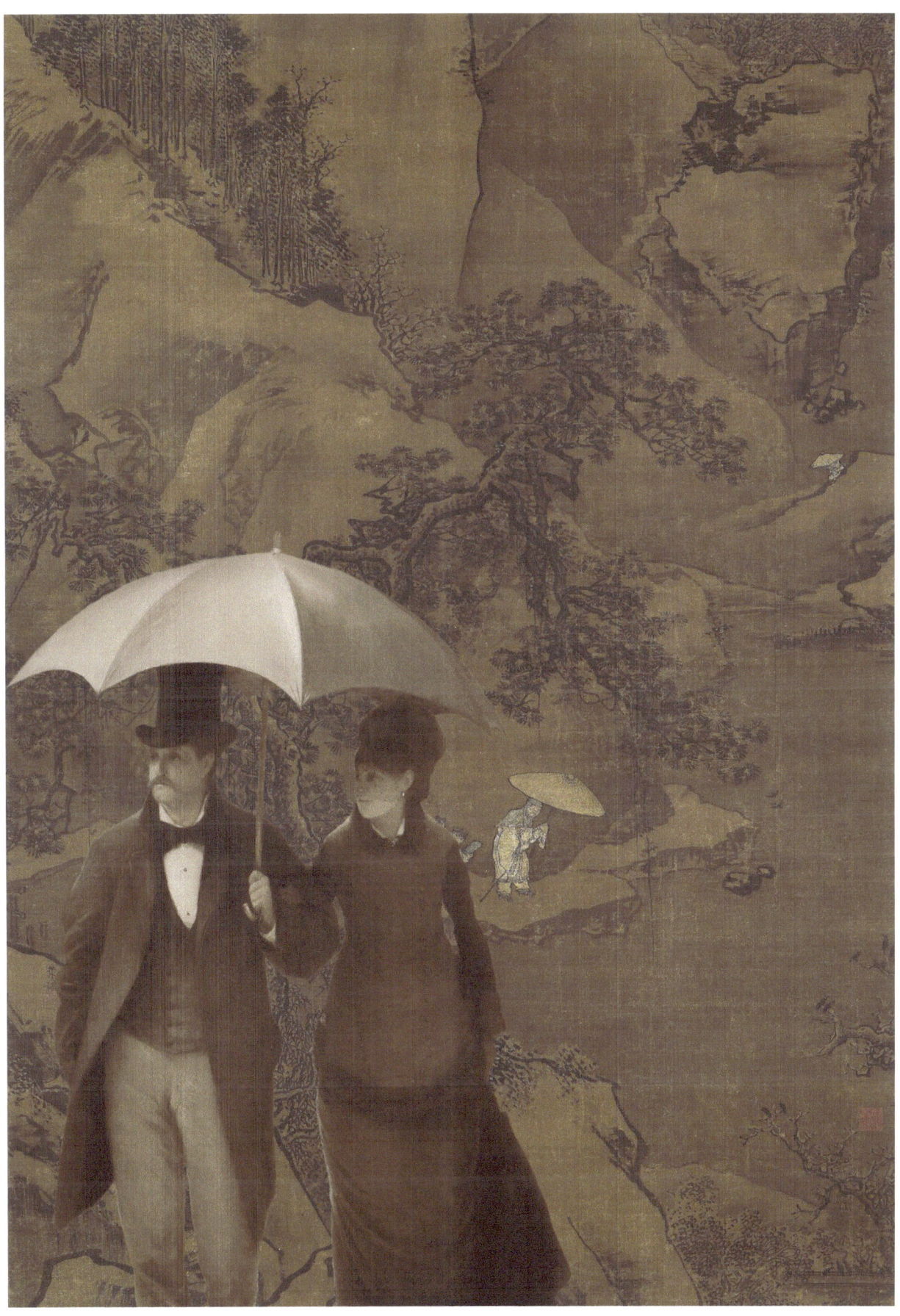

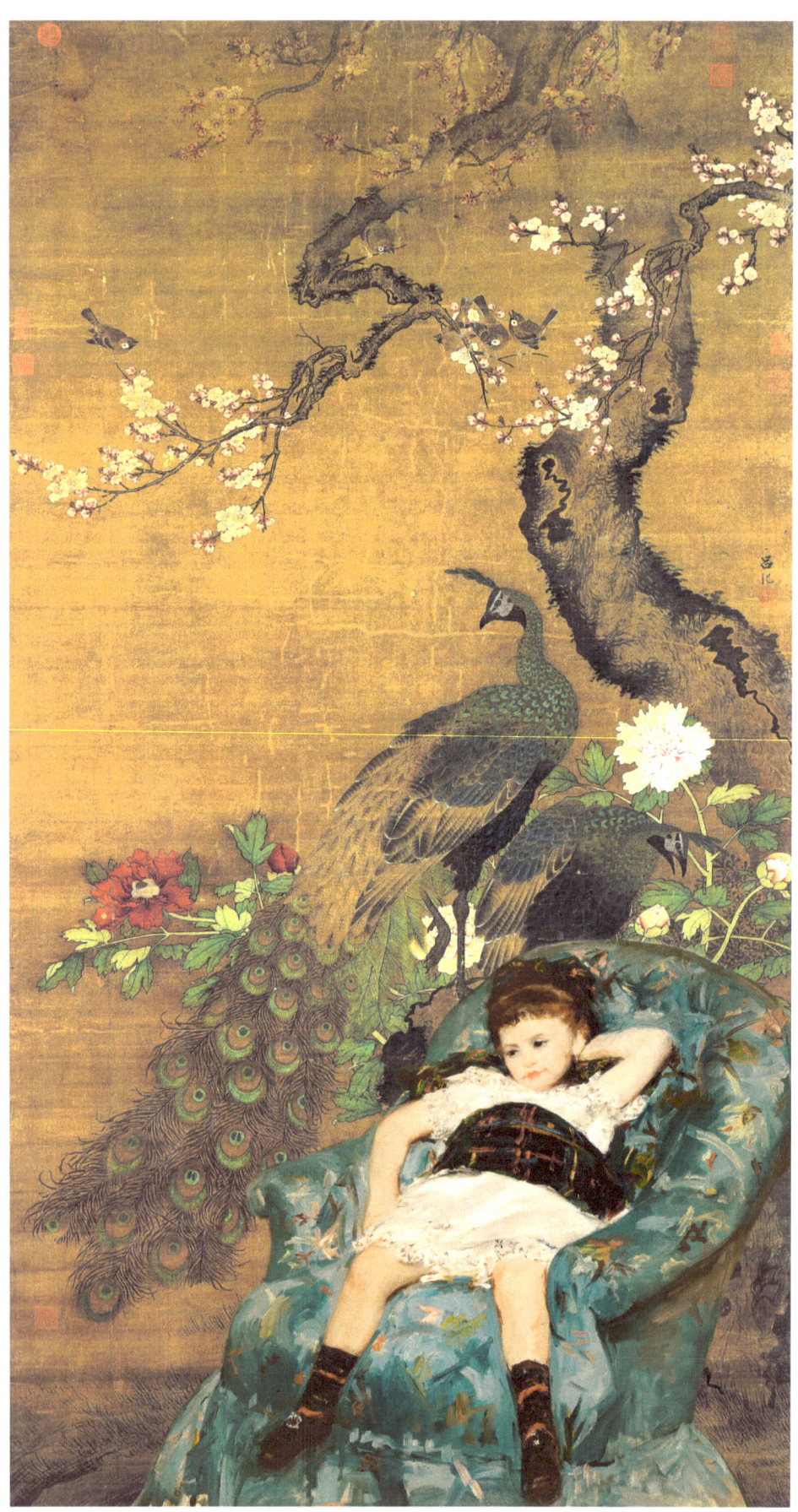

East #48

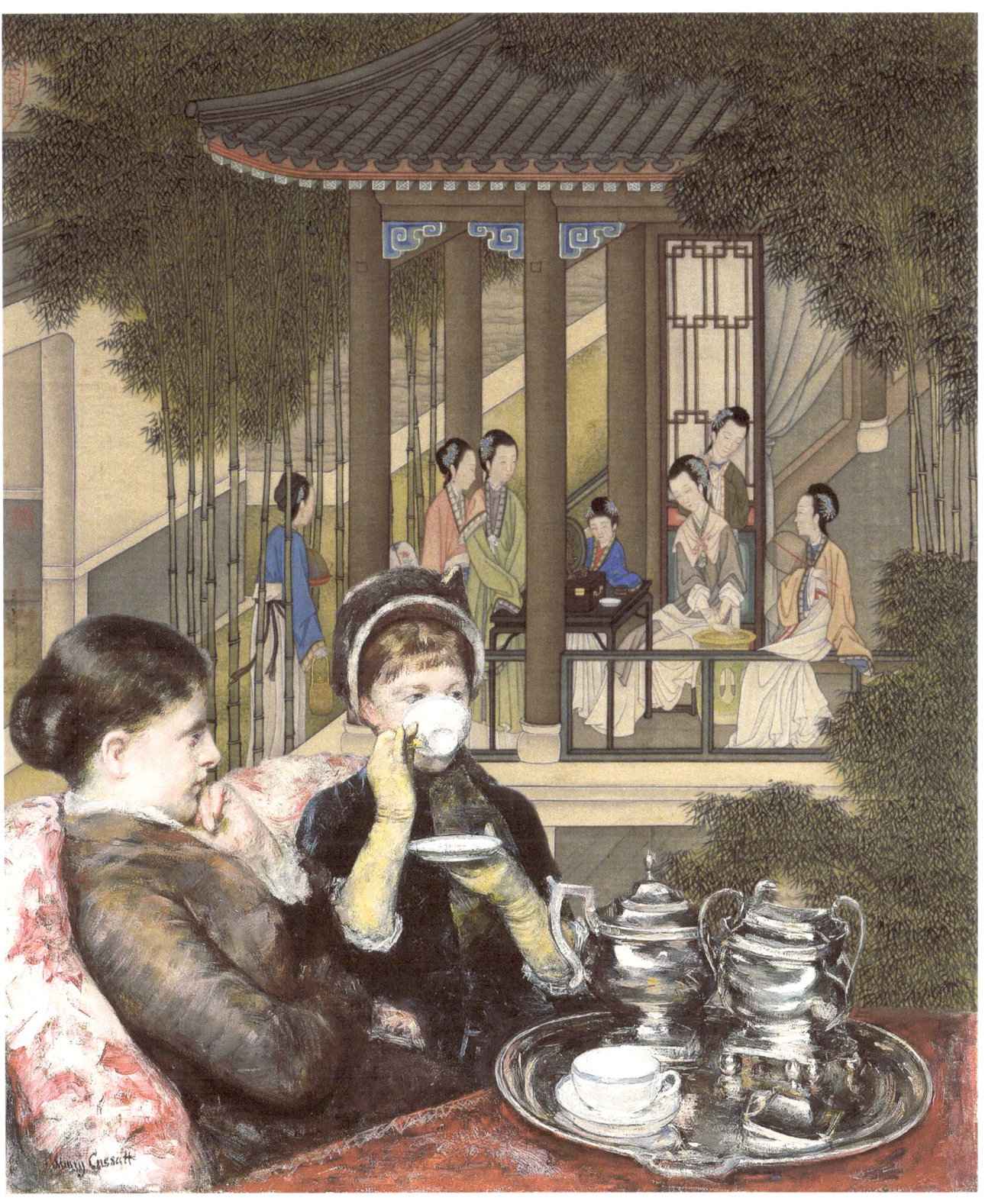

East #49

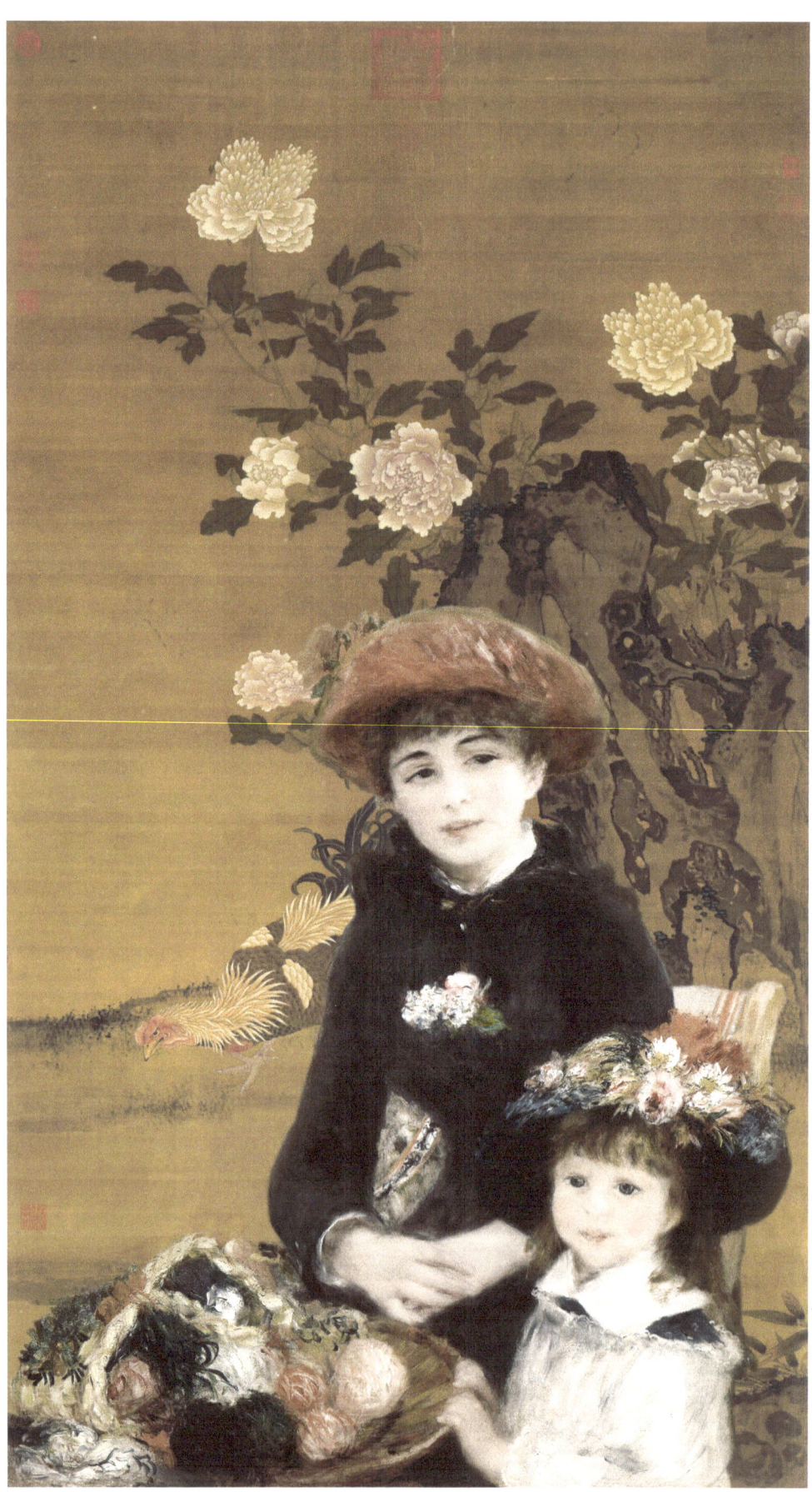

East #50

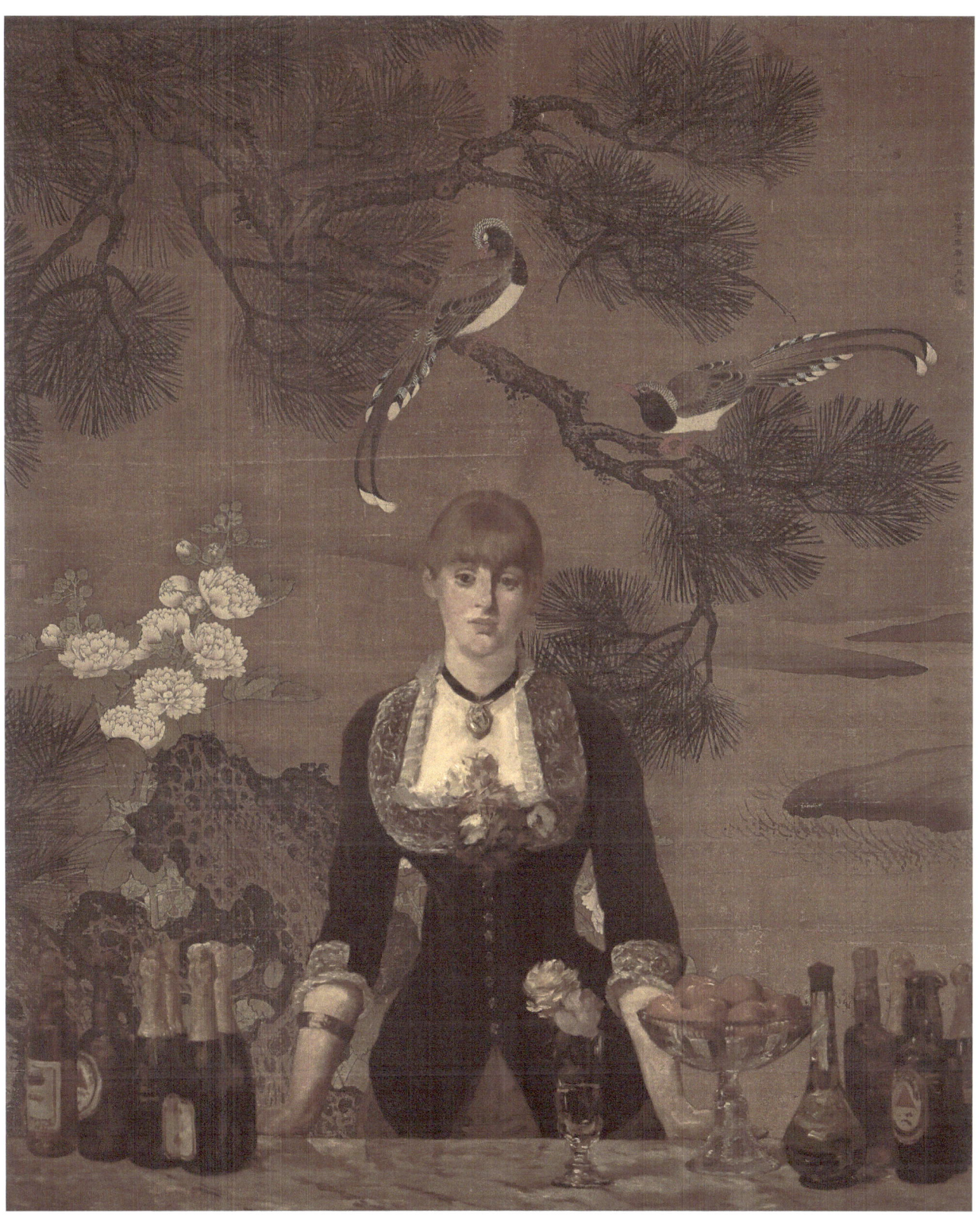

East #51

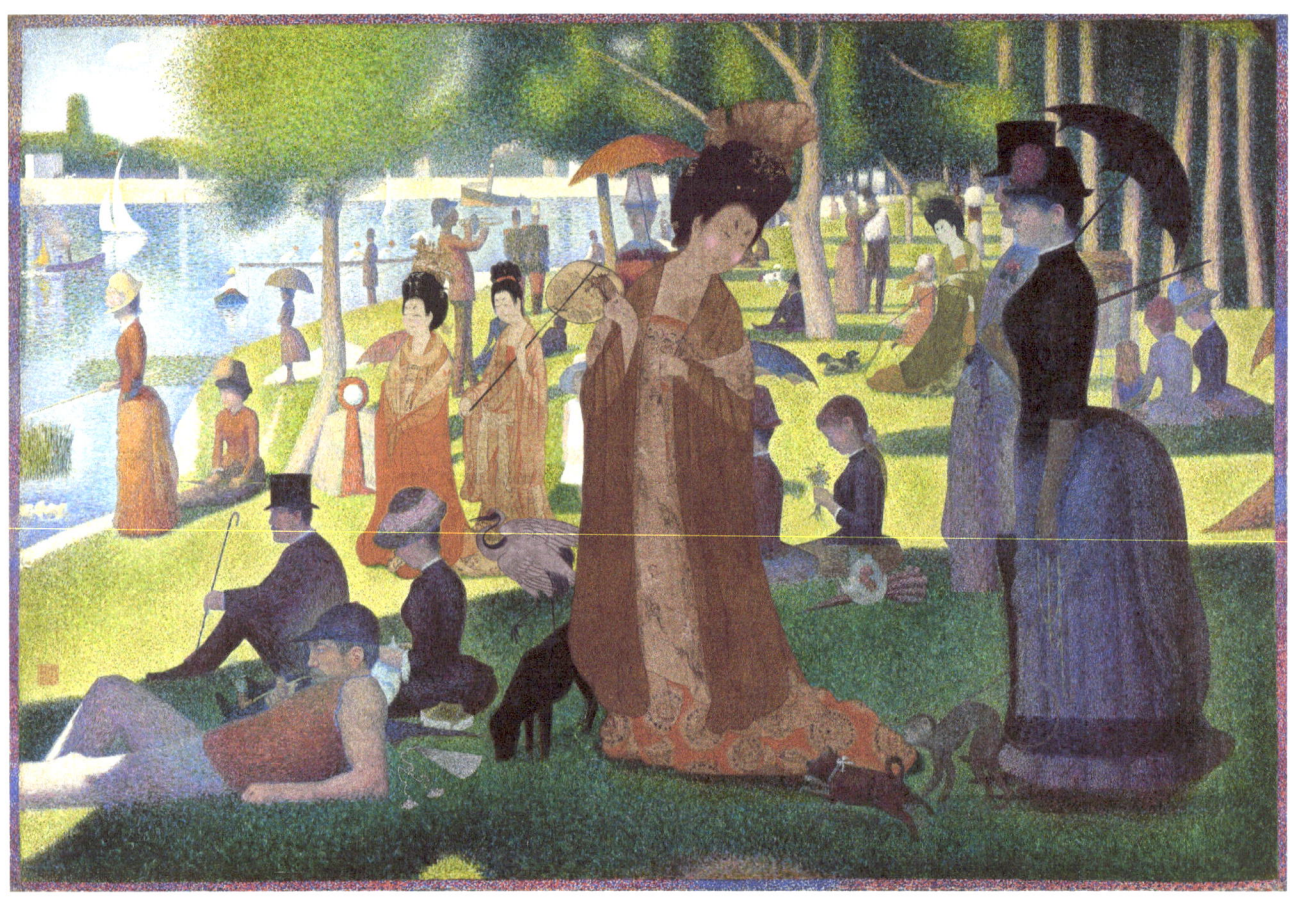

East #52

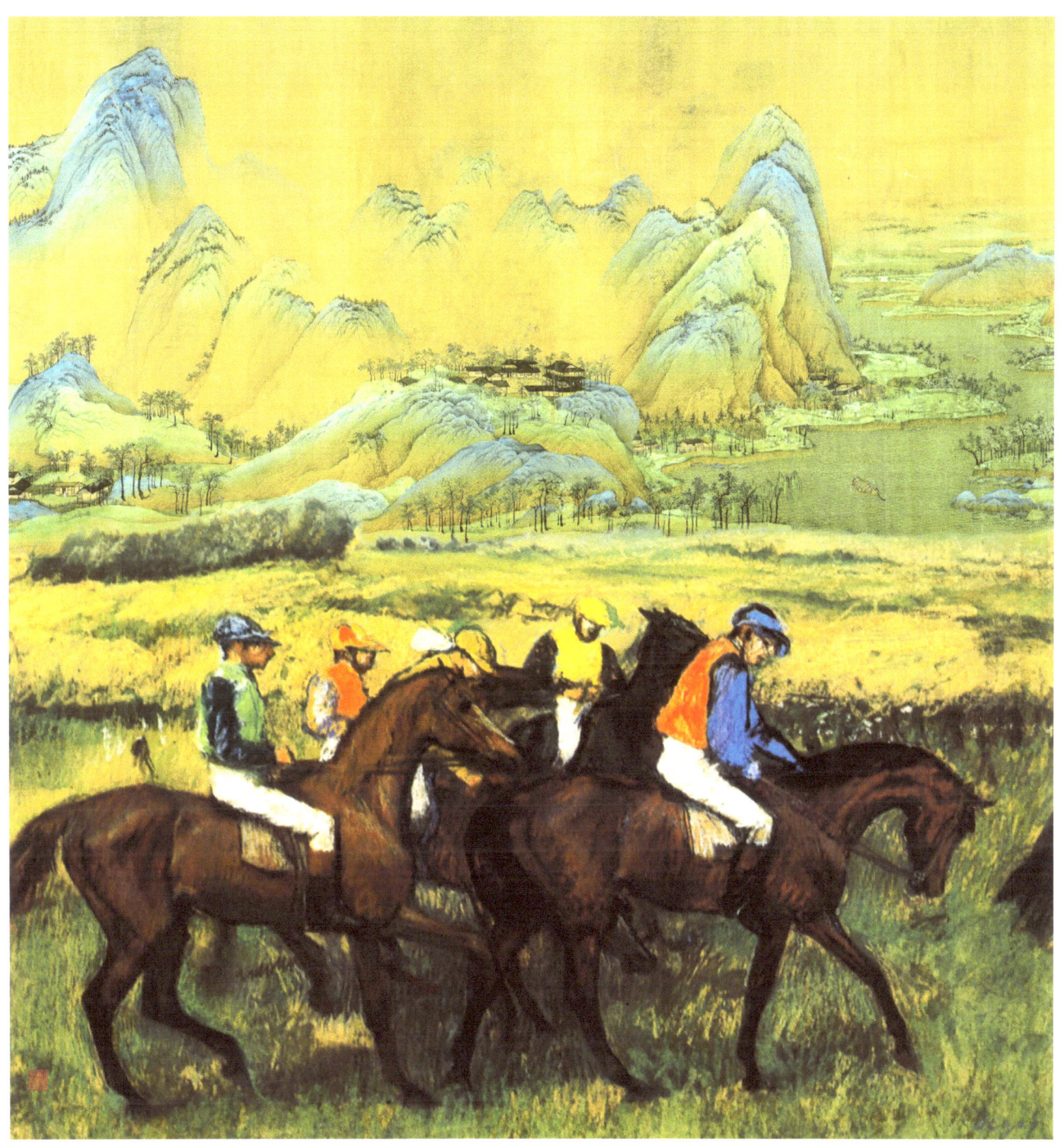

East #53

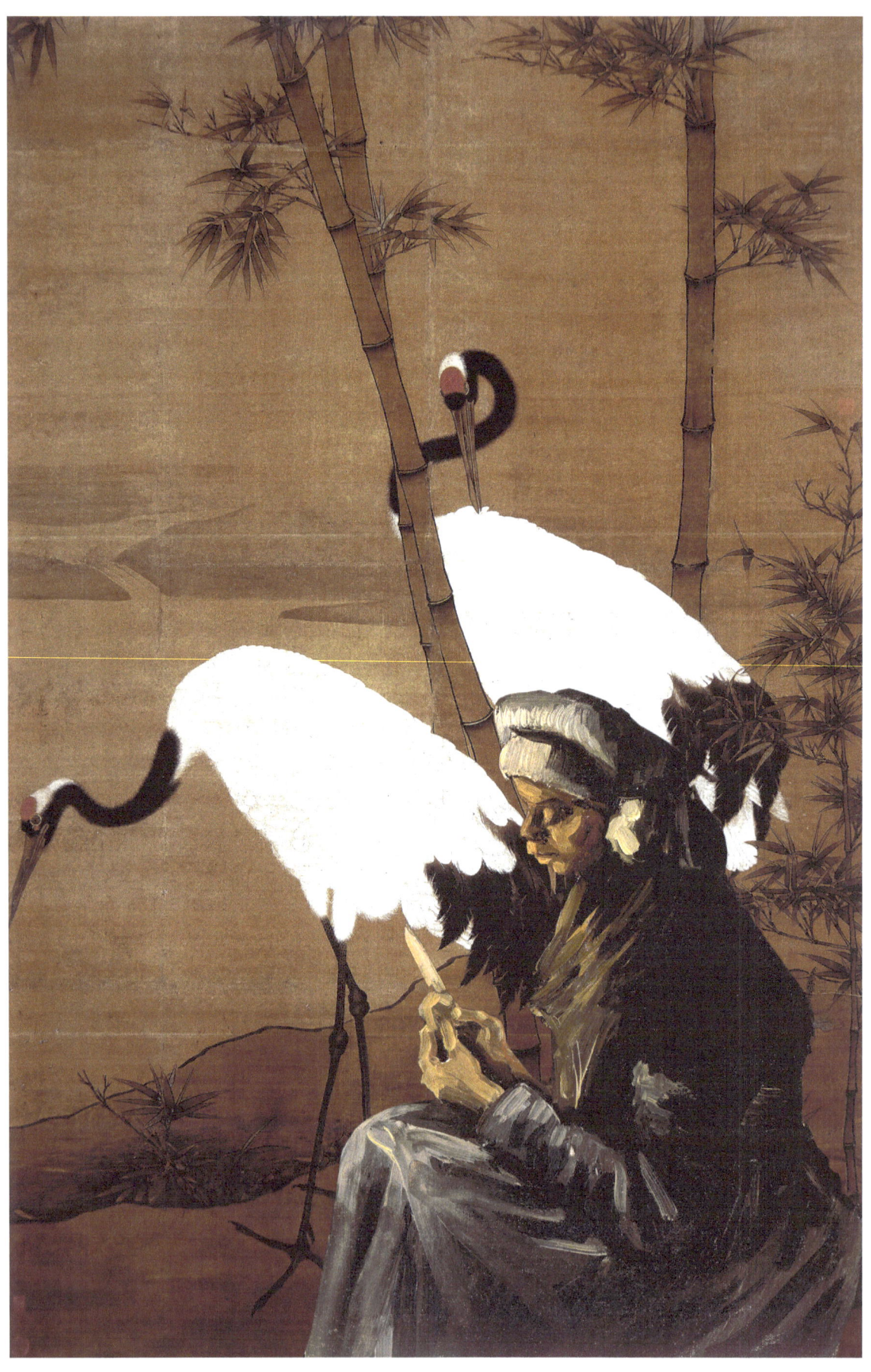

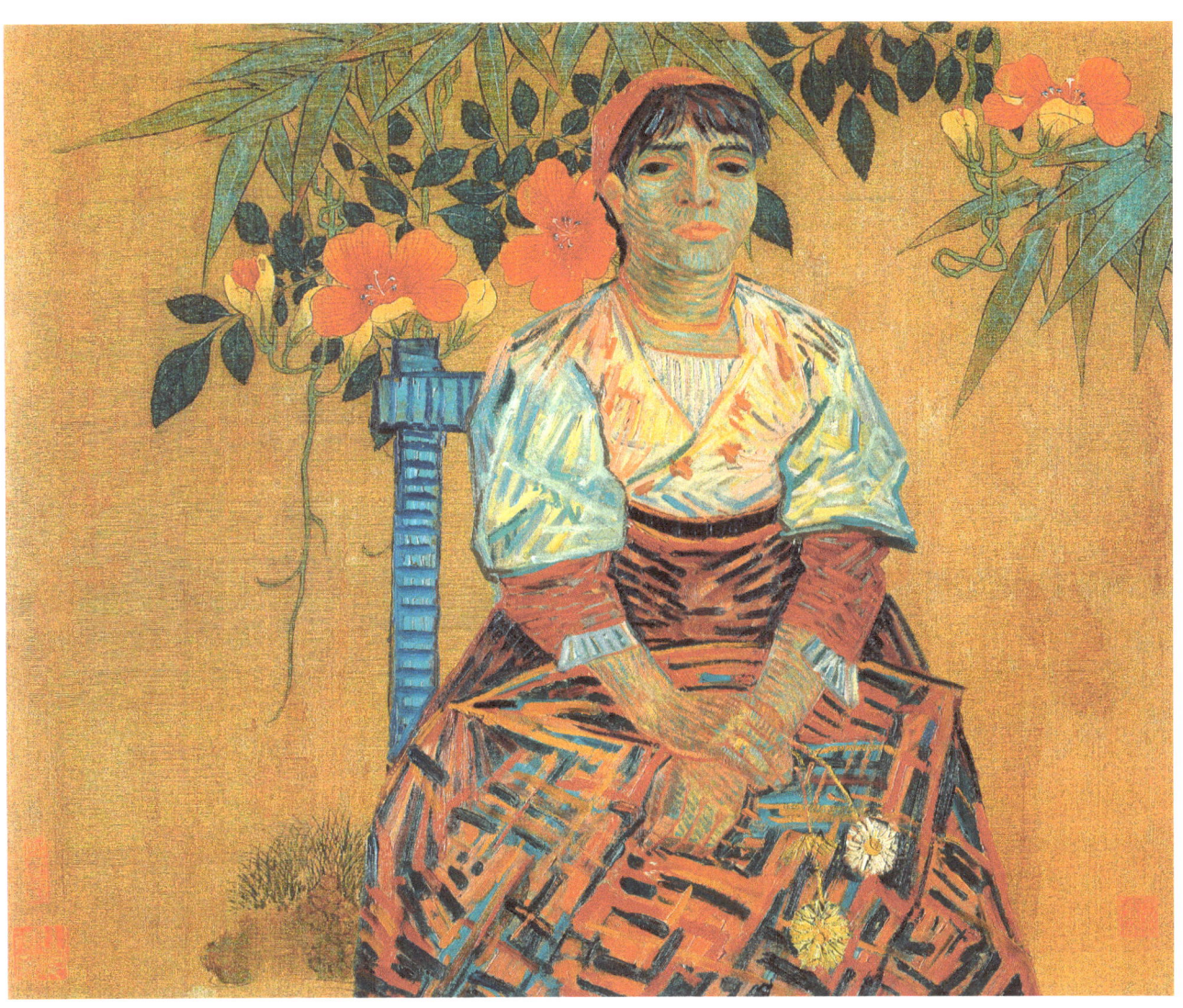

East #55

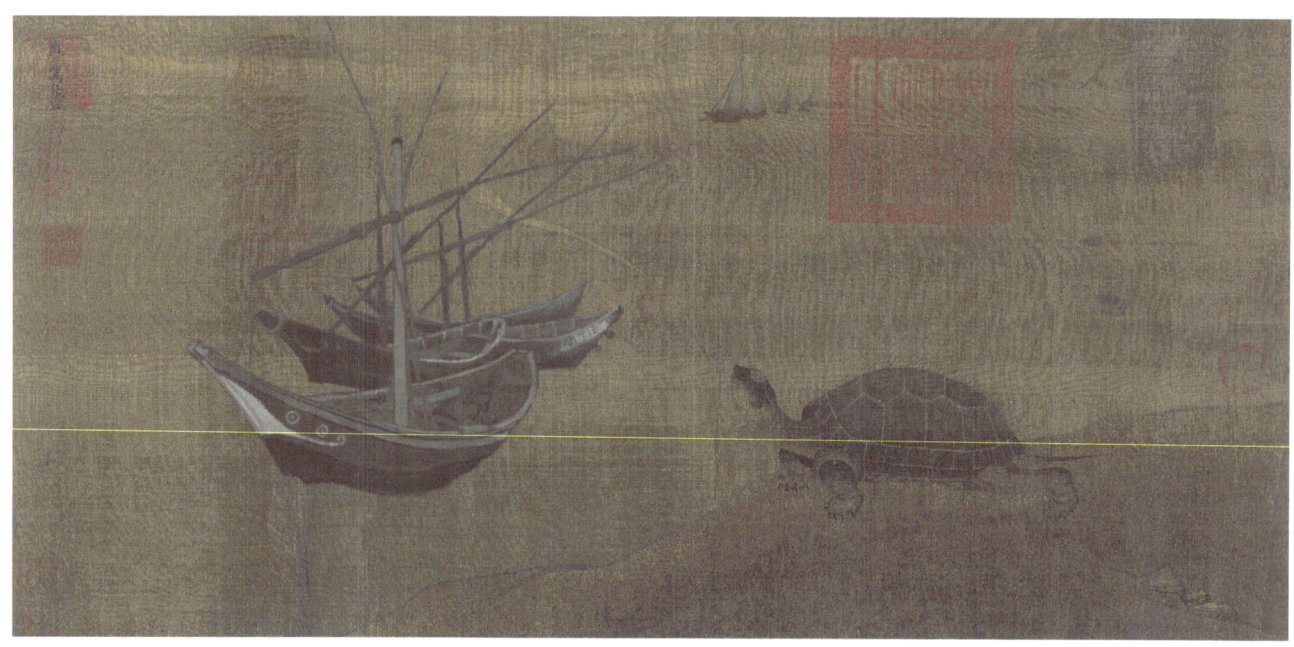

East #56

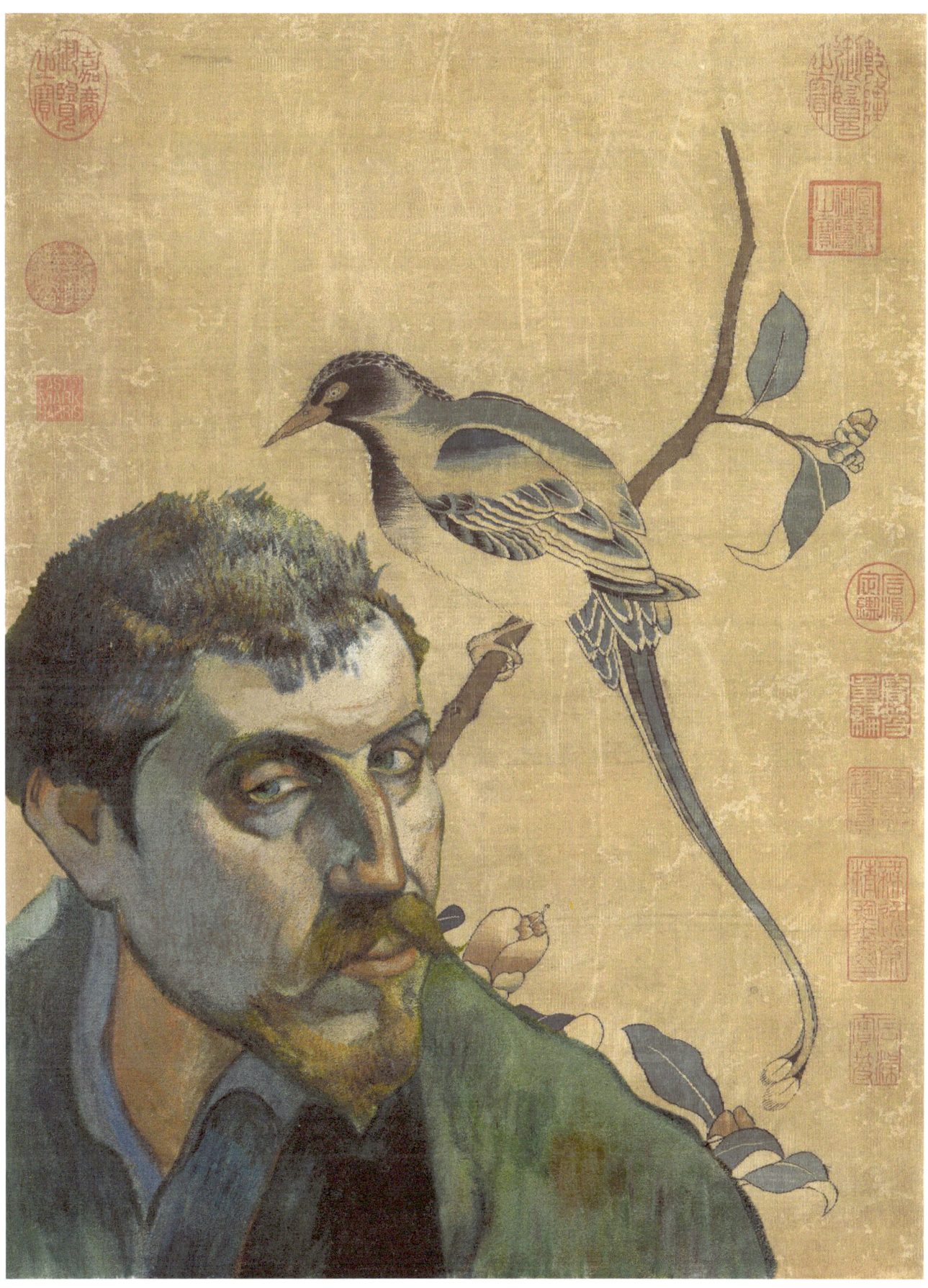

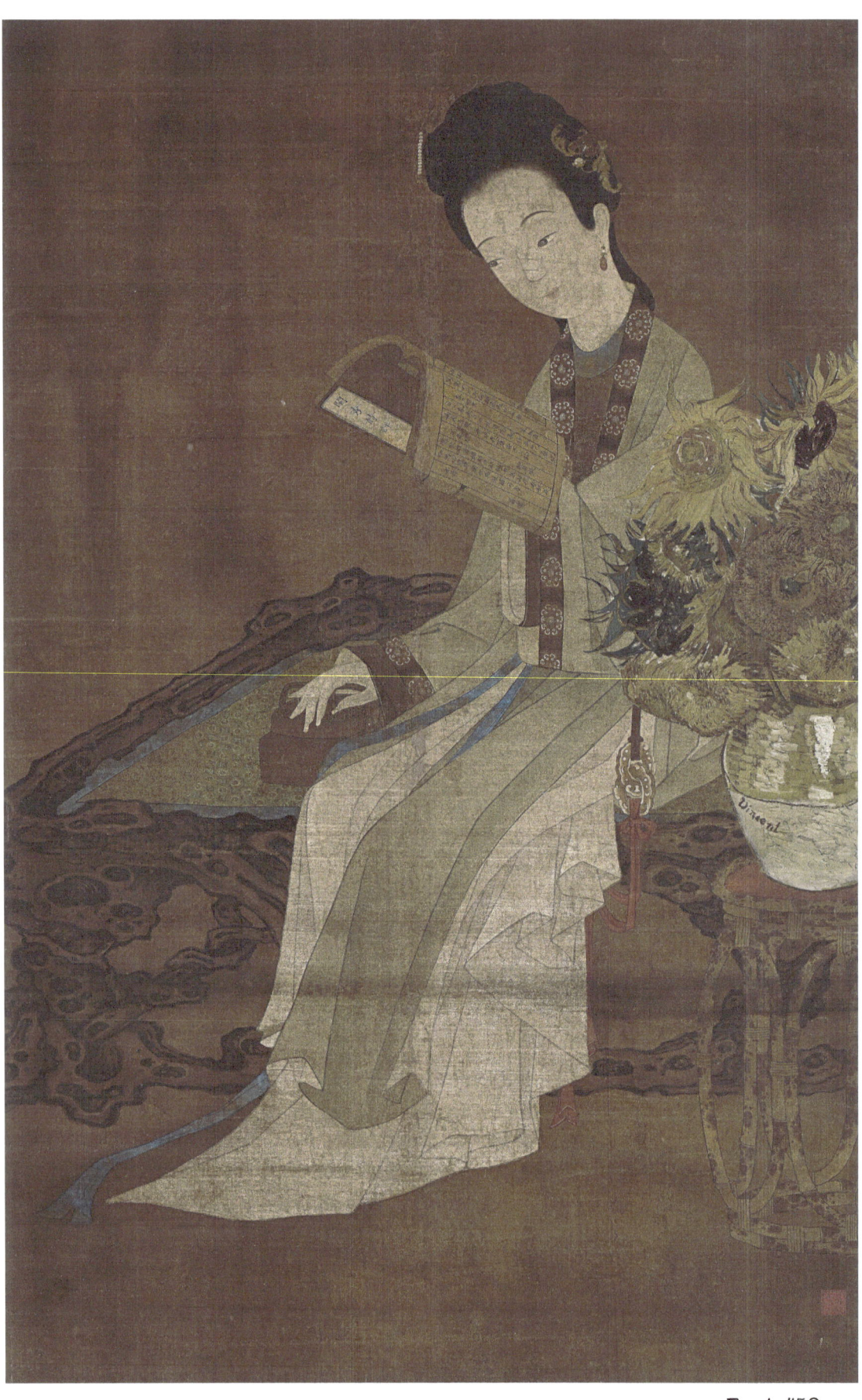

East #58

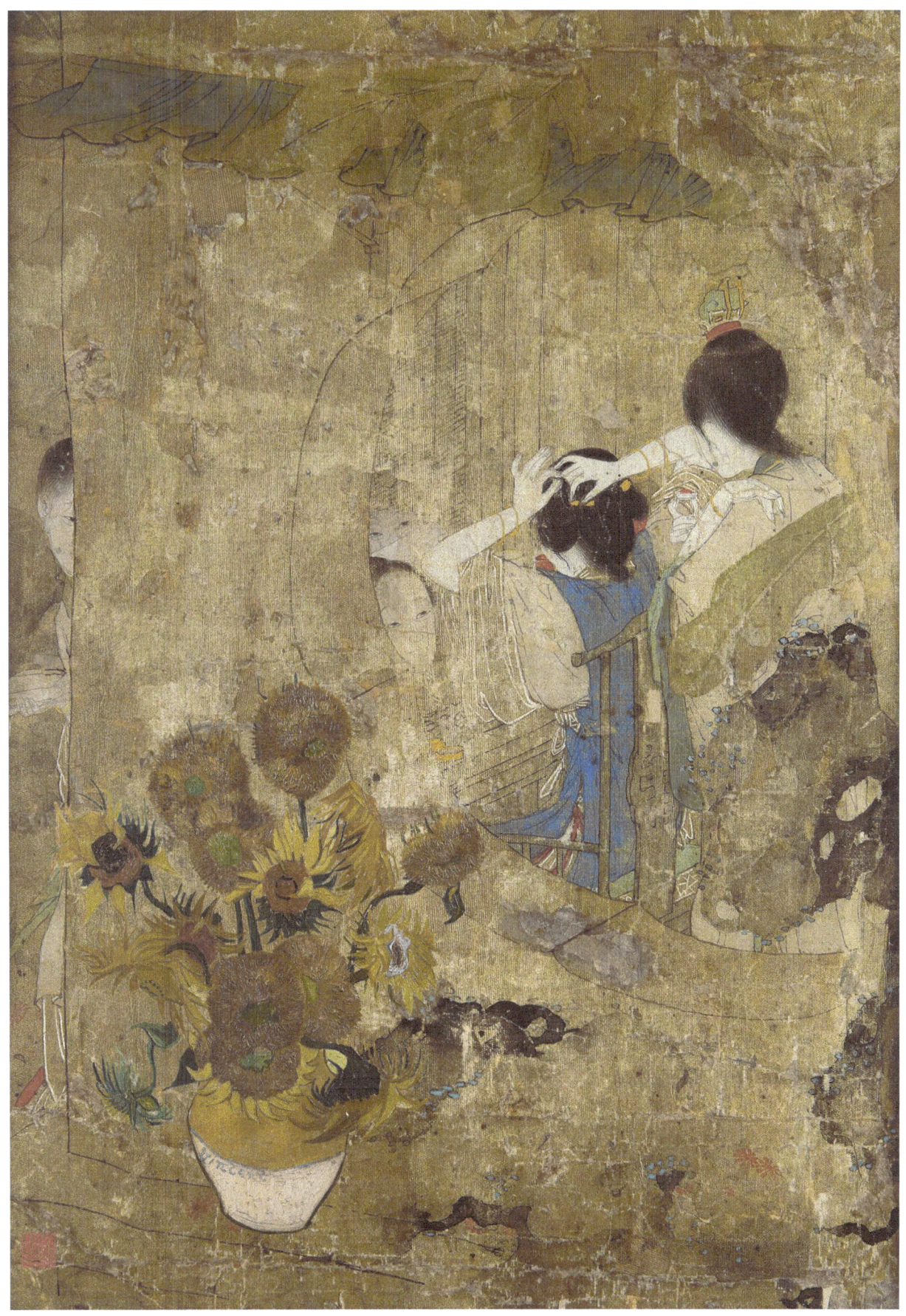

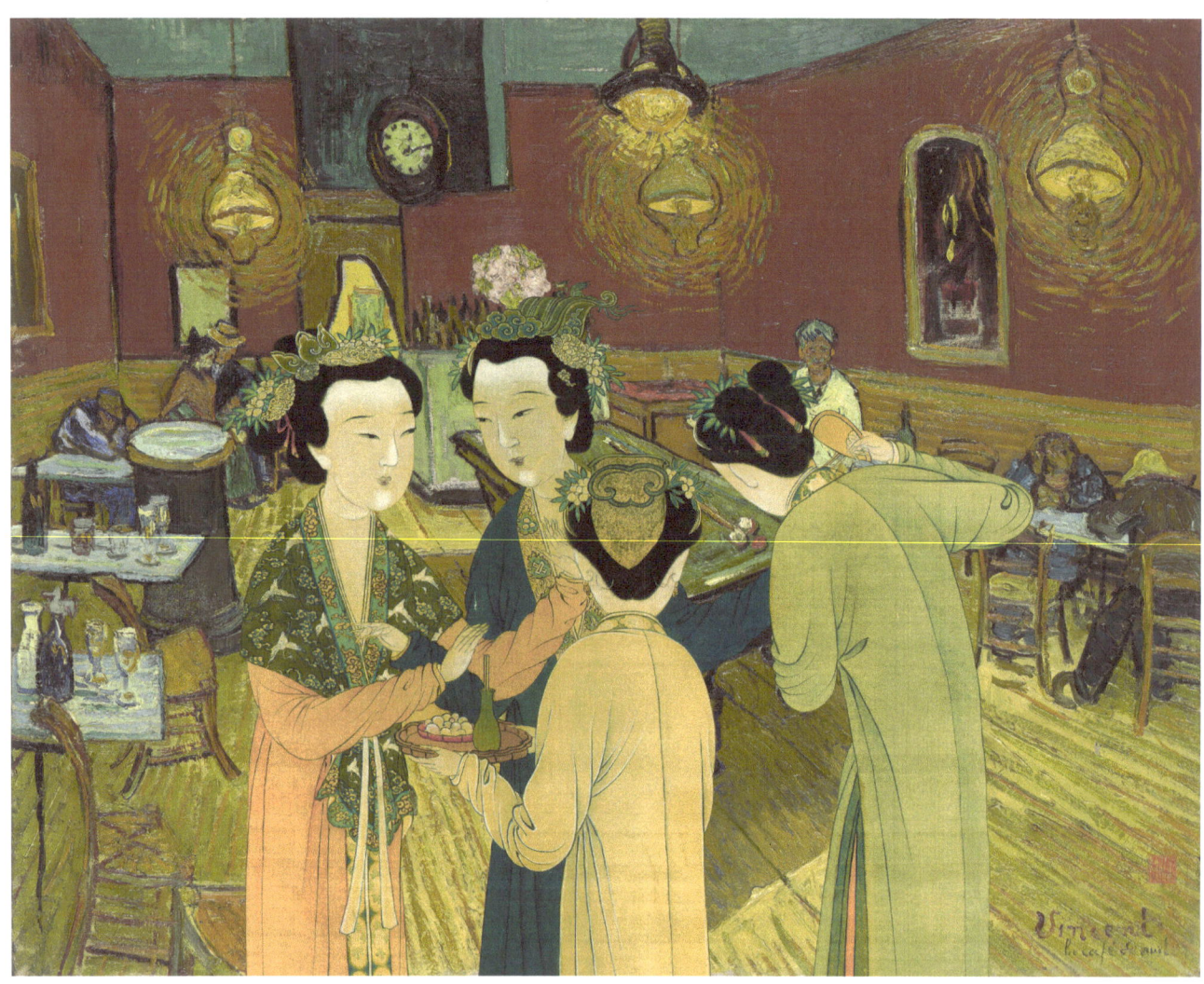

East #60

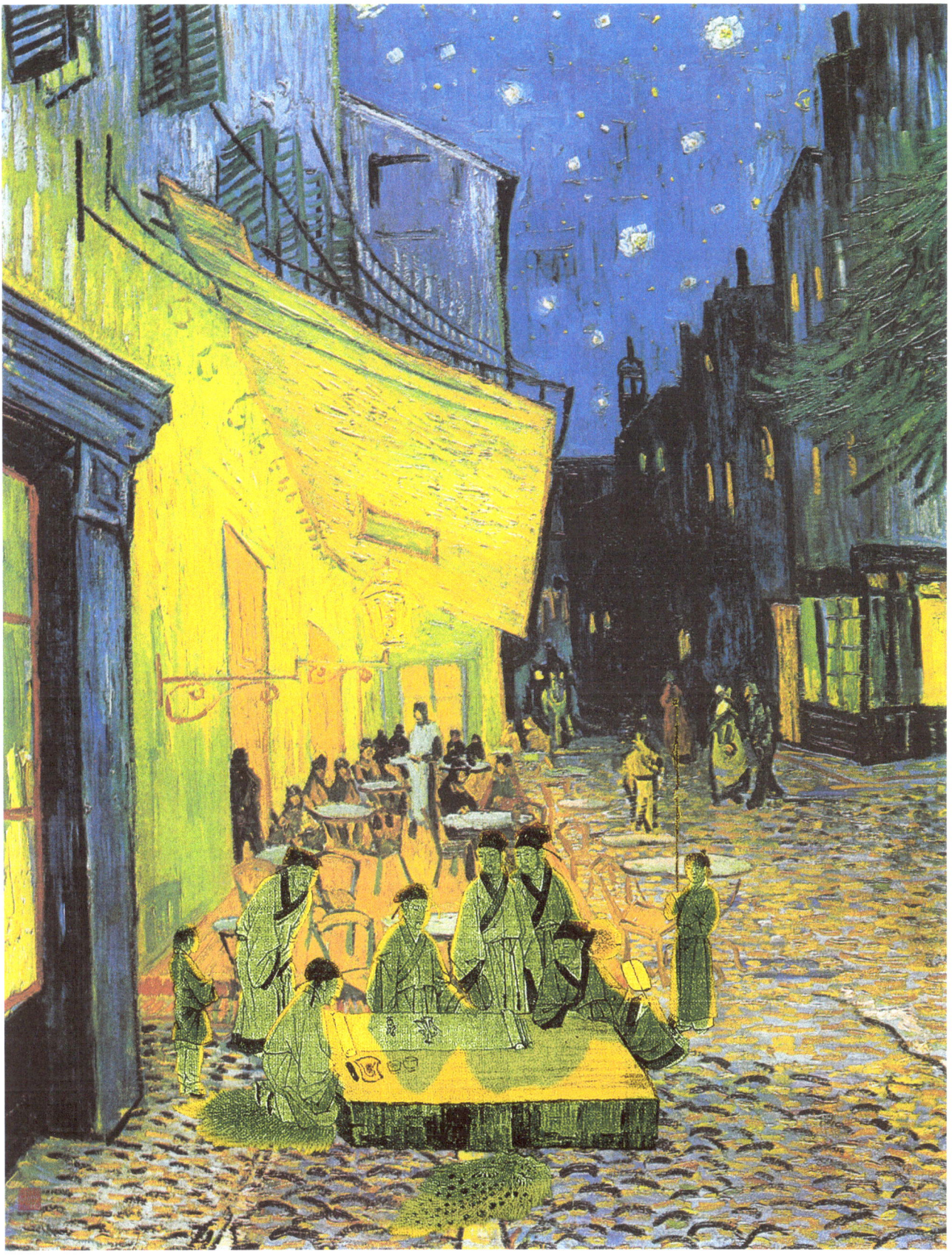

East #61

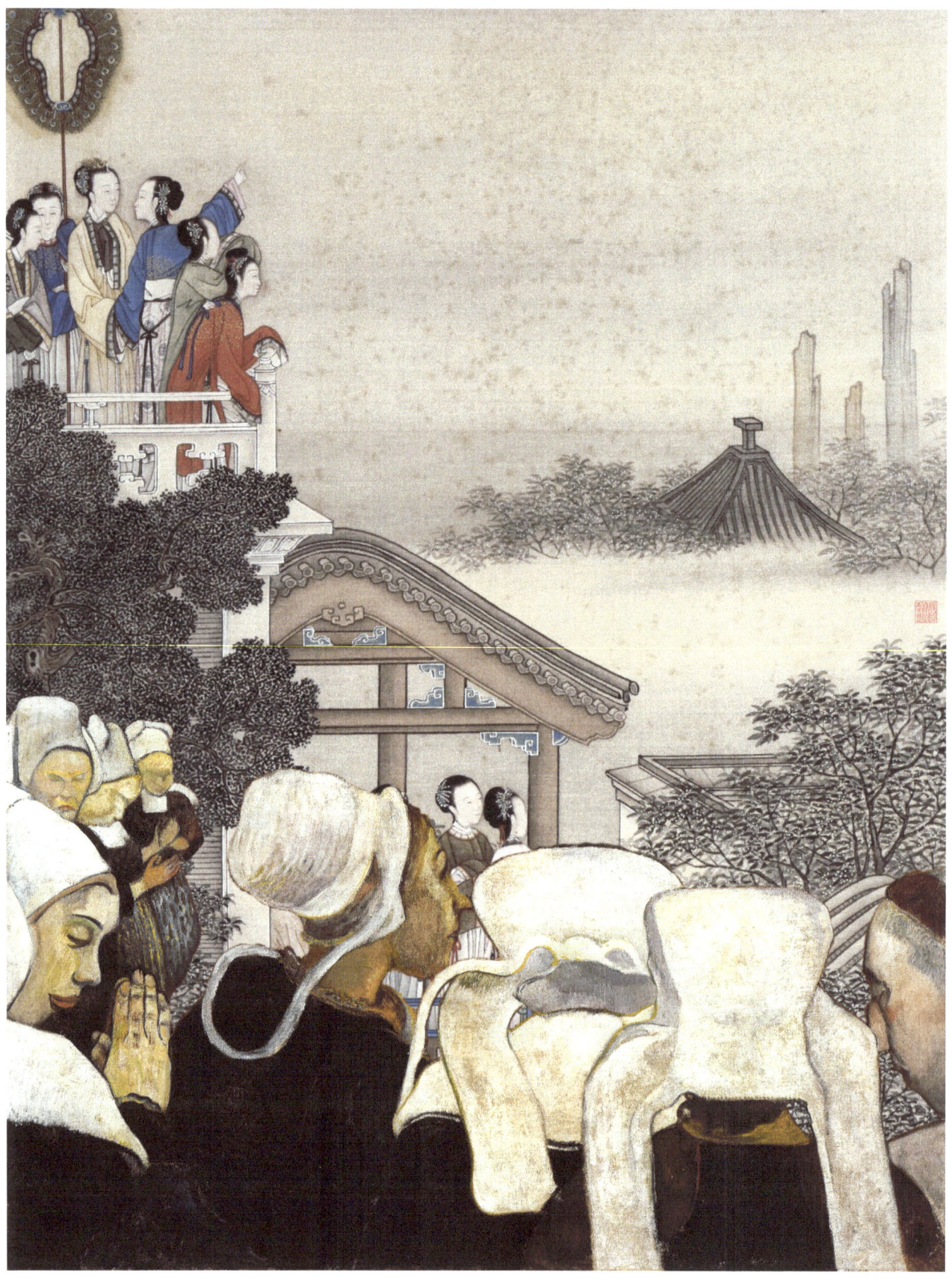

East #62

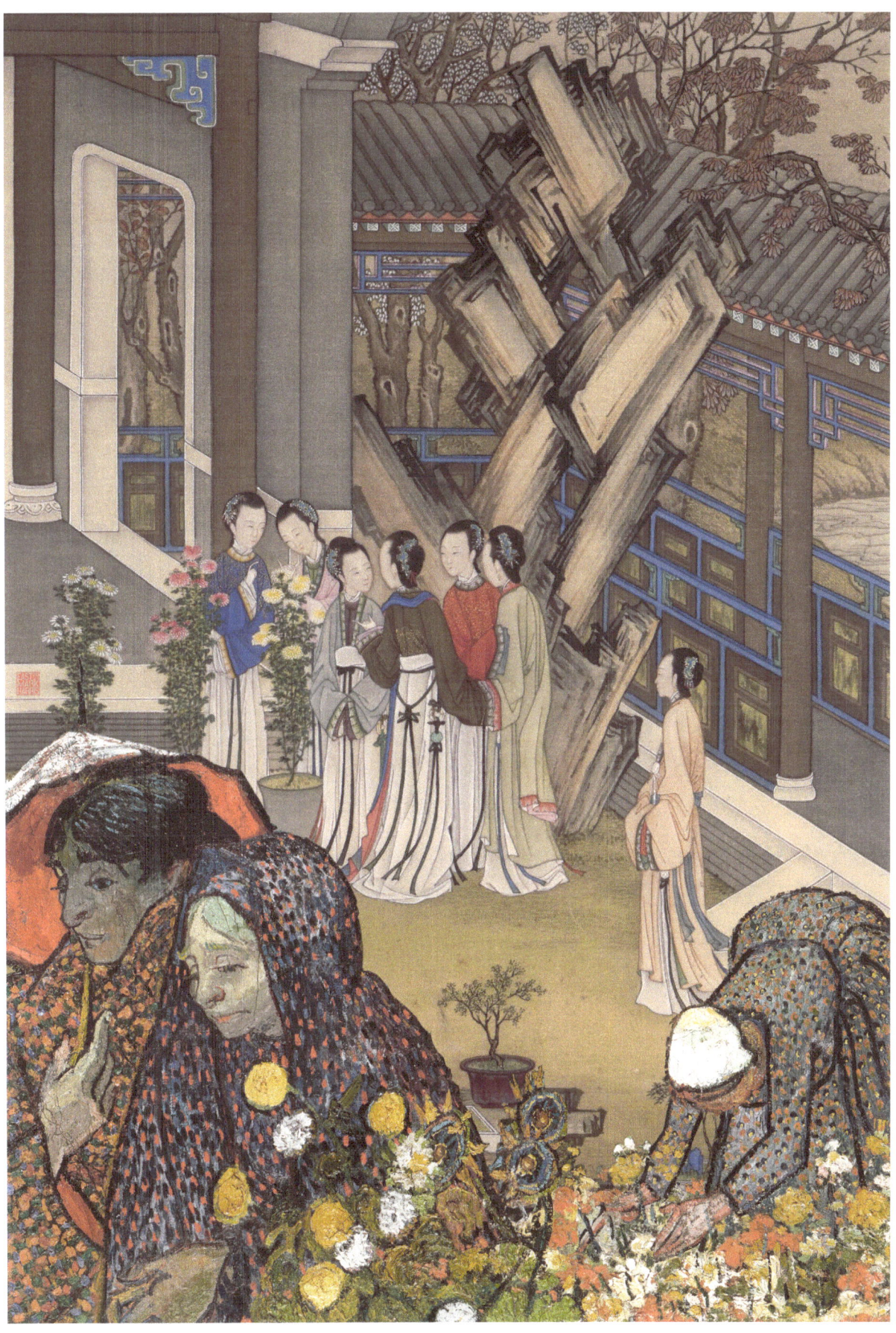

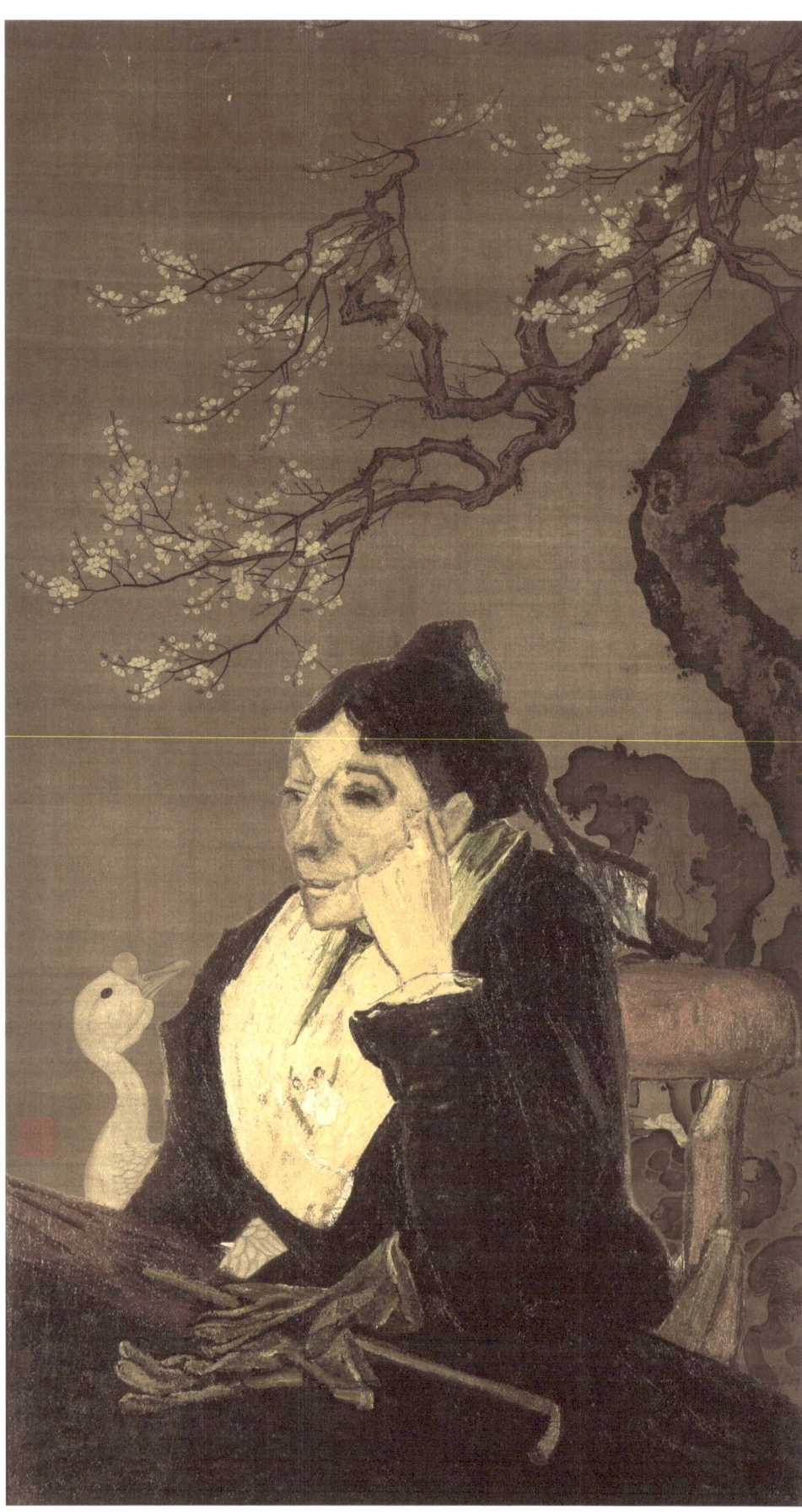

East #64

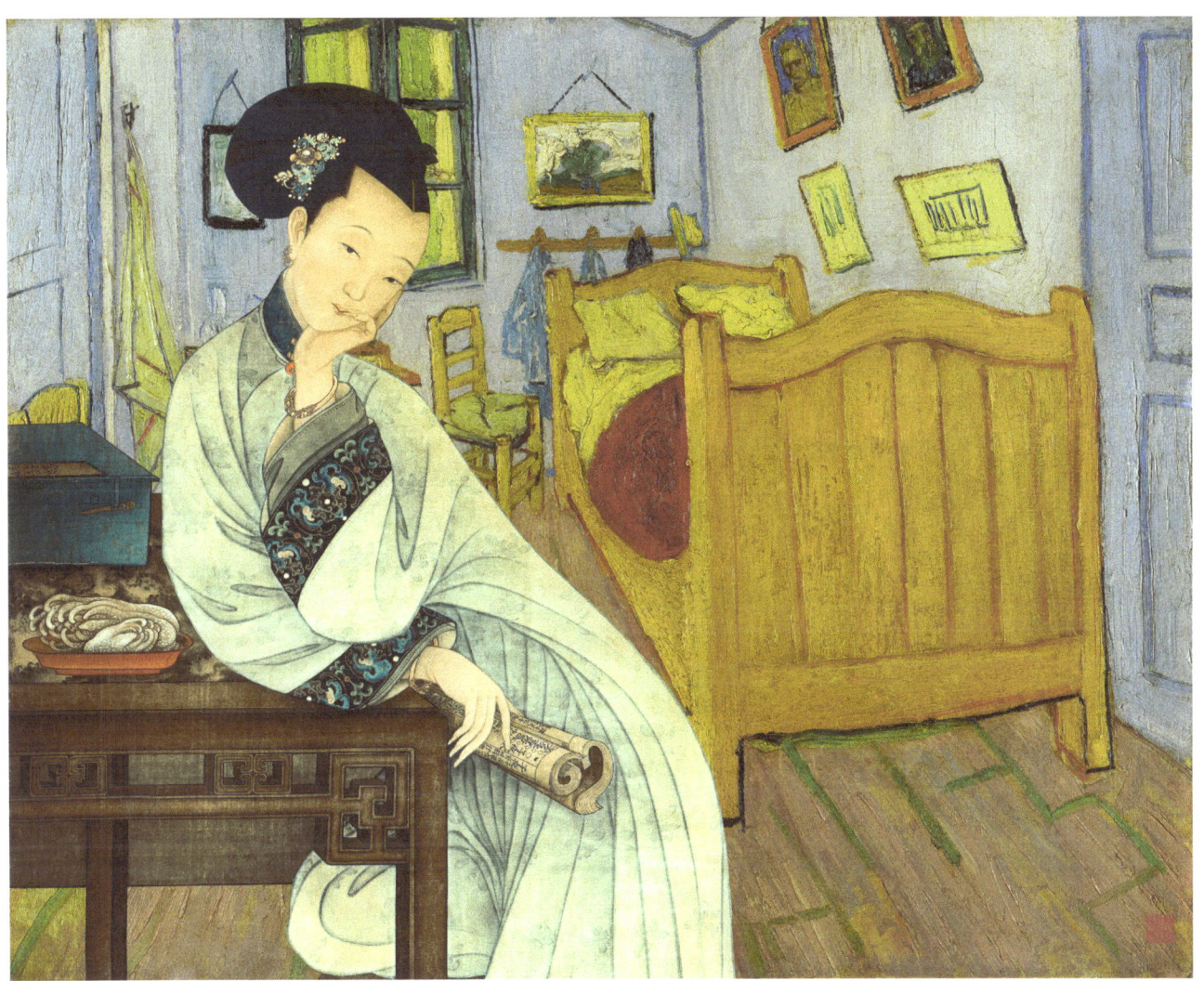

East #65

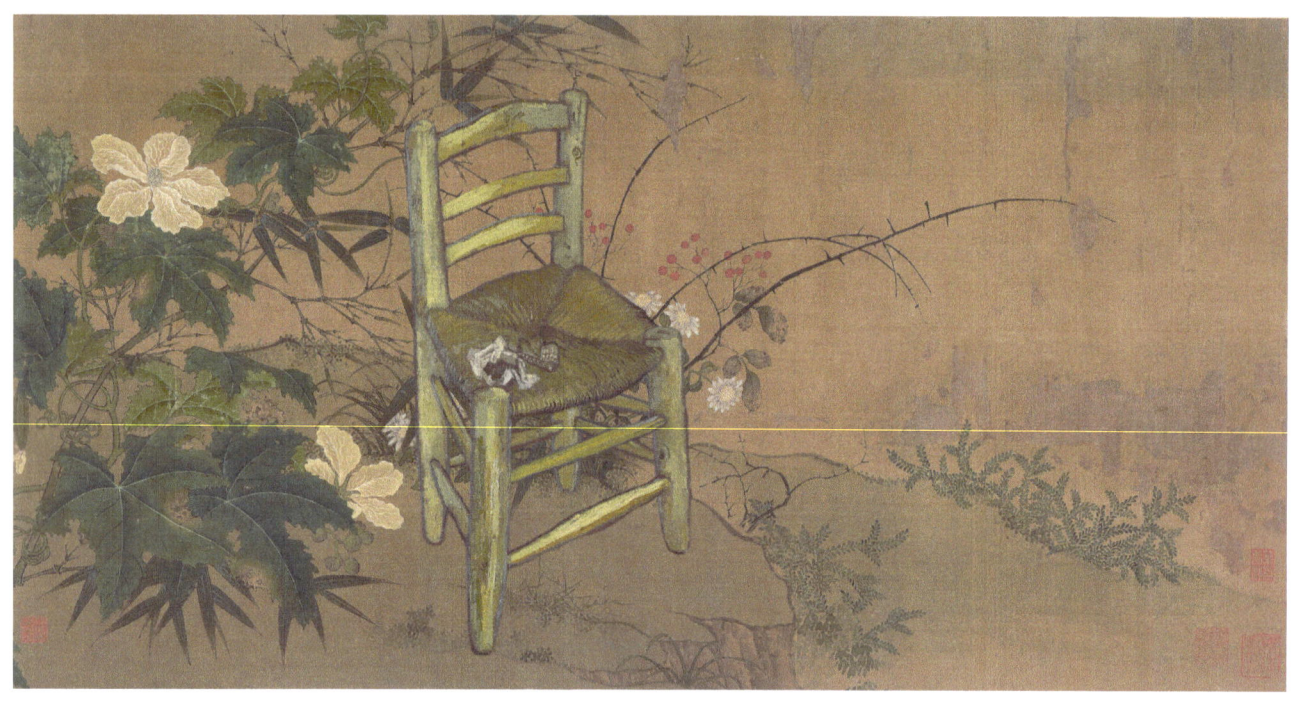

East #66

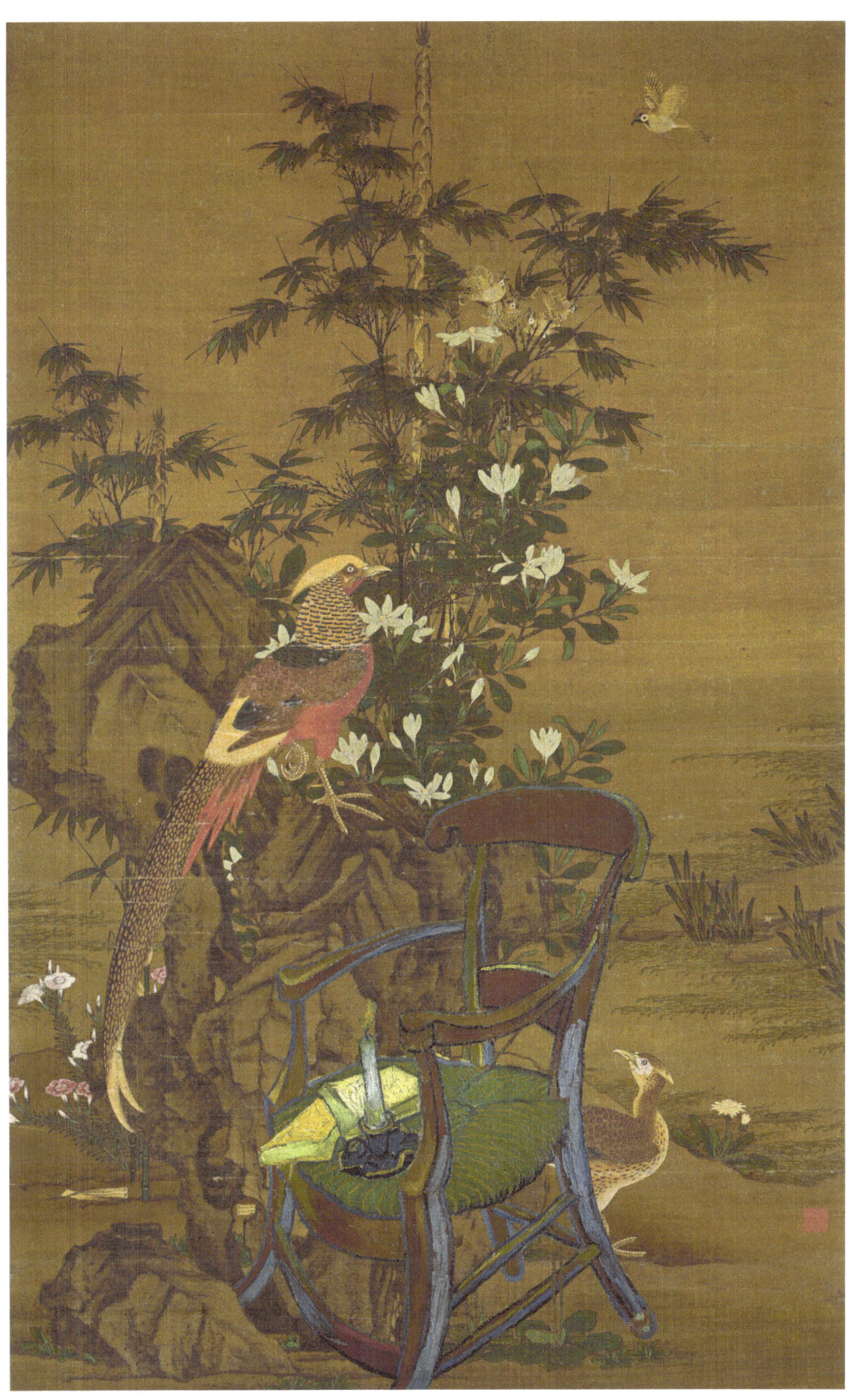

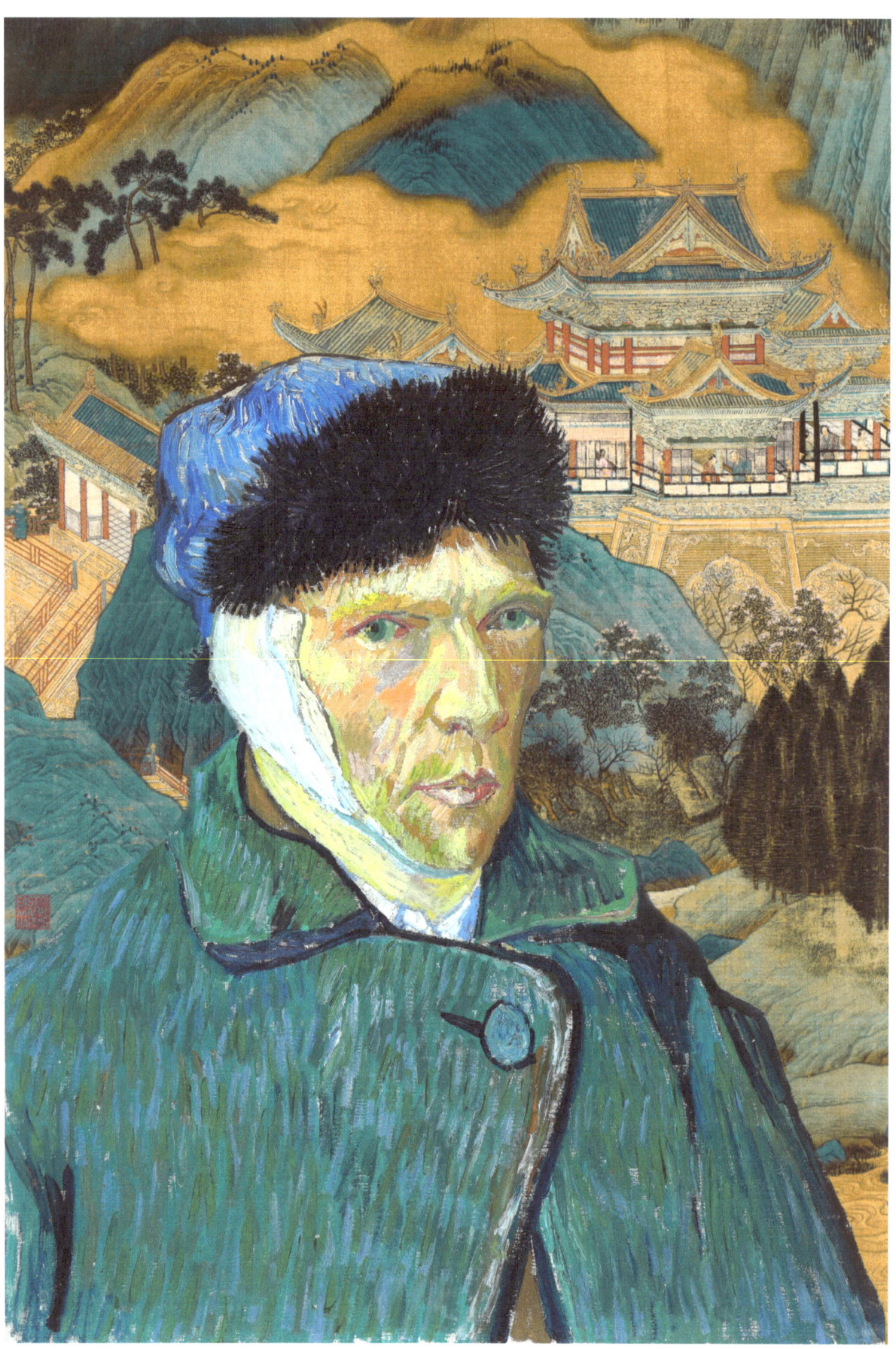

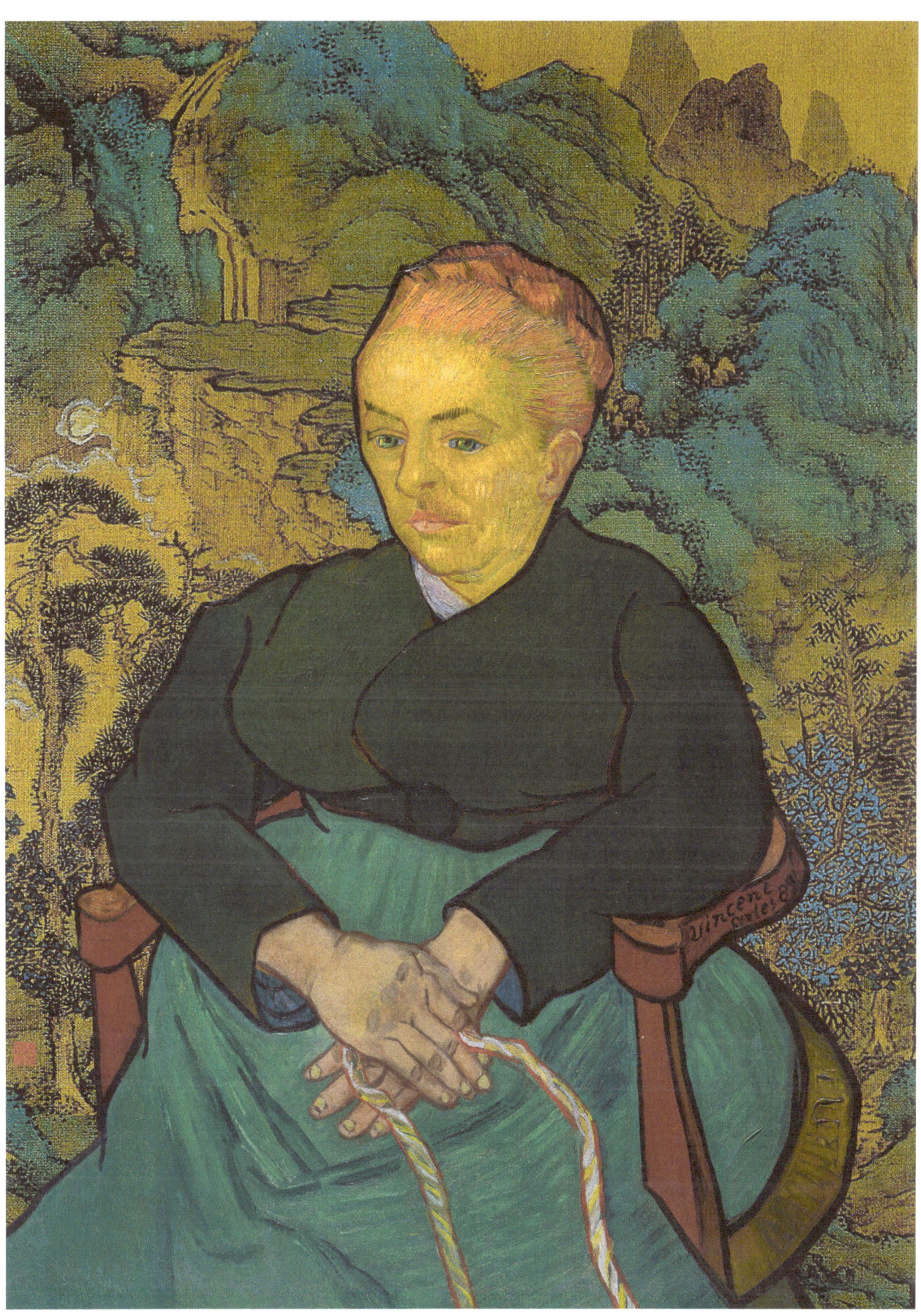

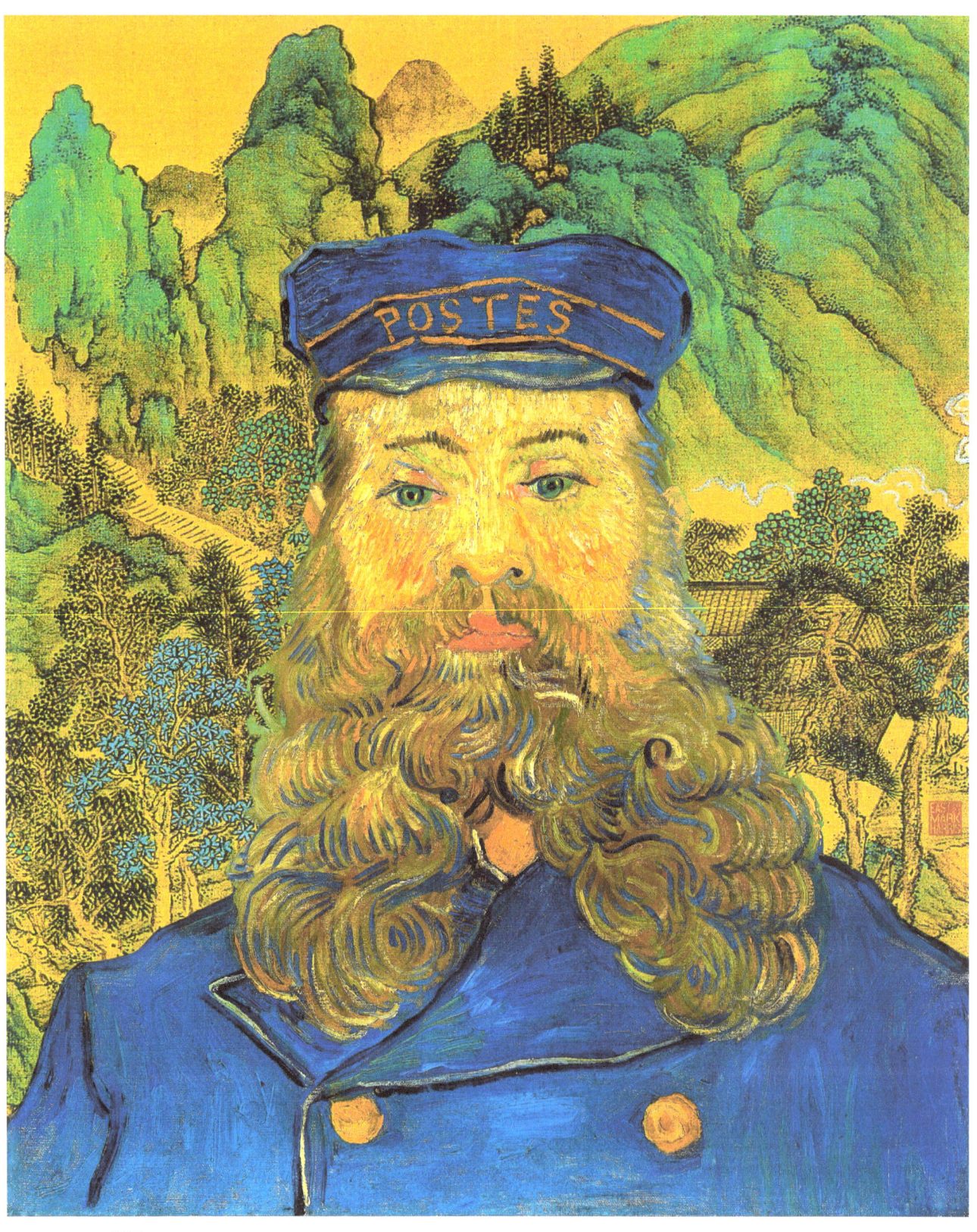

East #70

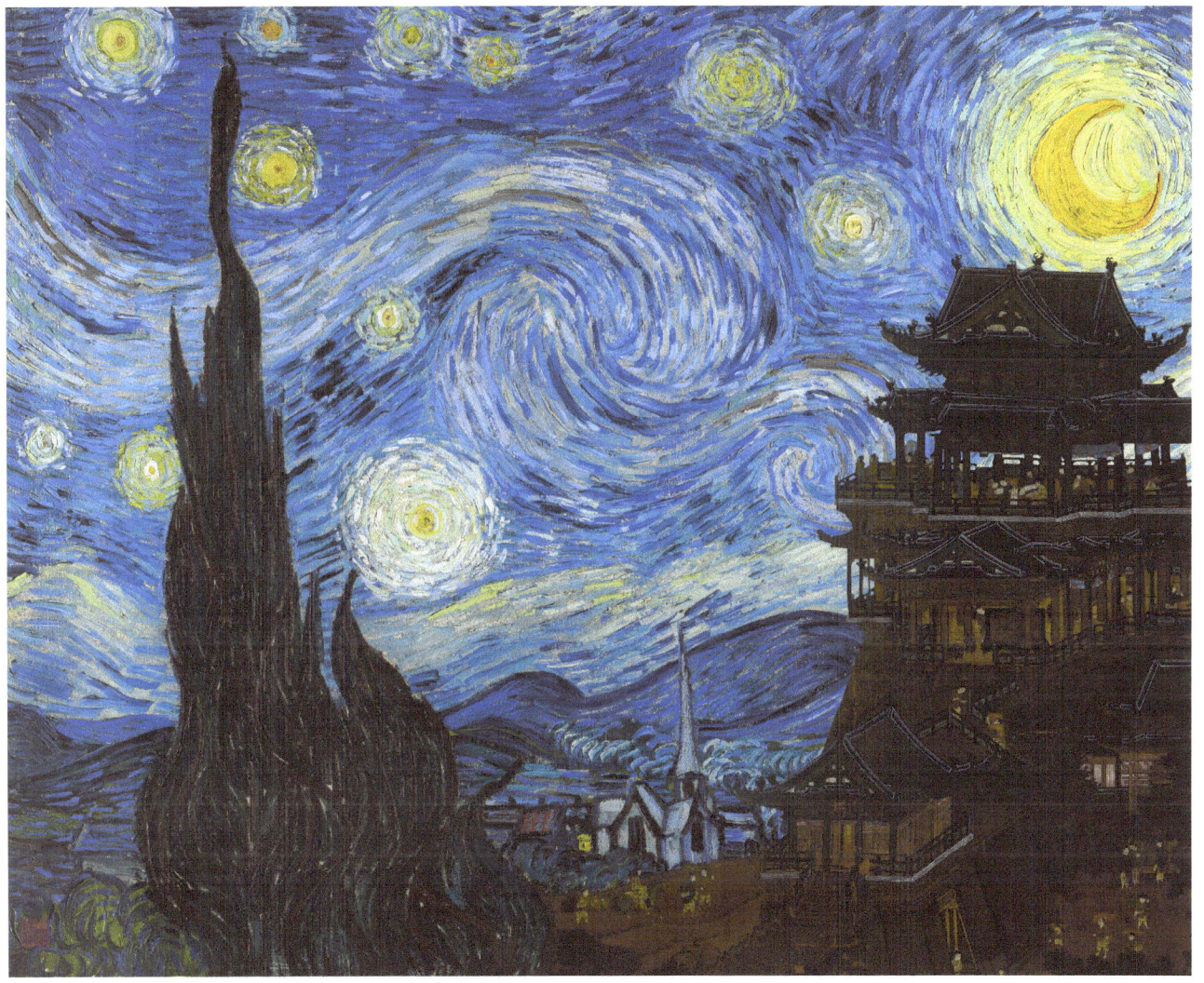

East #71

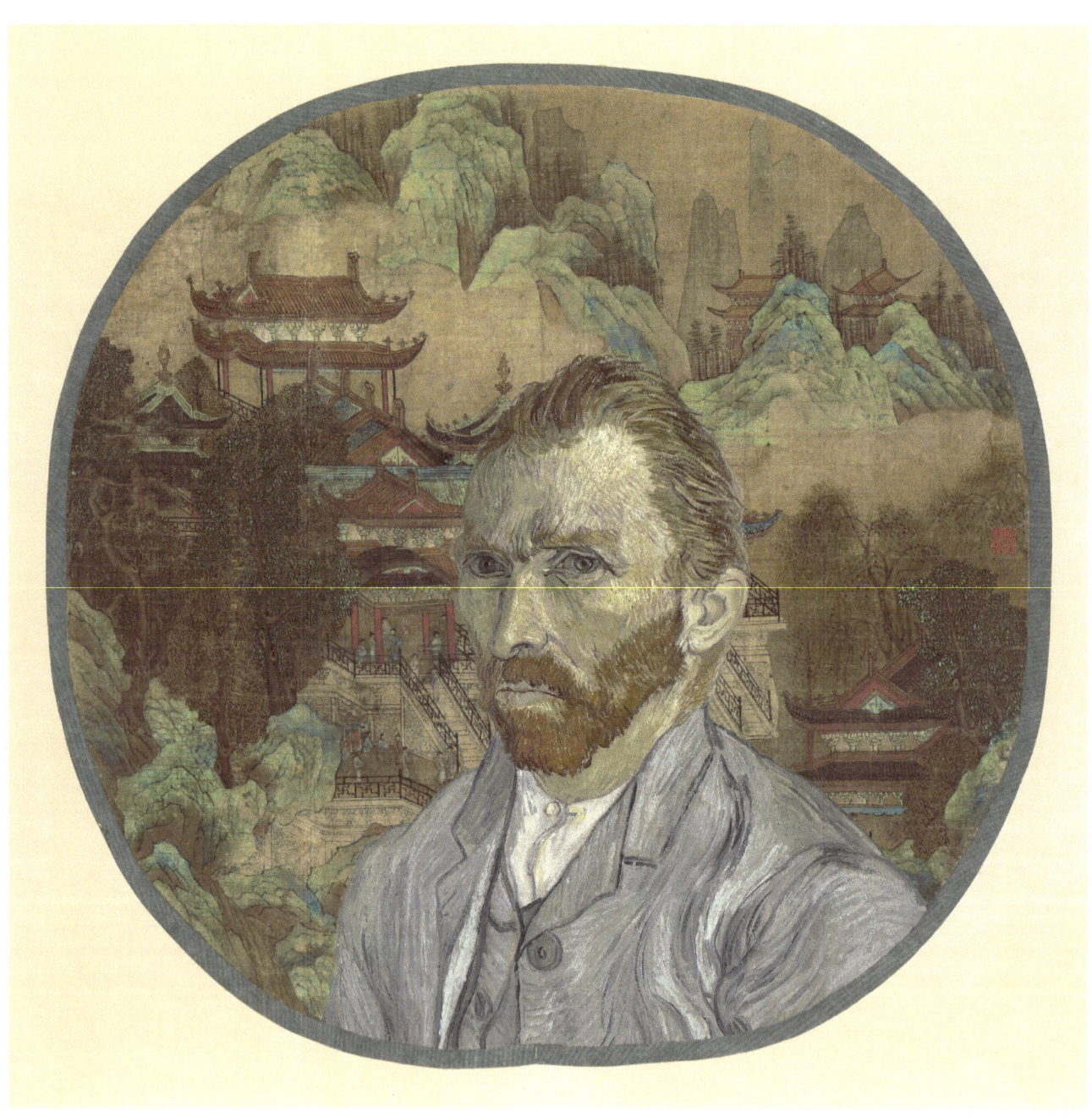

East #72

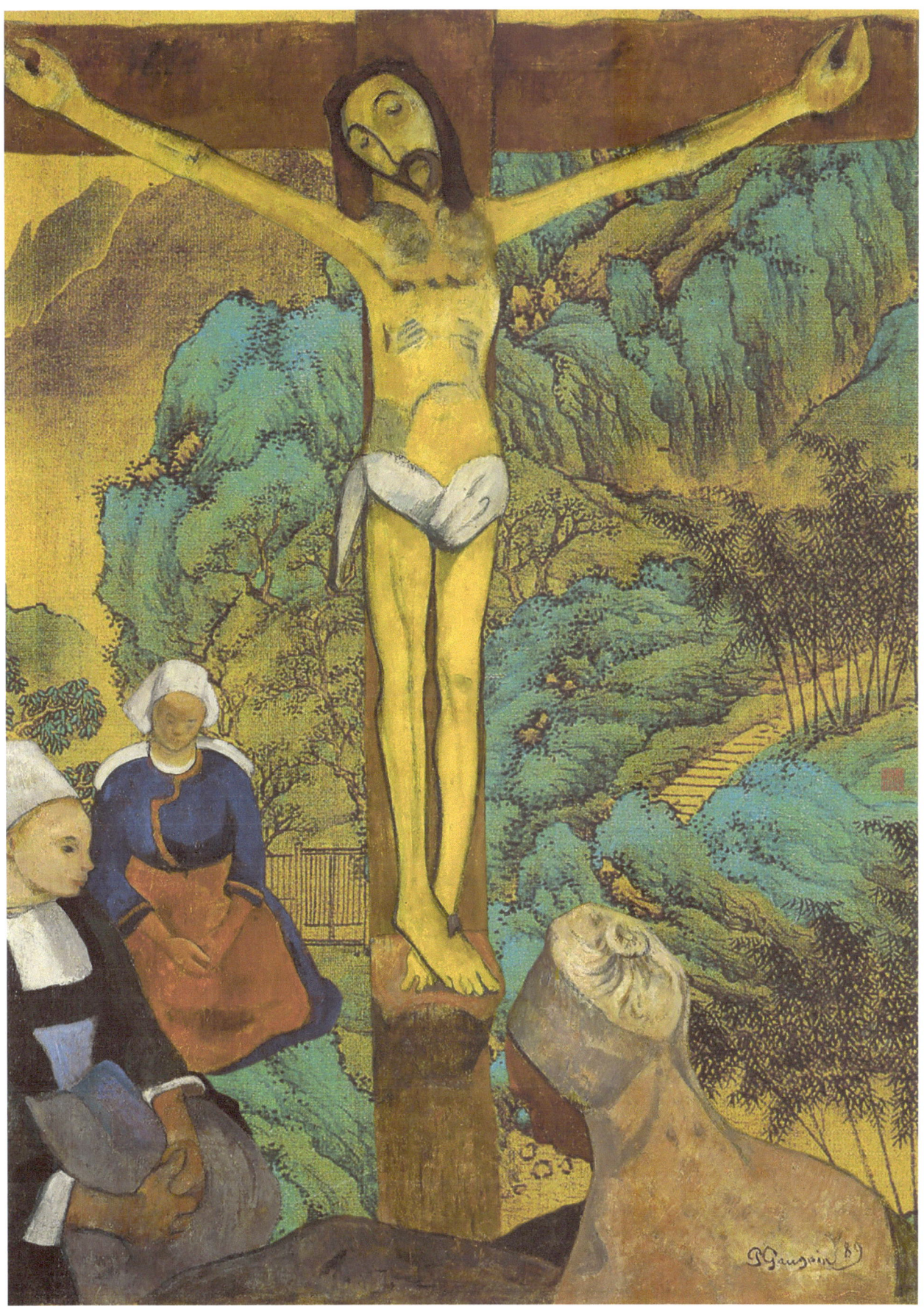

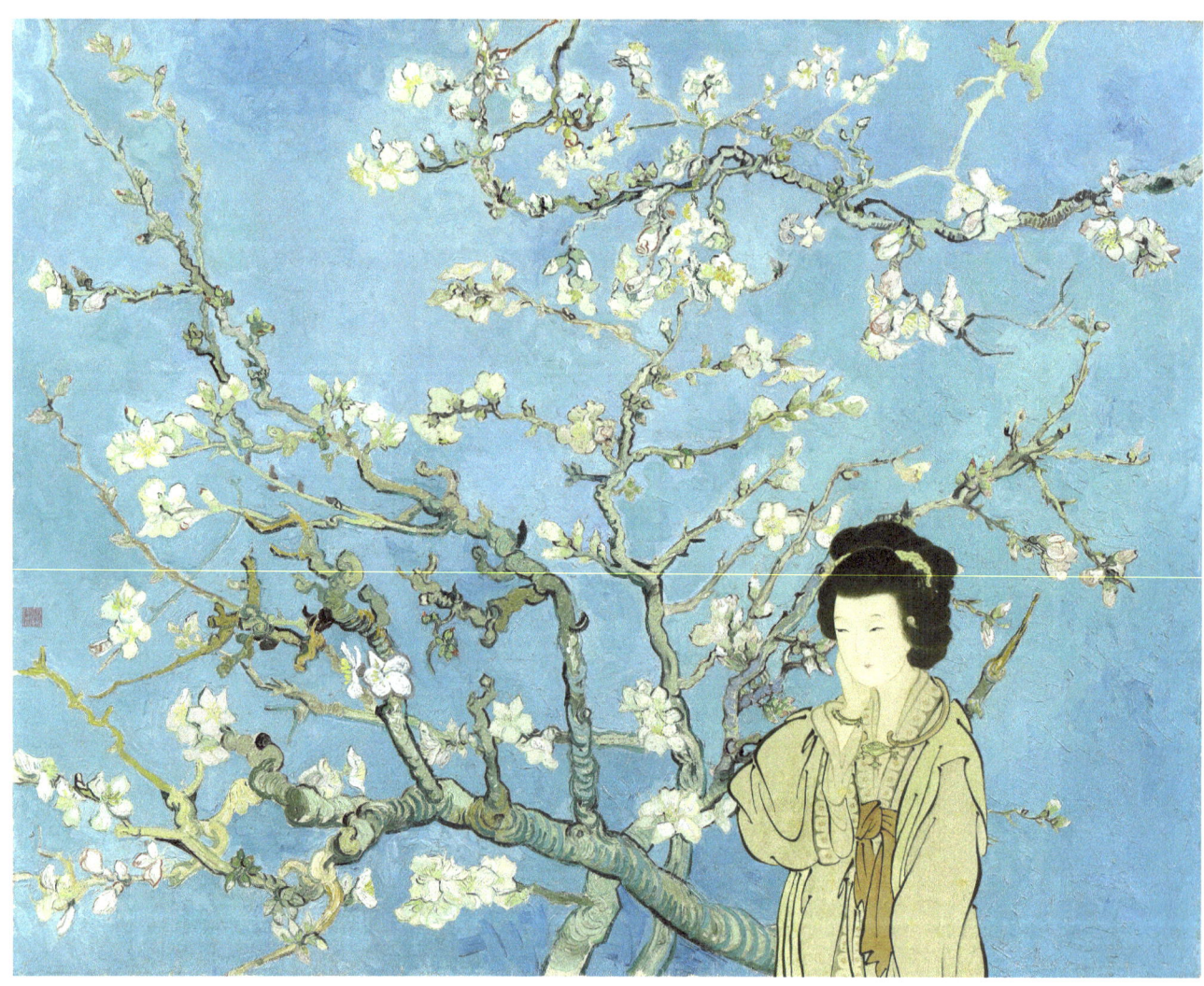

East #74

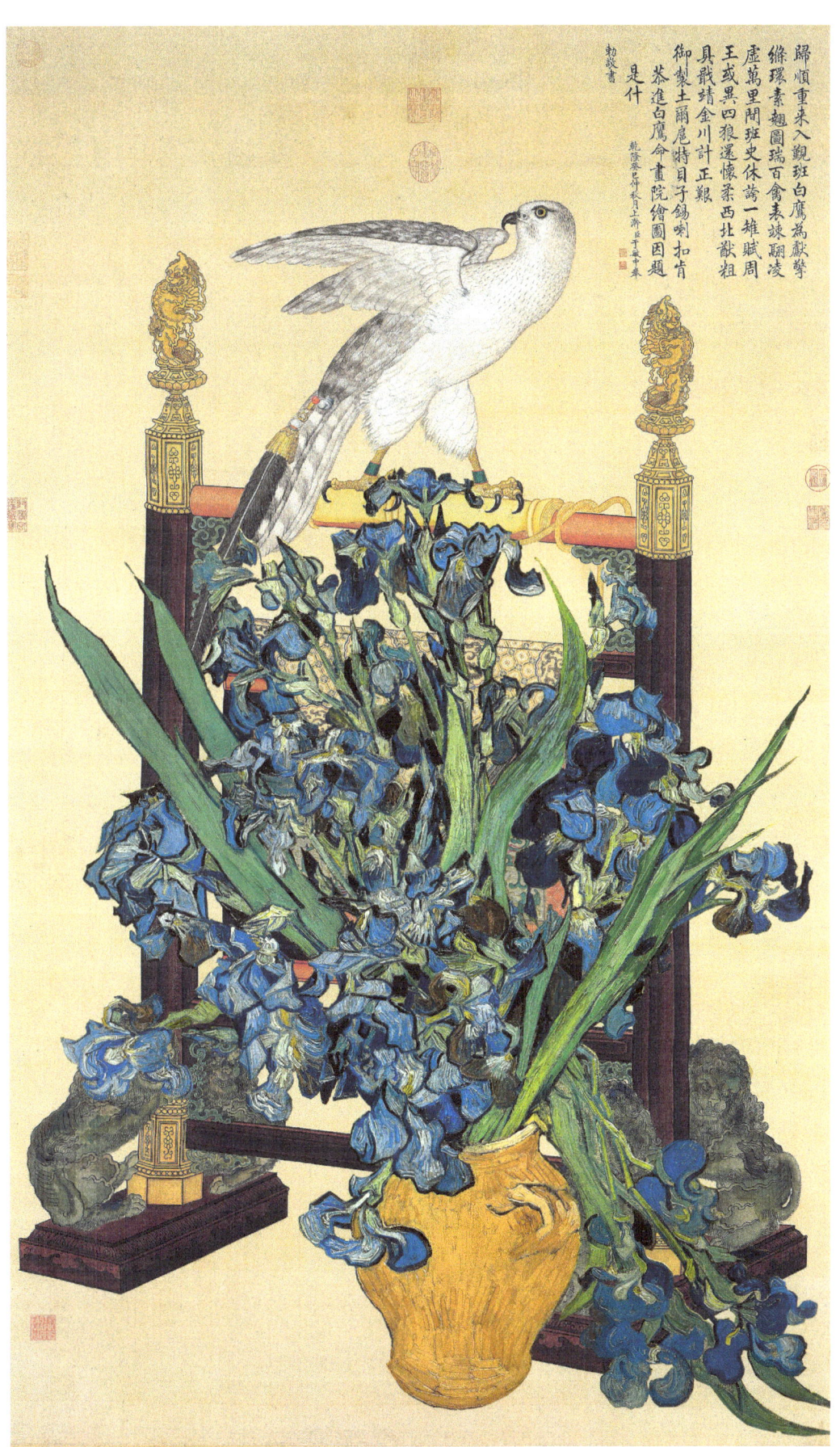

East #75

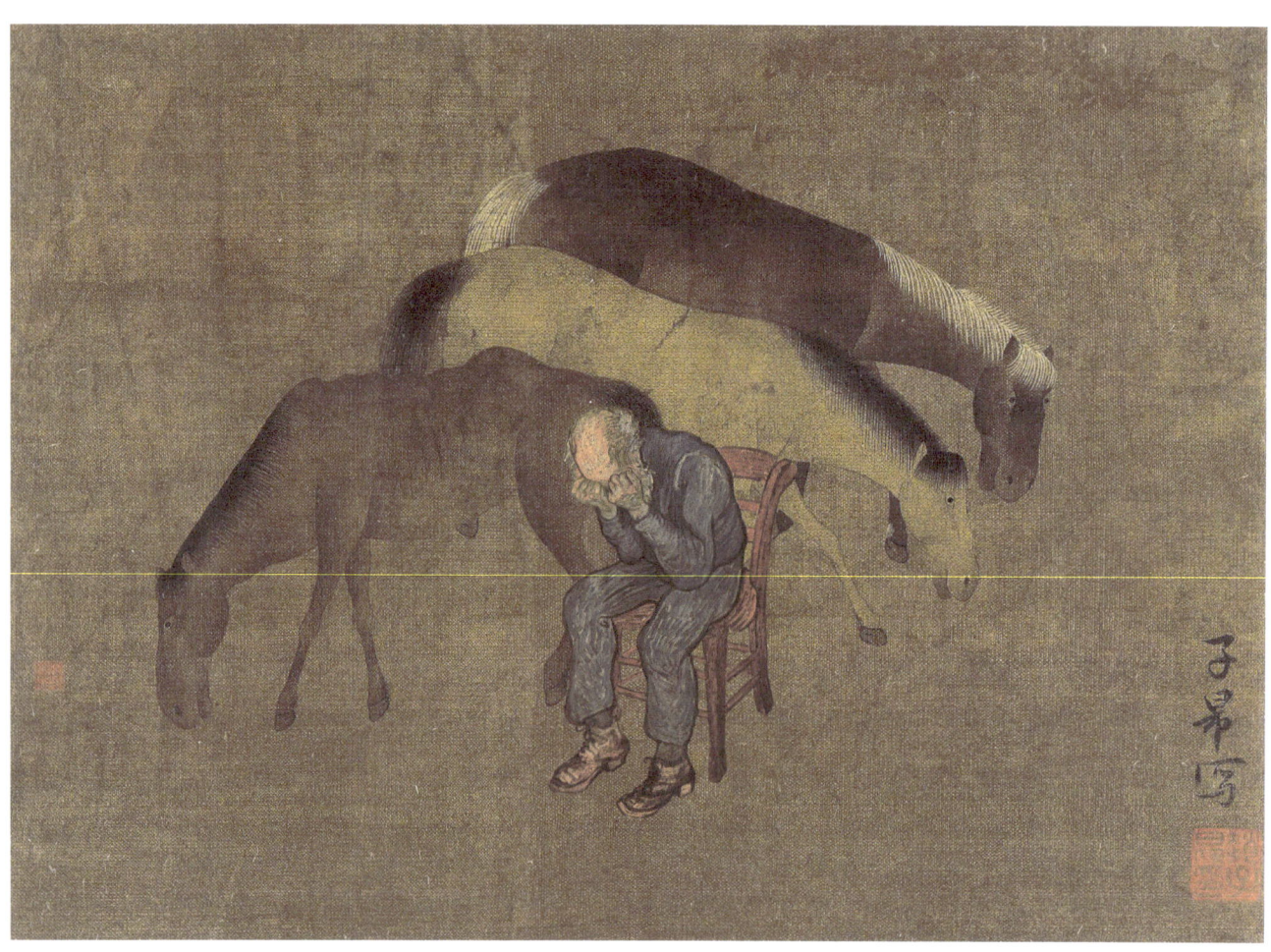

East #76

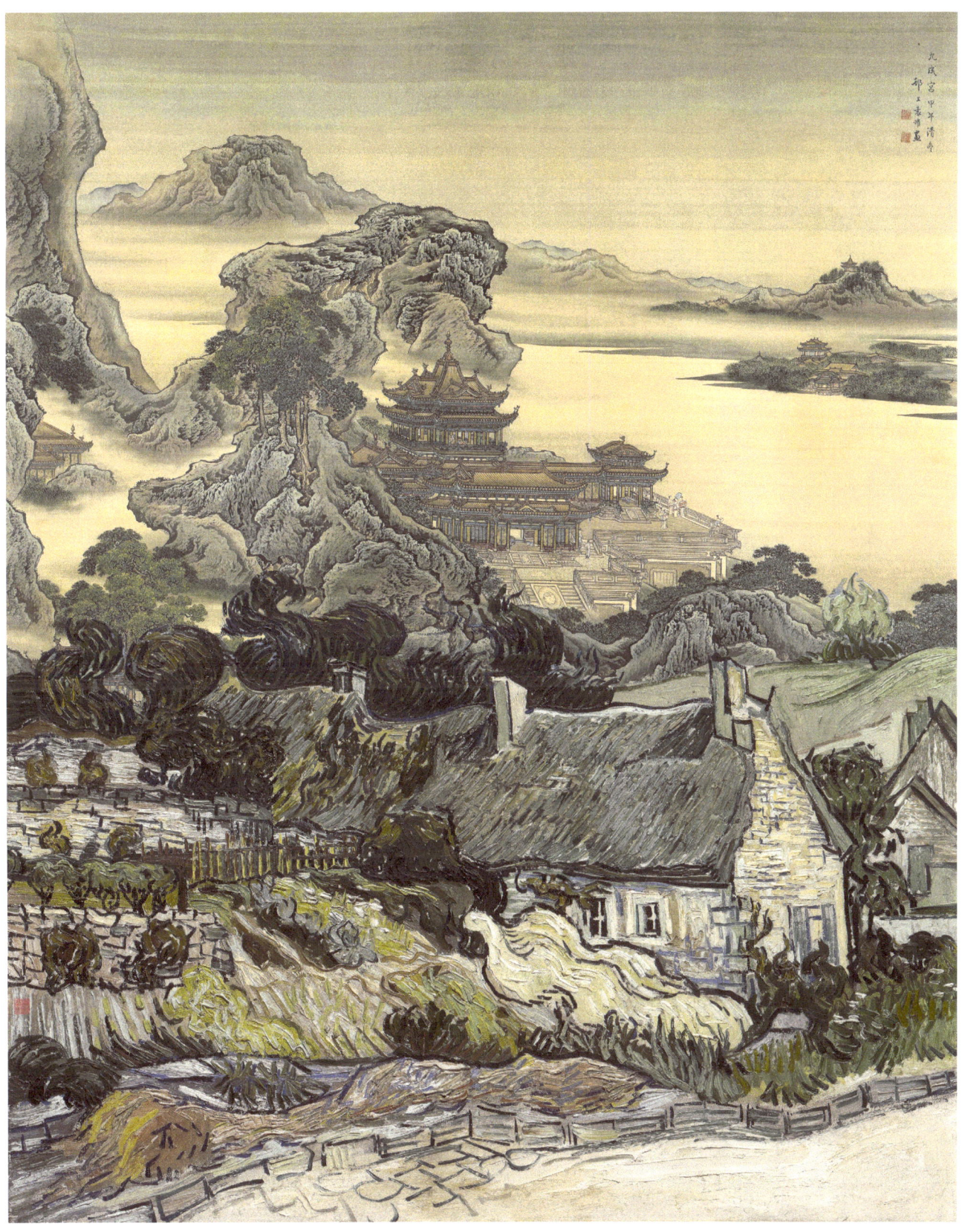

East #77

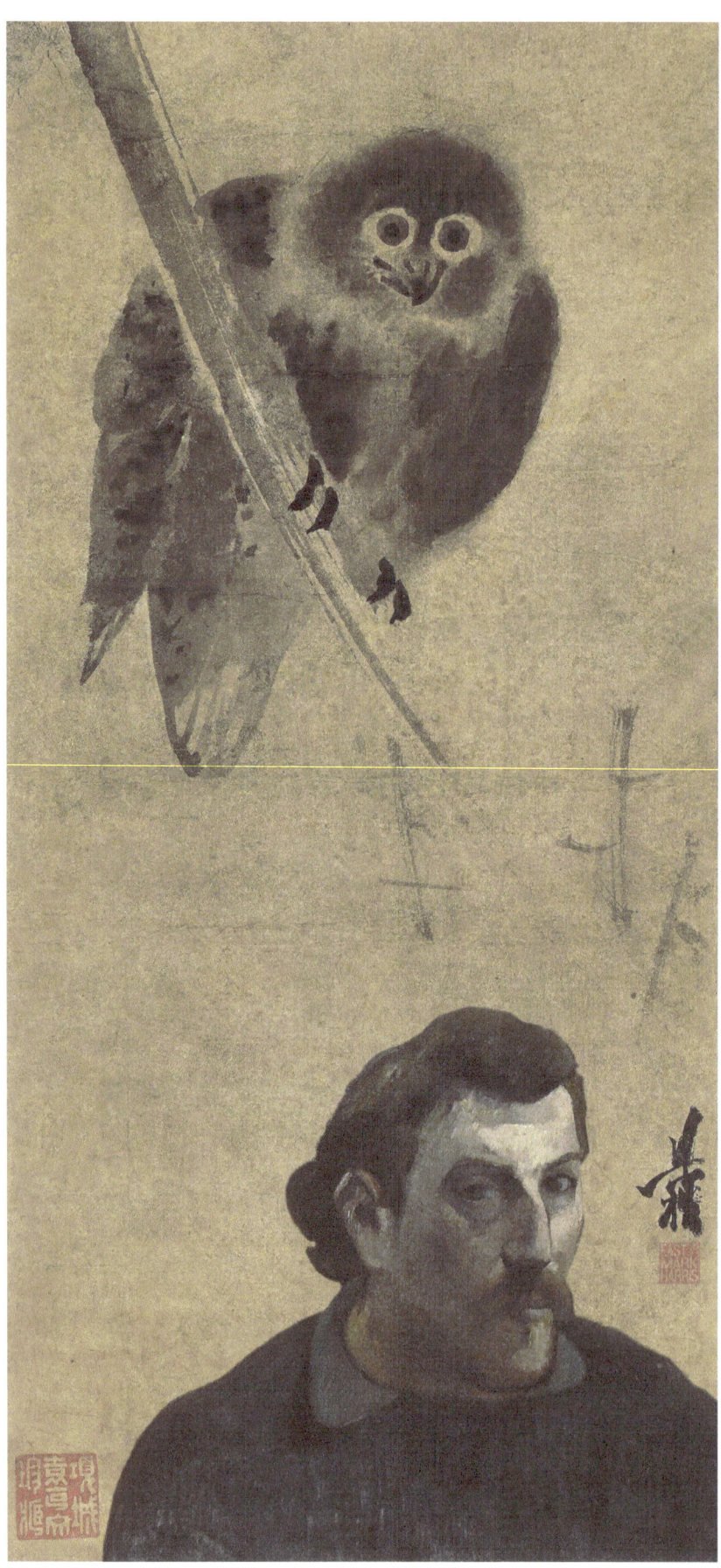

East #78

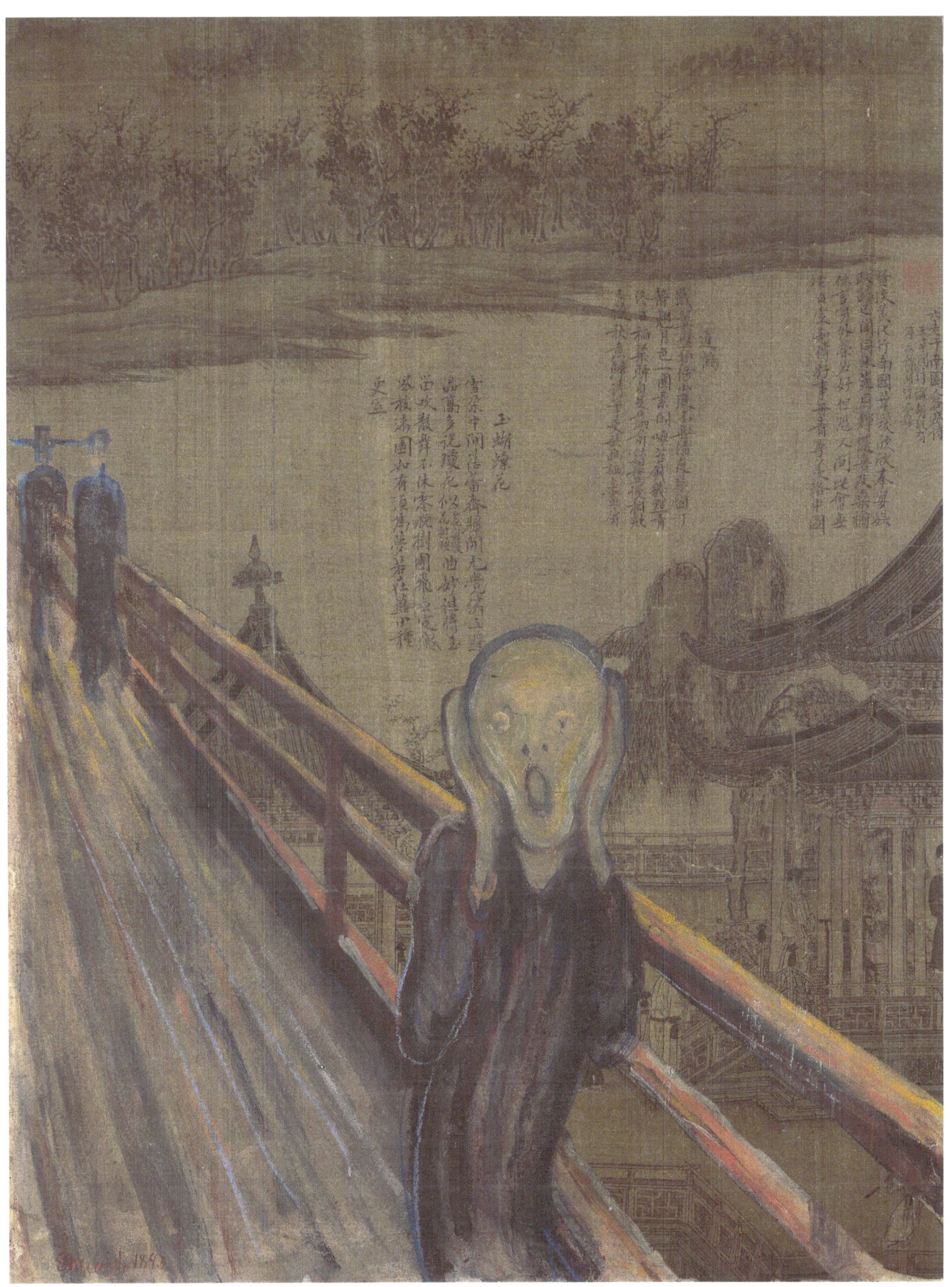

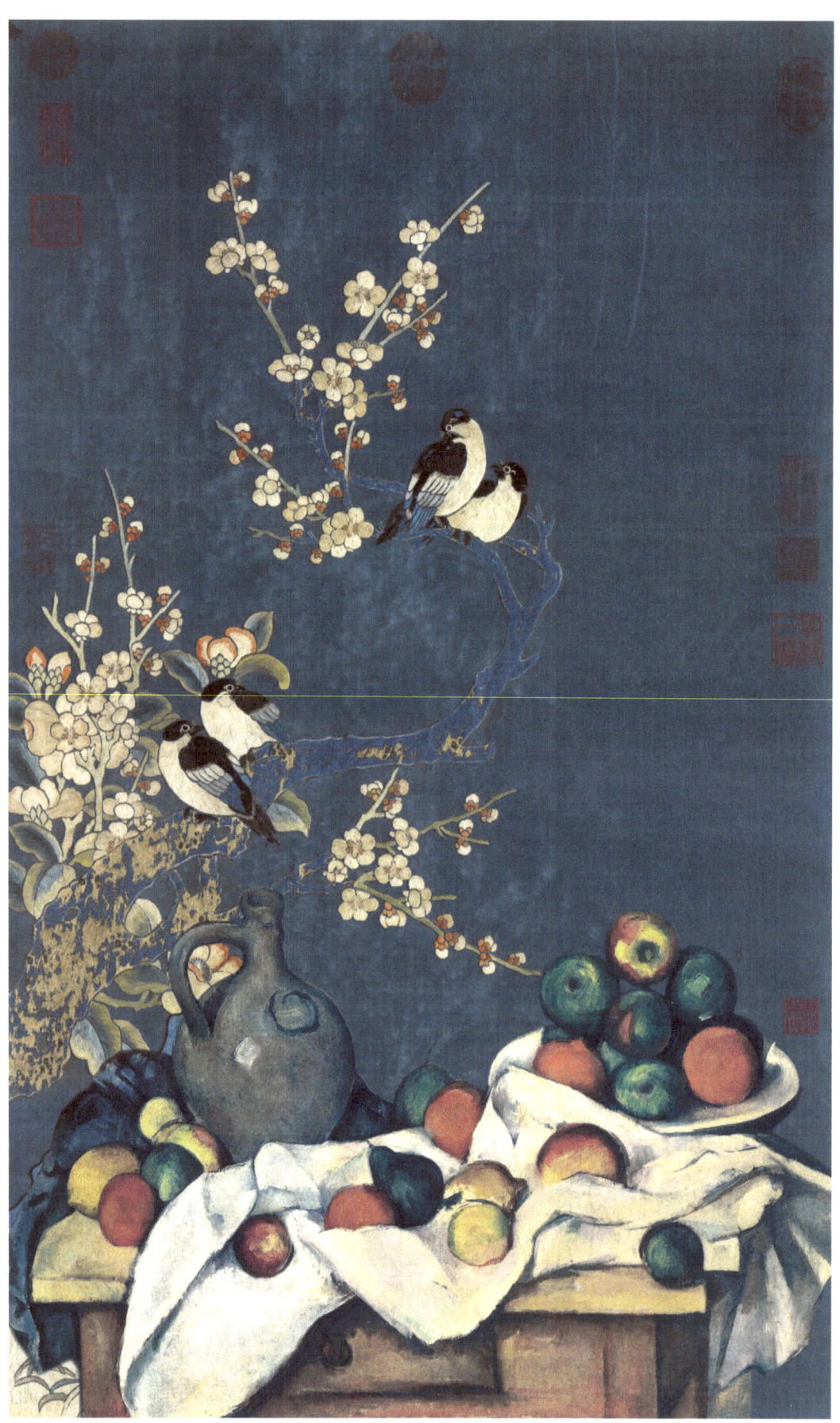

East #80

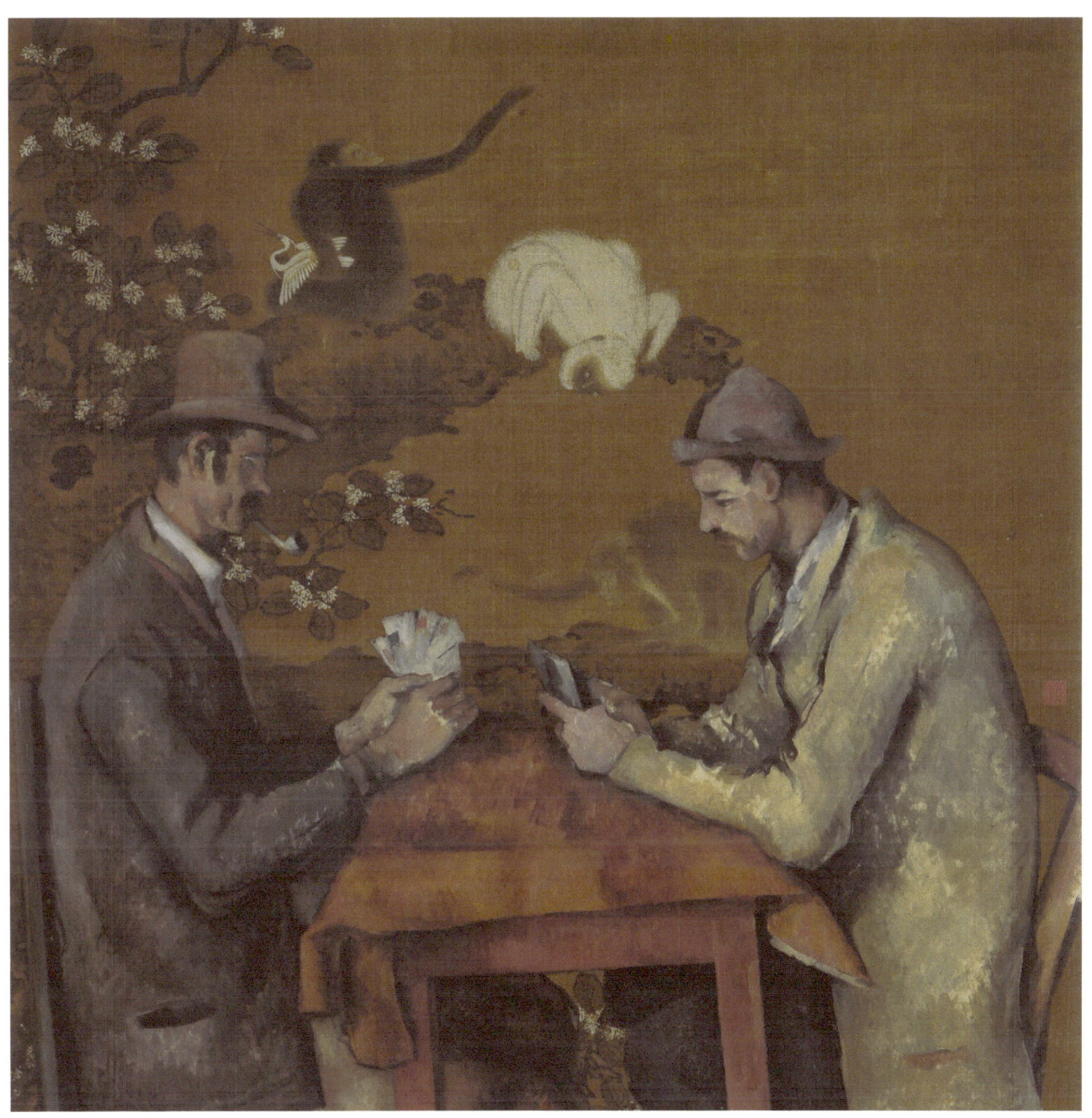

East #81

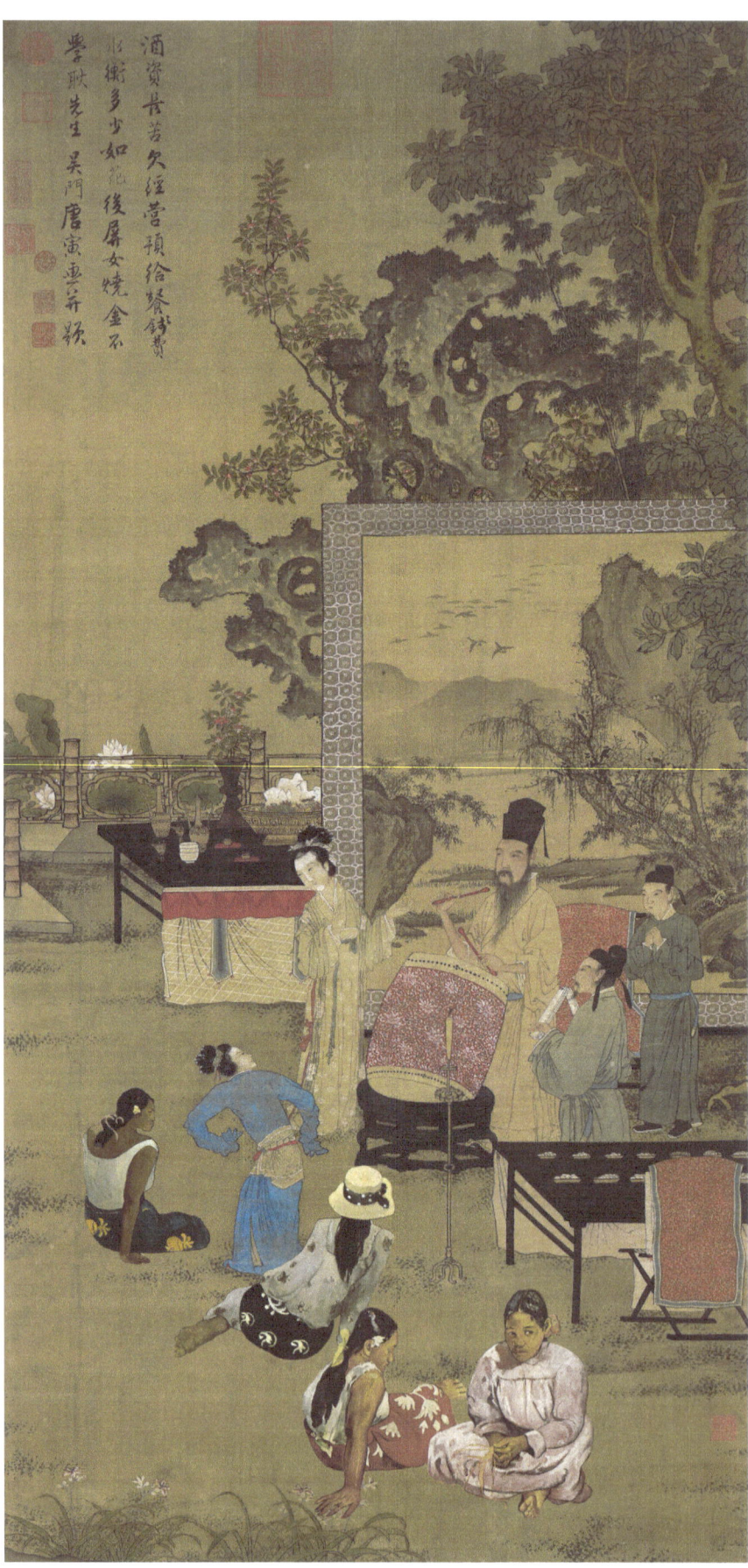

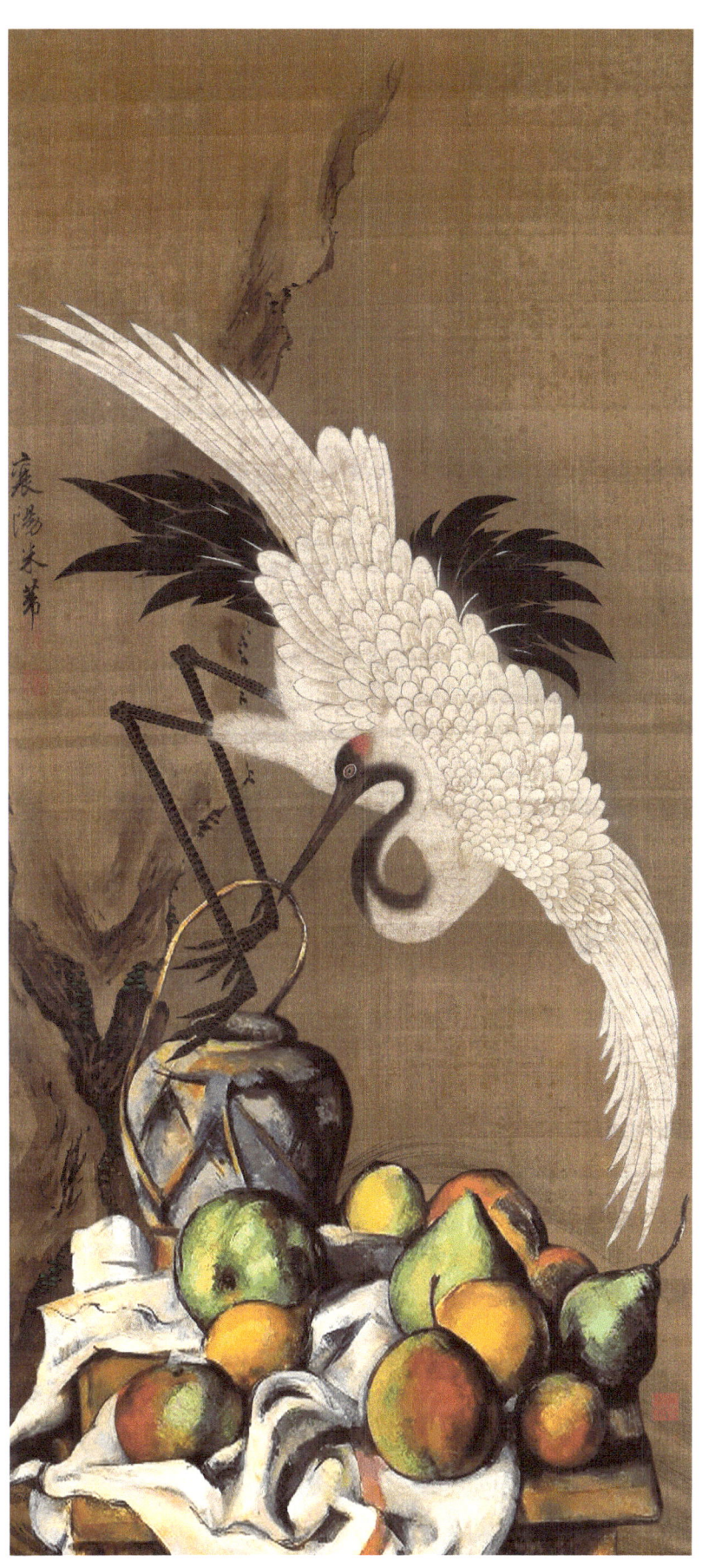

East #83

Mark Harris

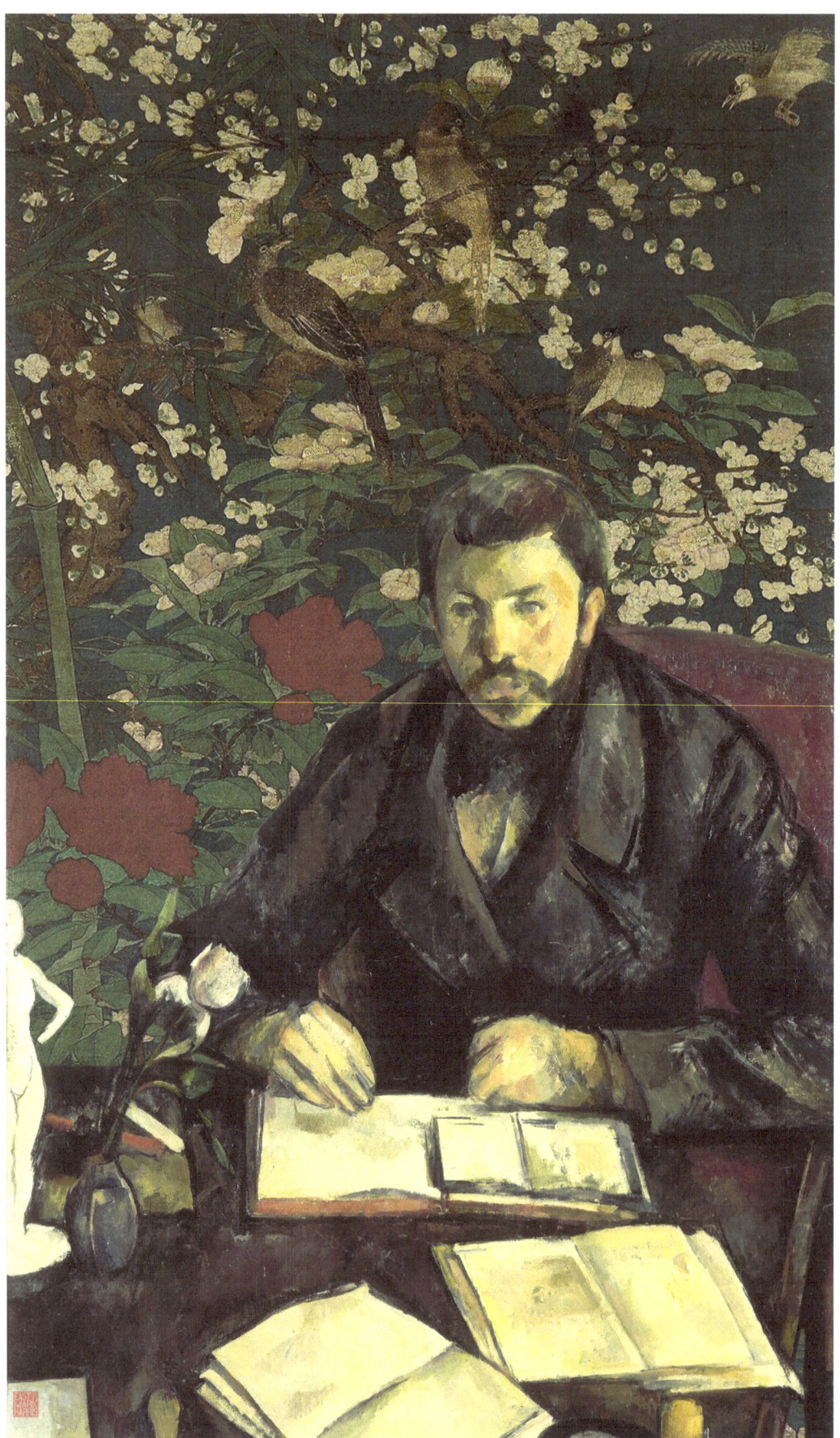

East #84

East #85

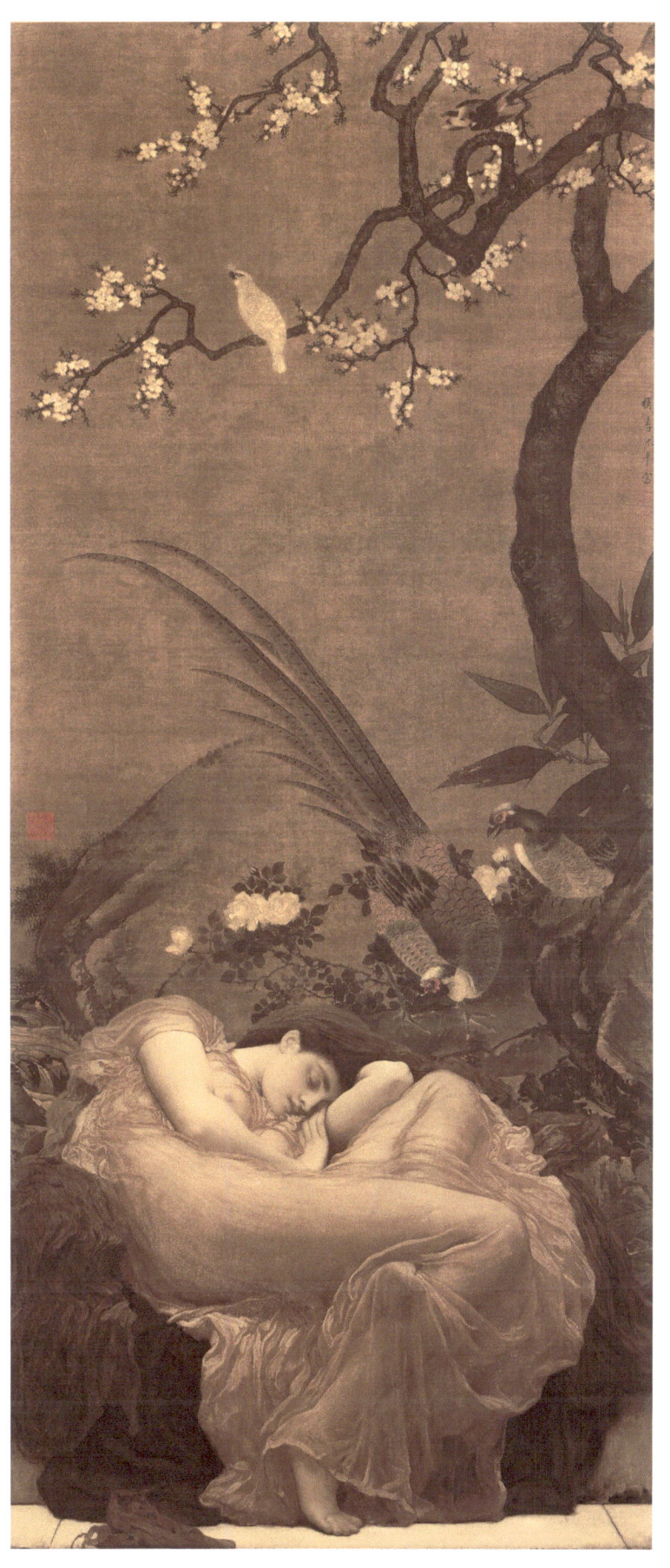

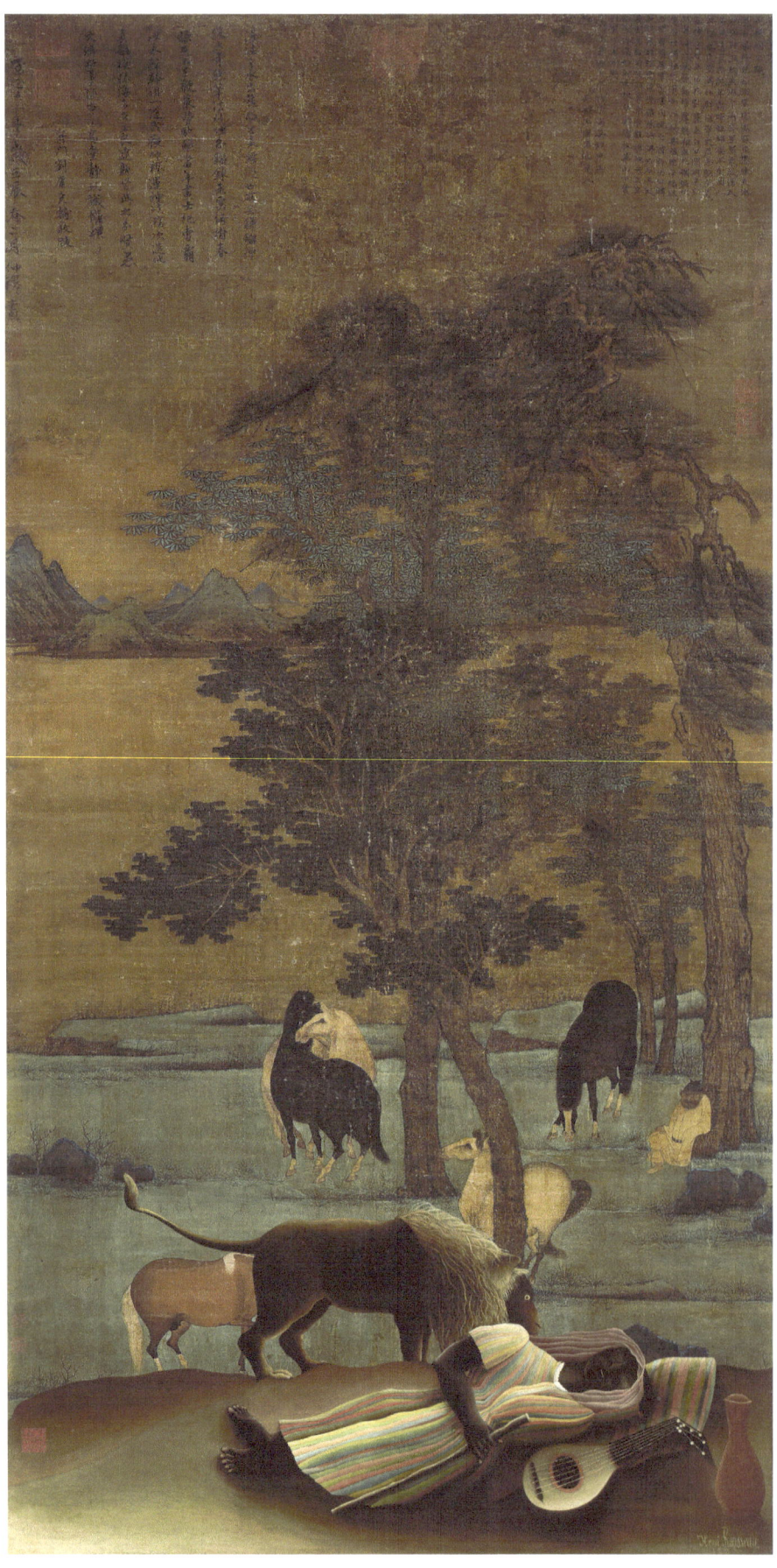

East #86

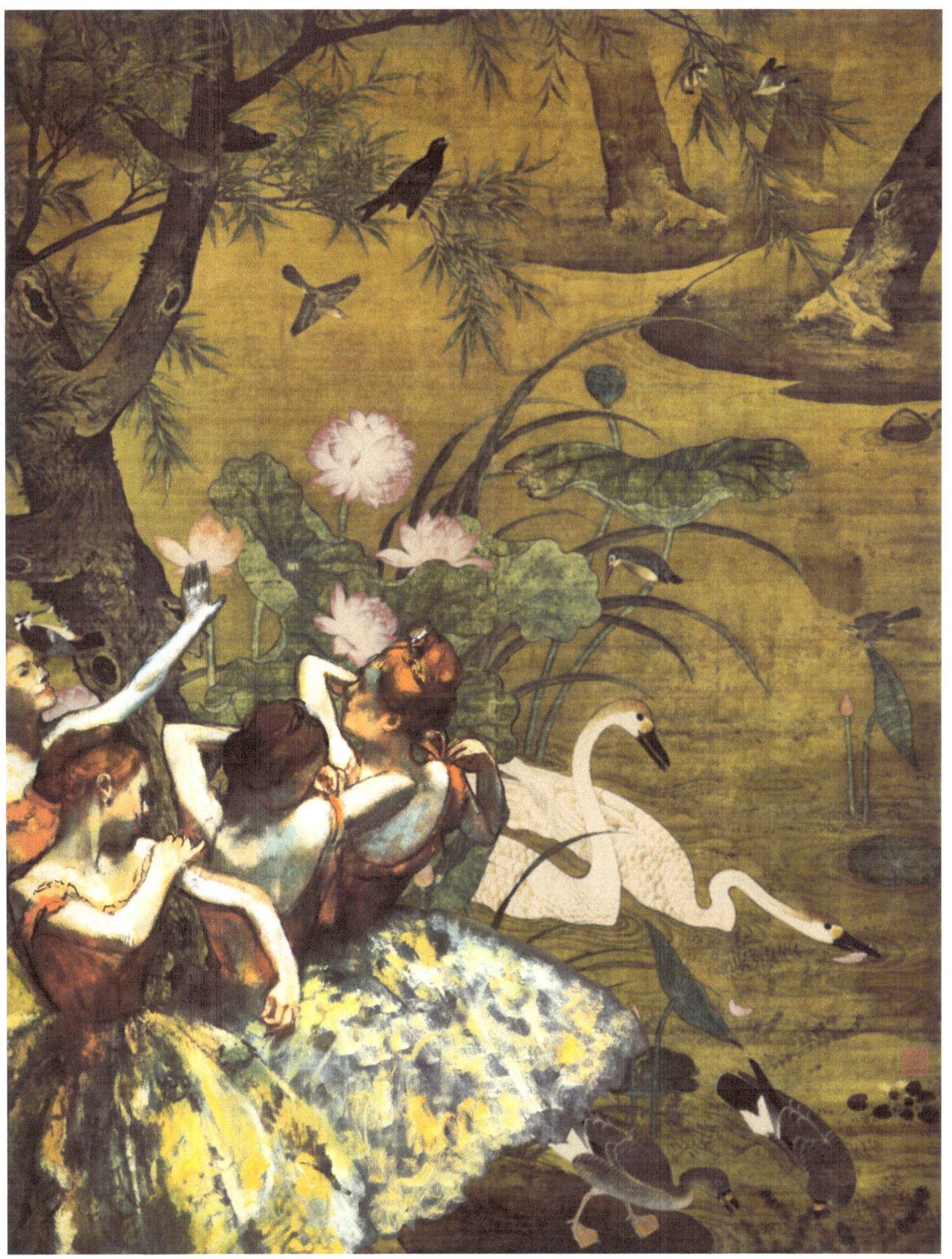

East #87

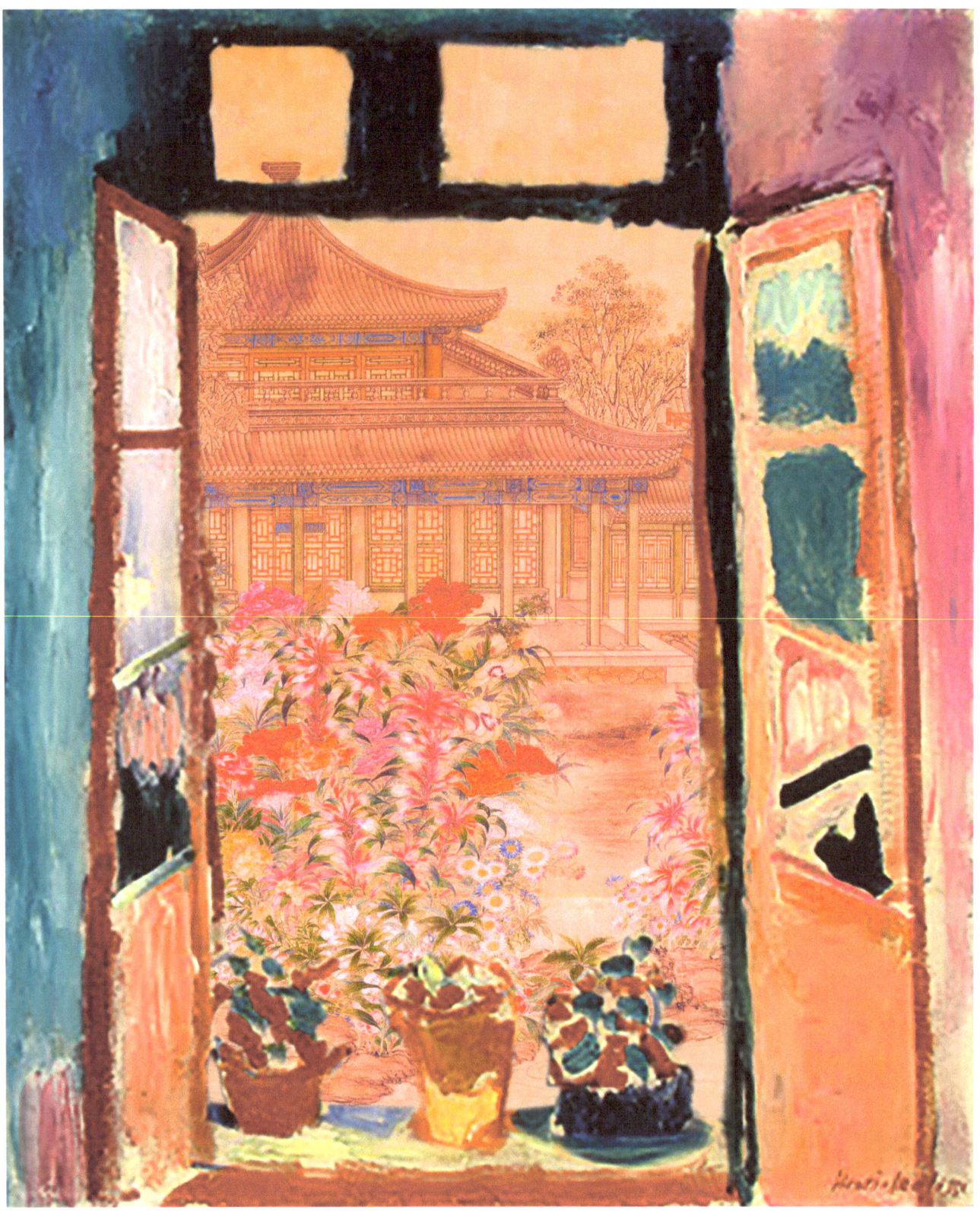

East #88

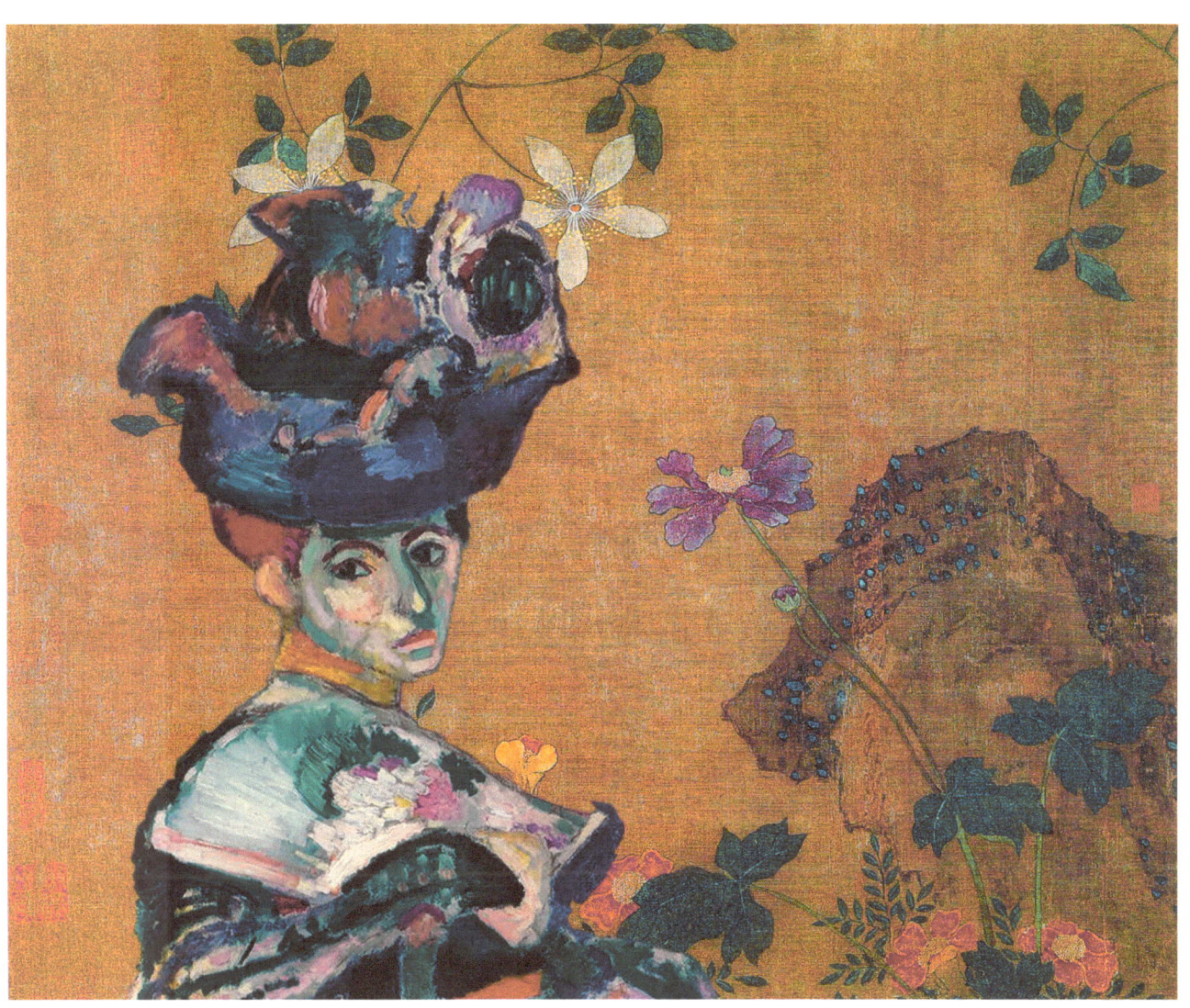

East #89

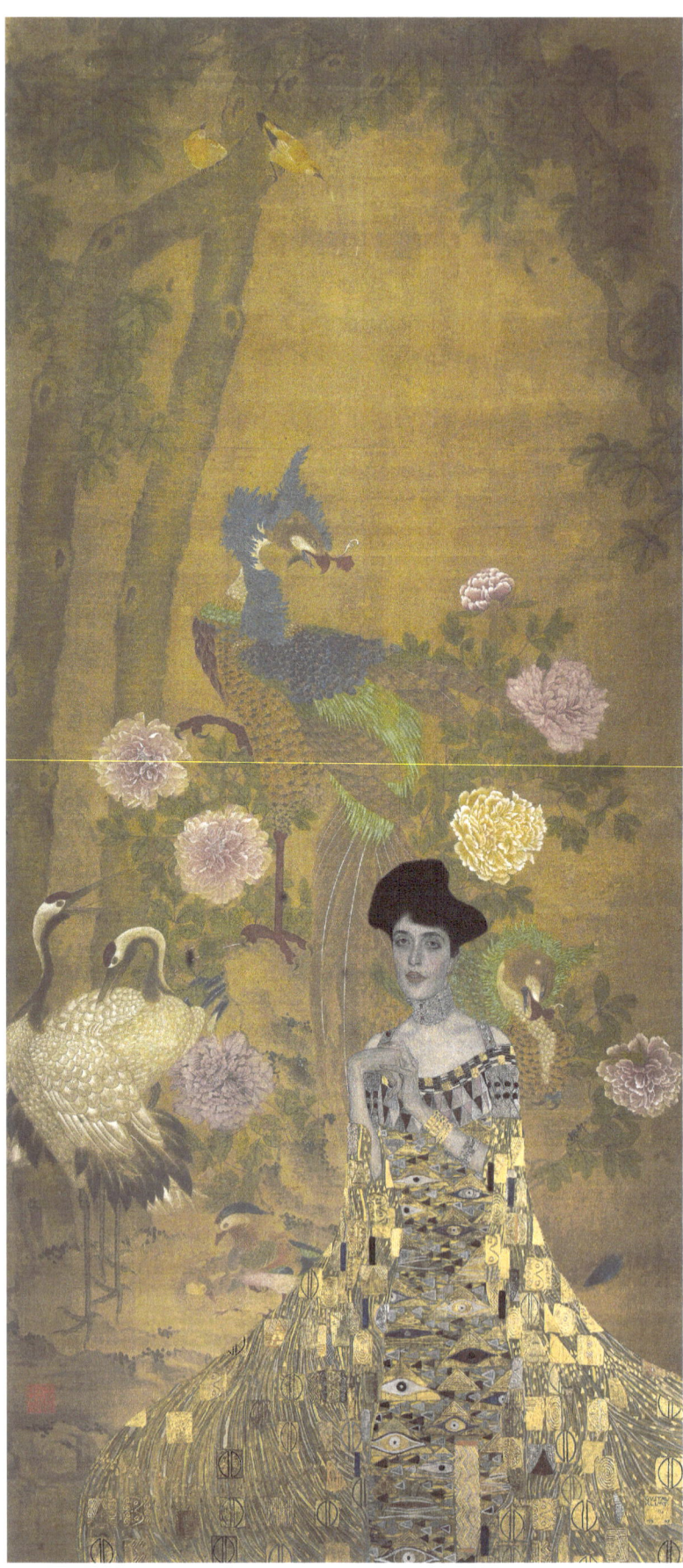

East #90

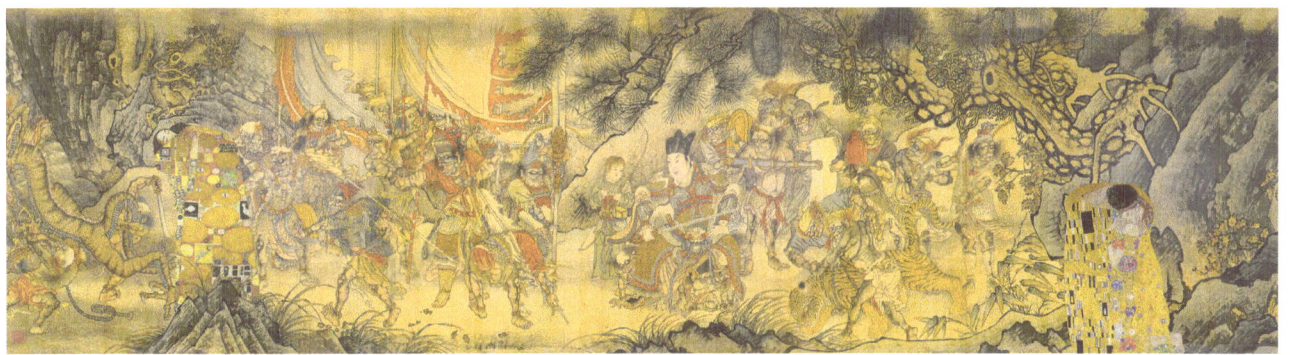

East #91

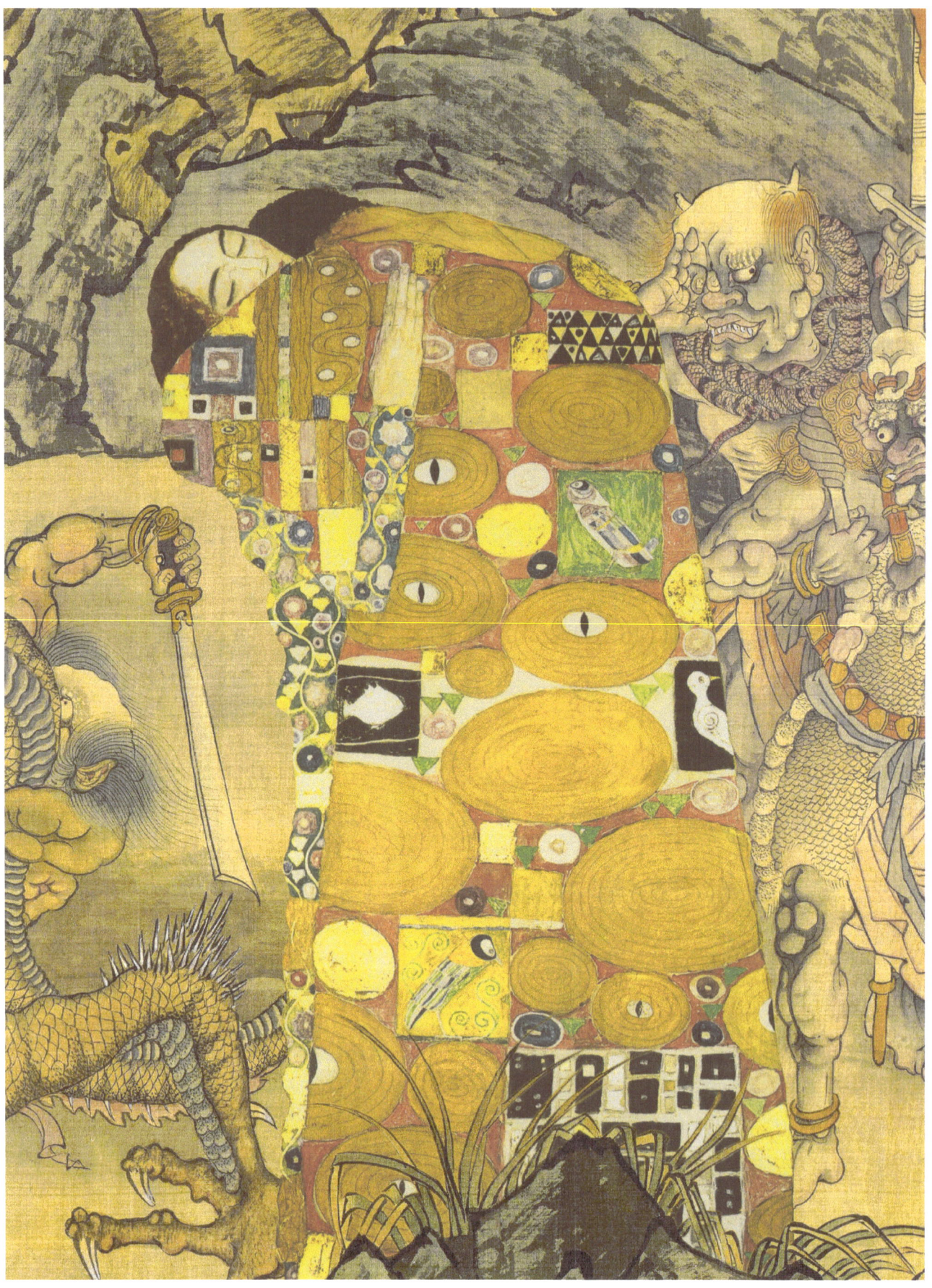

East #91 (detail 1)

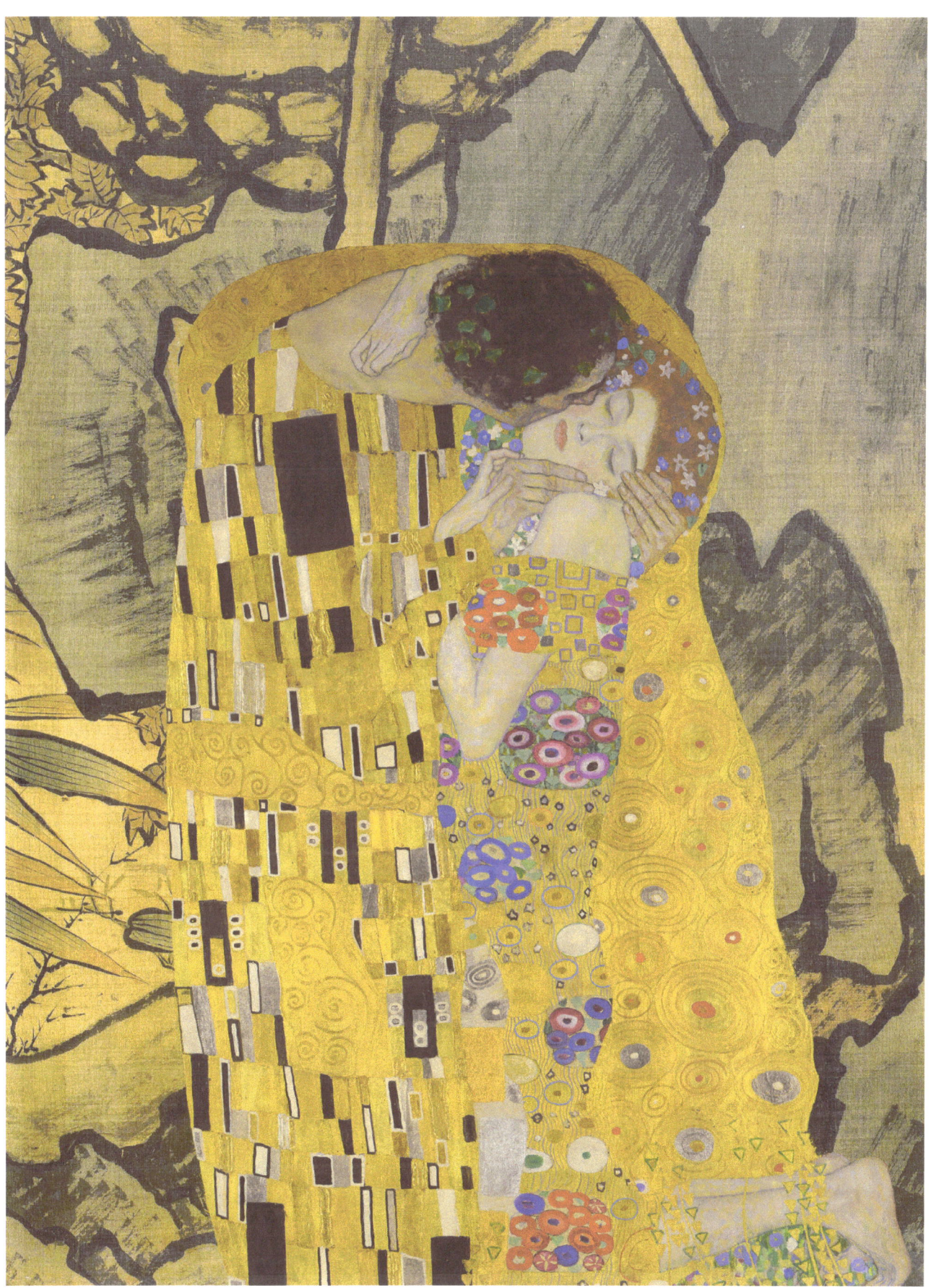

East #91 (detail 2)

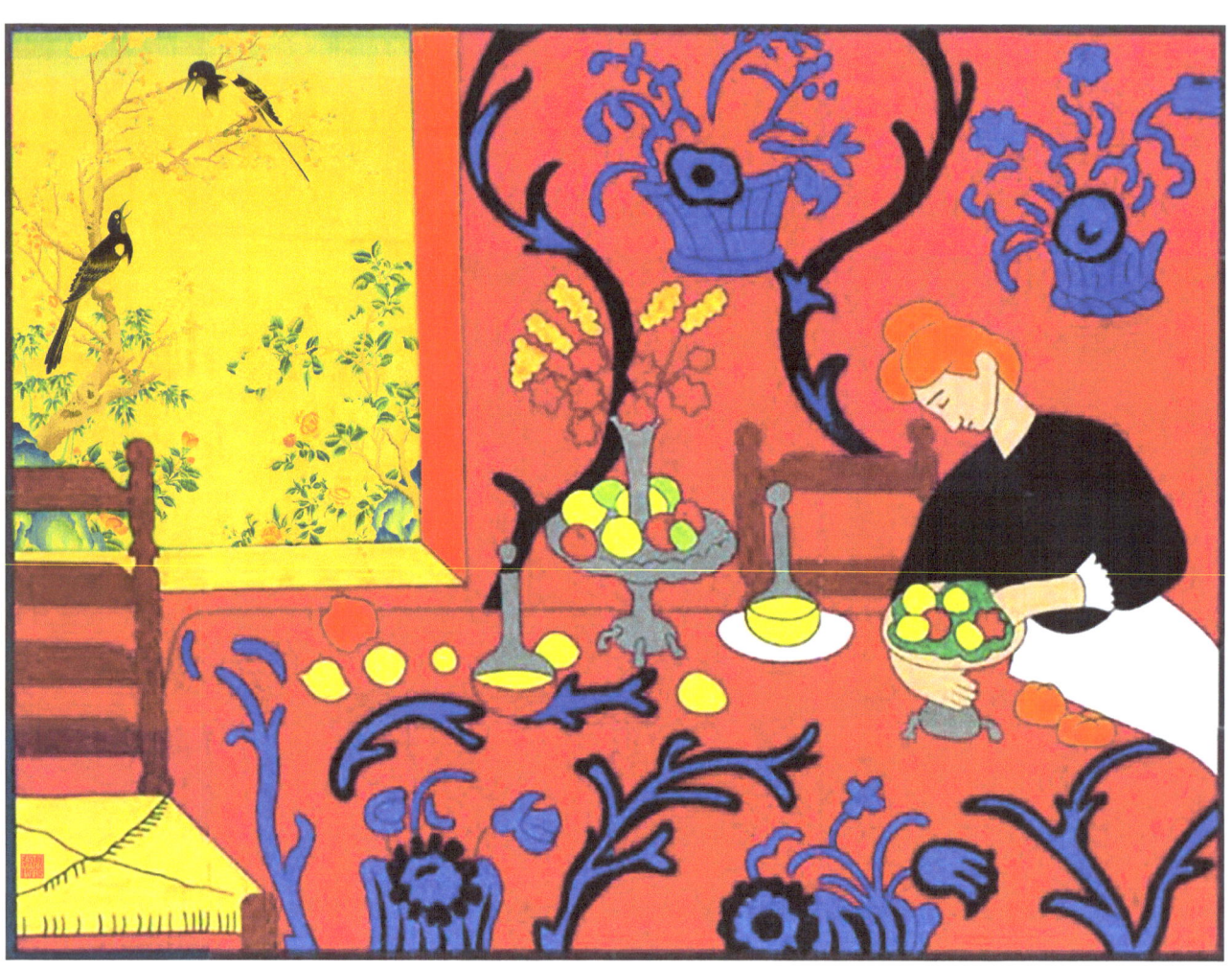

East #92

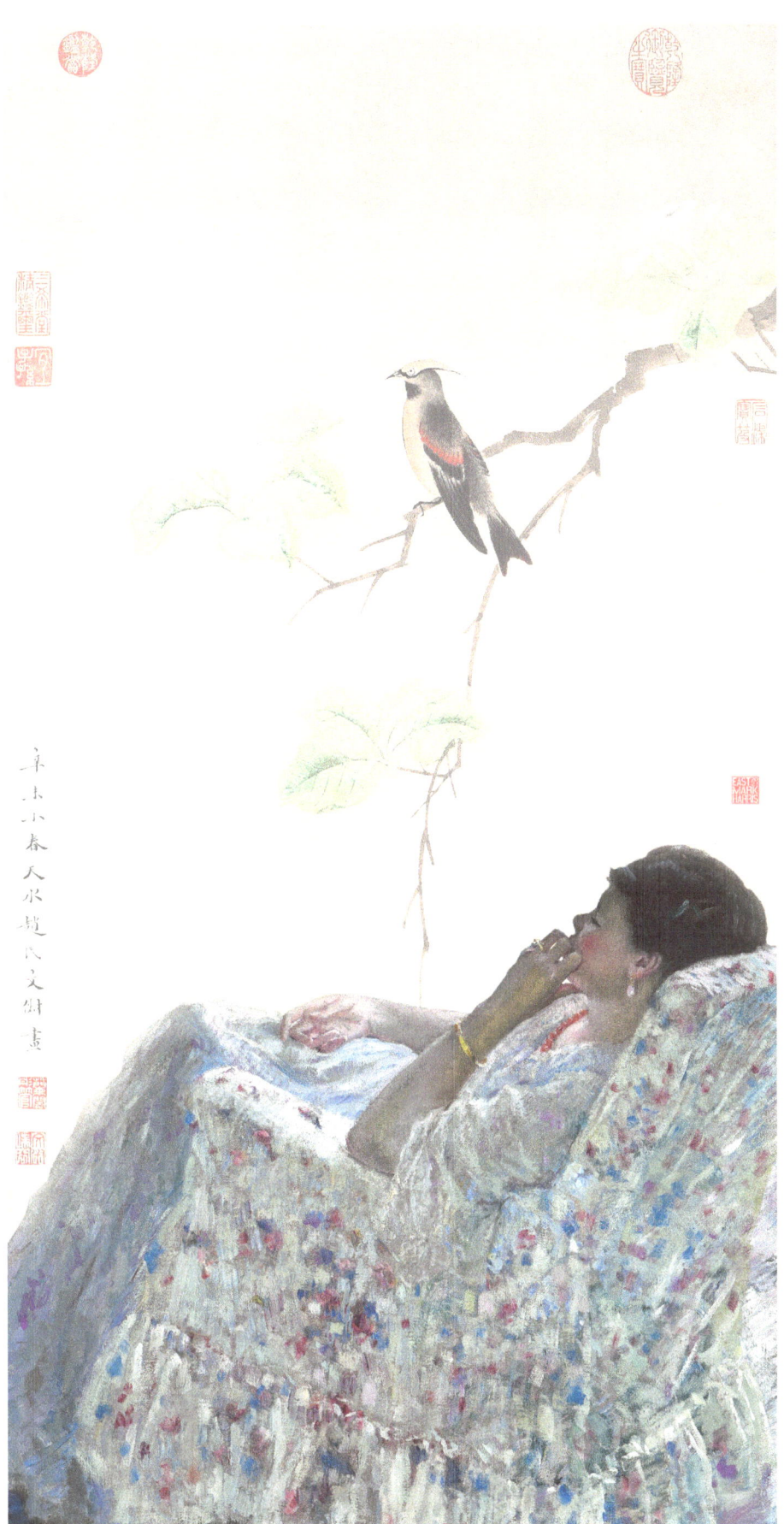

East #93

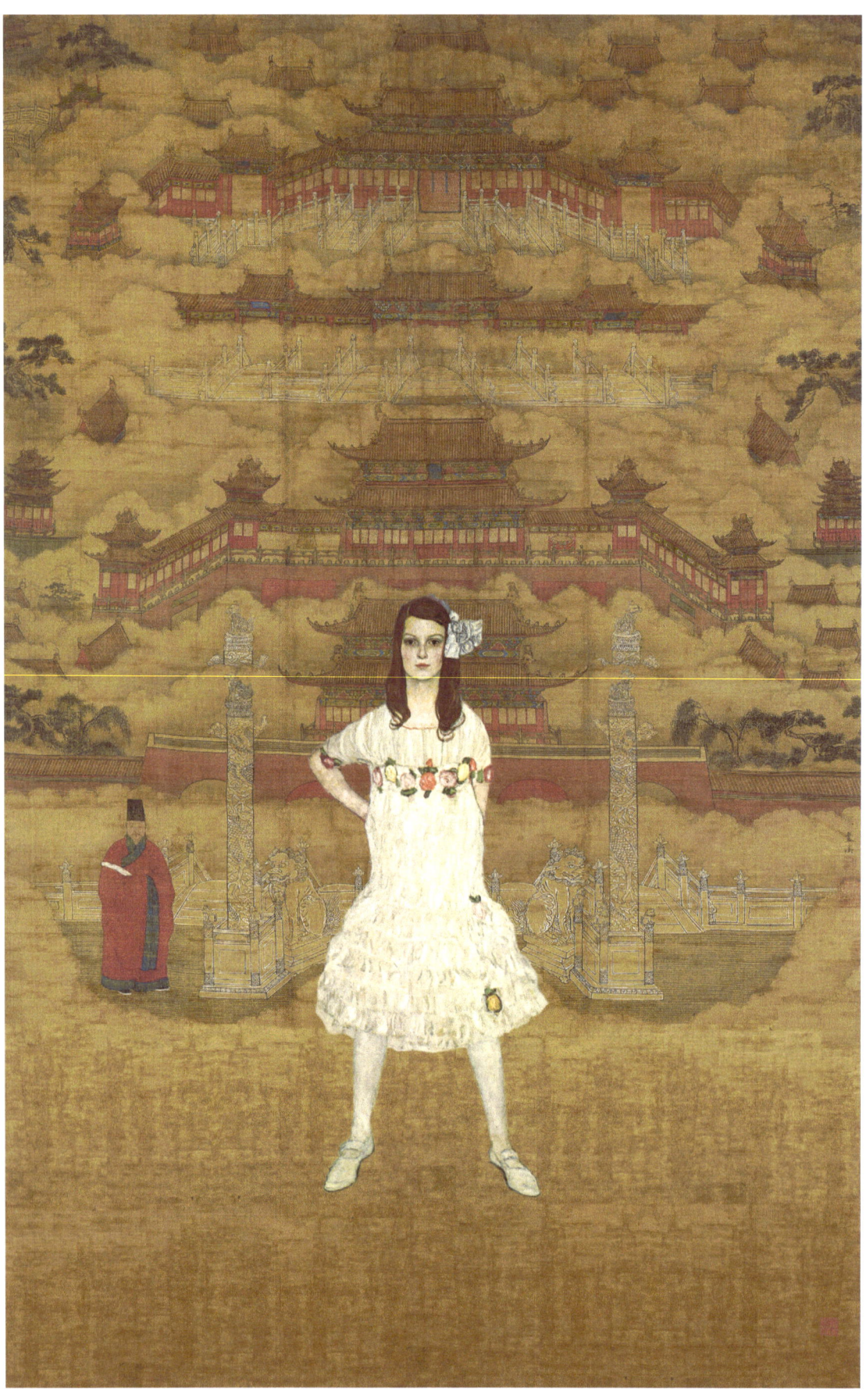

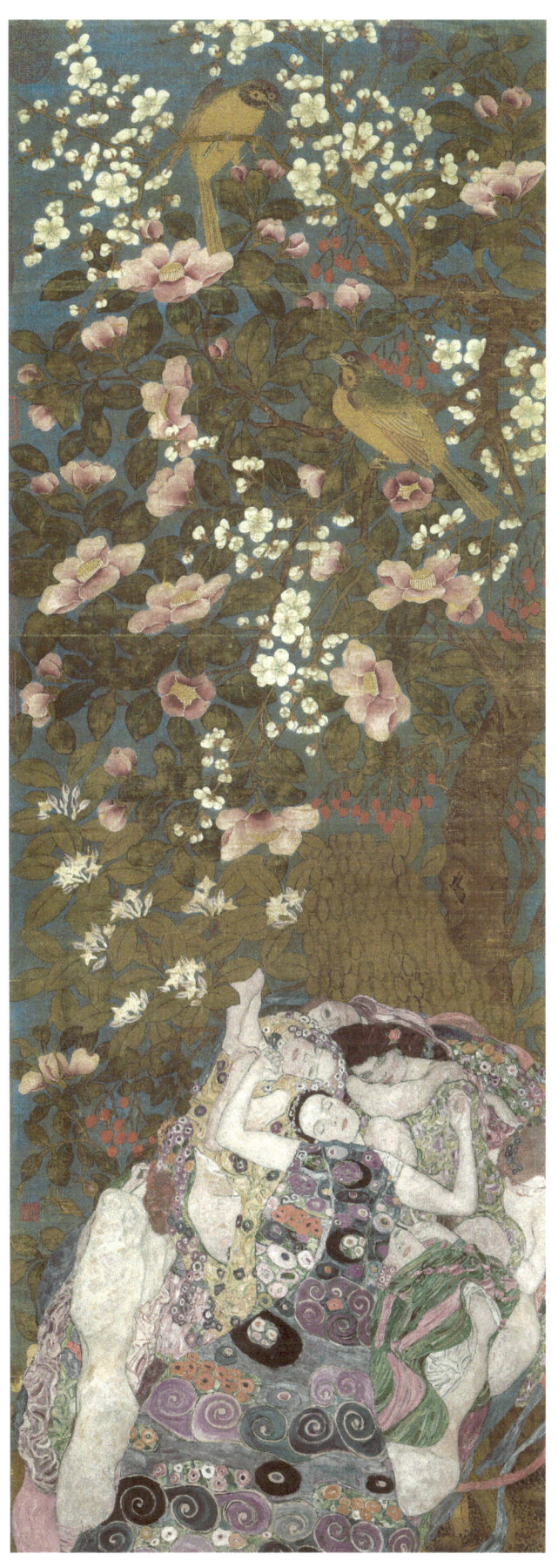

East #95

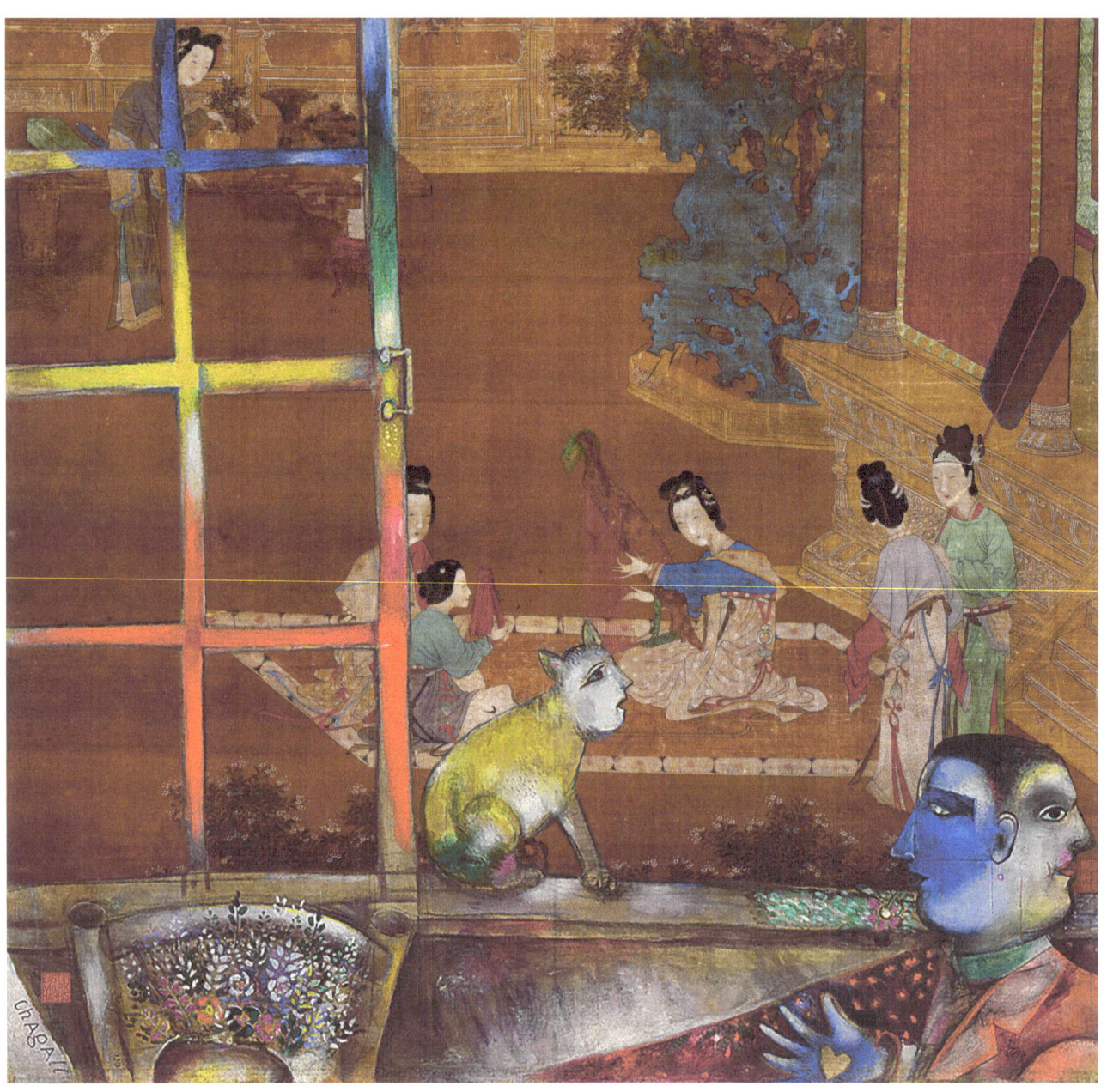

East #96

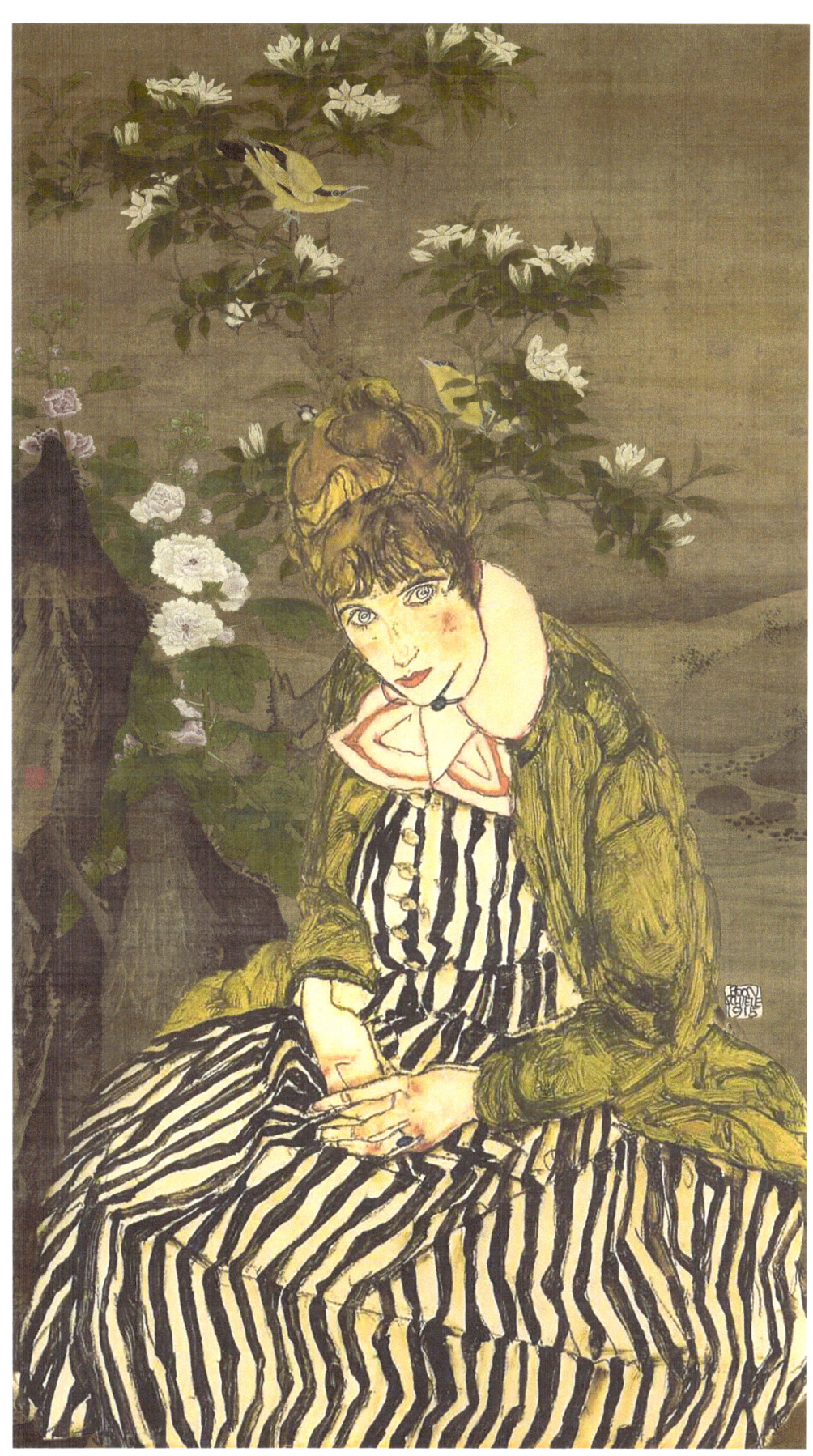
East #97

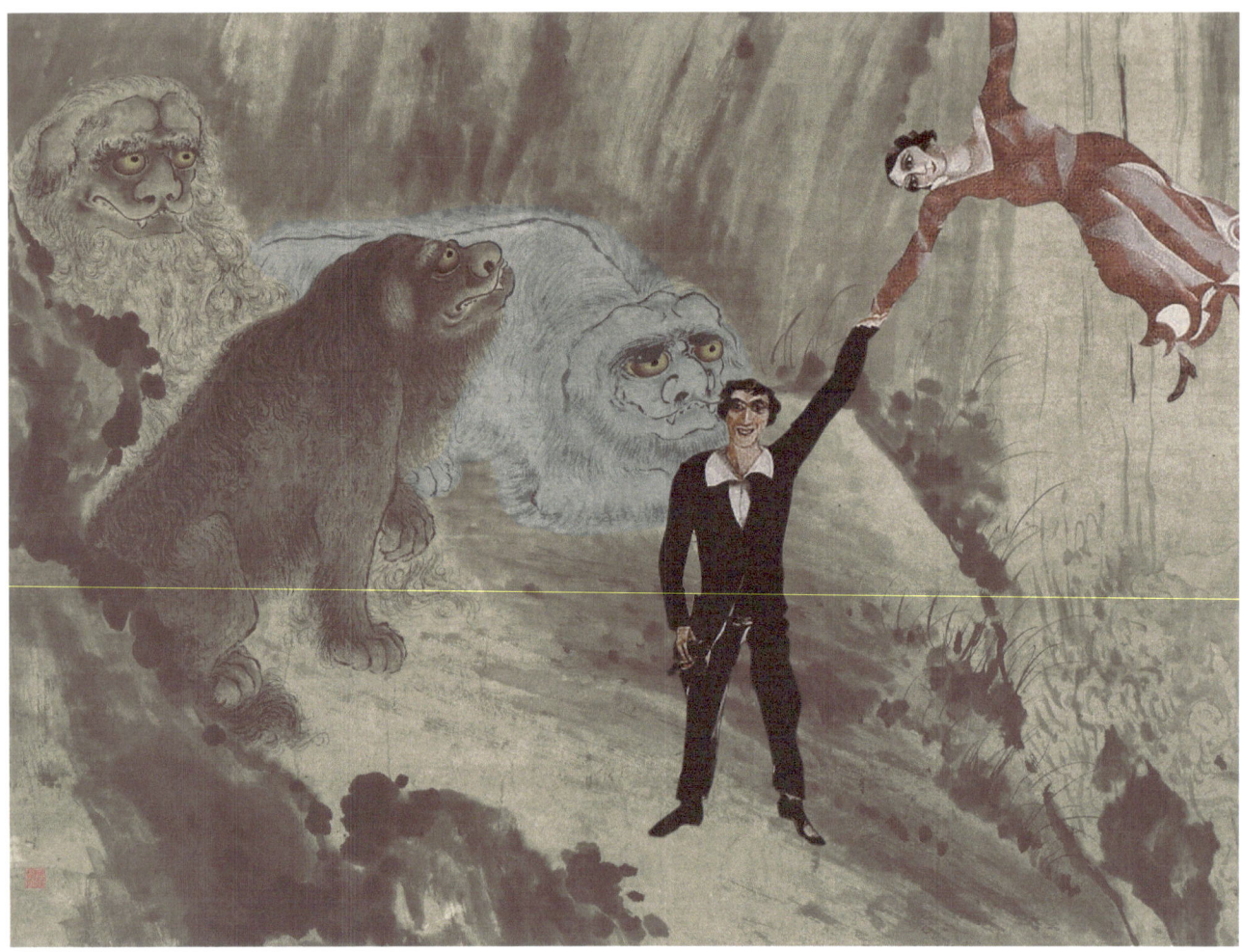

East #98

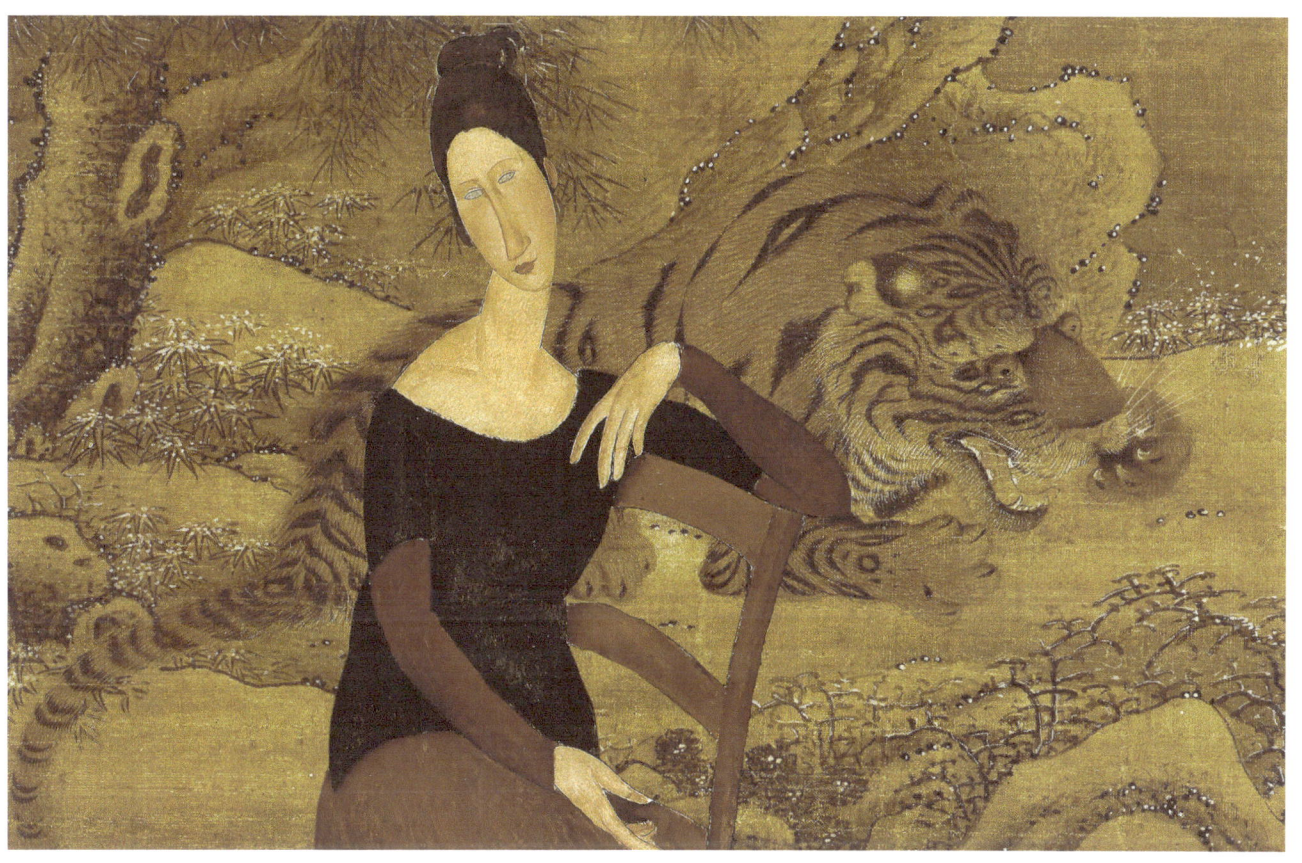

East #99

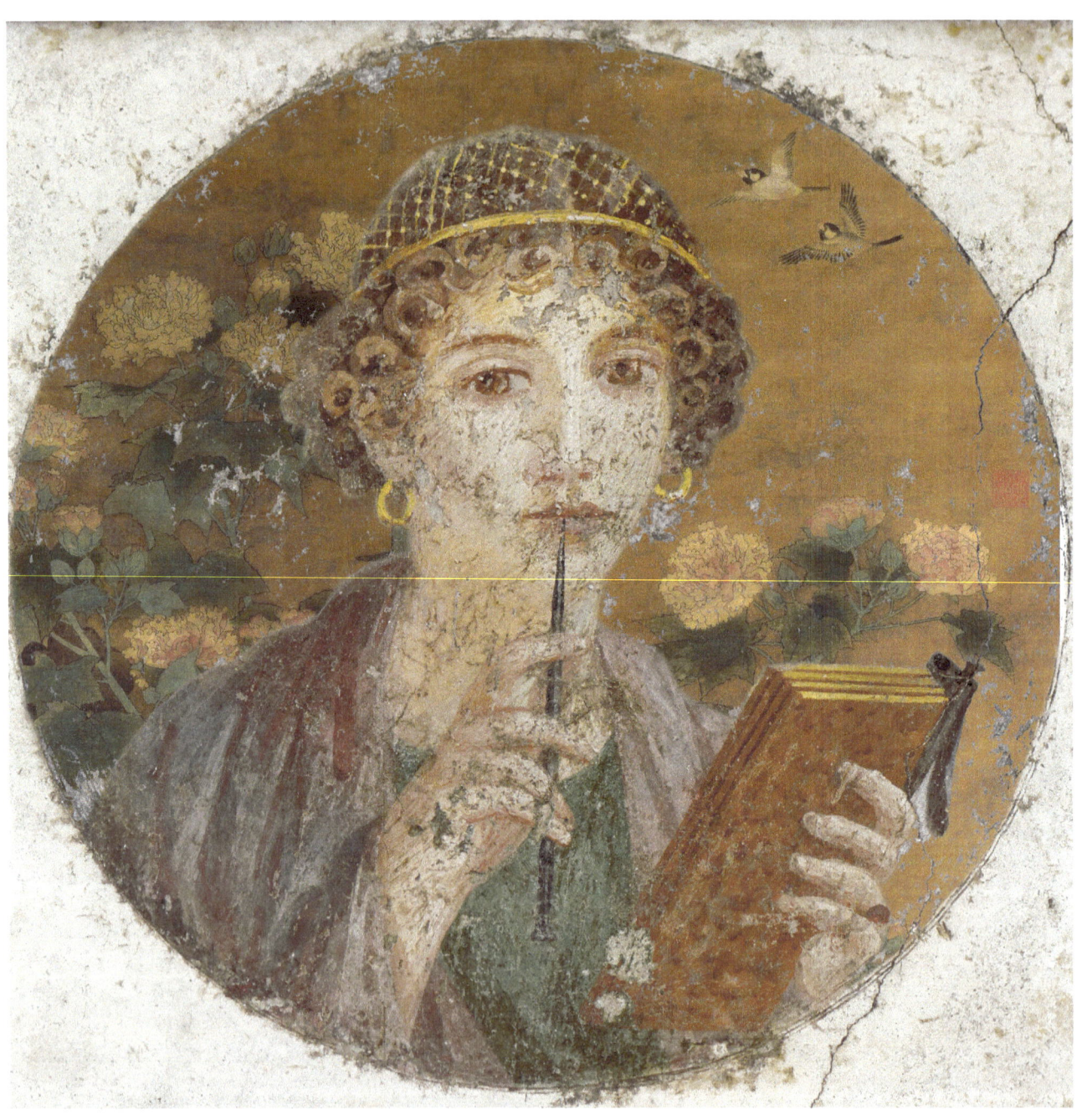

East 100

SOURCES

East #1   Jan van Eyck (1434), *The Arnolfini Portrait* [Oil on oak panel of 3 vertical boards]. National Gallery, London.
Lü Ji (15th century), *Autumn Egrets and Hibiscus* [Ink and color on silk]. National Palace Museum, Taipei.

East #2   Petrus Christus (c. 1470), *Portrait of a Young Girl* [Oil on oak wood]. Gemäldegalerie, Berlin.
Li Song (13th century), *Moon Night Bore Tide Viewing* [Ink and color on silk]. National Palace Museum, Taipei.

East #3   Paolo Uccello (c. 1470), *Saint George and the Dragon* [Oil on canvas]. National Gallery, London.
Zhou Wenju (10th century), *United by Music* [Ink and color on silk]. The Art Institute of Chicago, Chicago.

East #4   Sandro Botticelli (late 1470s or early 1480s), *Primavera* [Tempera on panel]. Uffizi Gallery, Florence.
Anonymous (c. 17th century-20th century), *To Live a Long Life Like a Tortoise or a Crane*.

East #5   Leonardo da Vinci (c.1474-1478), *Ginevra de' Benci* [Oil on panel]. National Gallery of Art, Washington, D.C..
Anonymous (1271-1368), *Court Ladies in the Imperial Palace* [Ink and color on silk]. Cleveland Museum of Art, Cleveland.

East #6   Sandro Botticelli (c. 1480-1485), *Portrait of a Young Woman* [Tempera on wood]. Städel Museum, Frankfurt.
Sun Wen (c. 1867-1903), *Dream of the Red Chamber: Celebrating Grandmother Jia's 80th Birthday at Jia's House* [Ink and color on silk]. Lüshun Museum, Dalian.

East #7   Sandro Botticelli (c. 1484-1486), *The Birth of Venus* [Tempera on canvas]. Uffizi Gallery, Florence.
Anonymous (c. 12th century-13th century), *Lotus and Birds* [Kesi]. National Palace Museum, Taipei.

East #8   Michelangelo (c. 1487-1488), *The Torment of Saint Anthony* [Oil and tempera on panel]. Kimbell Art Museum, Fort Worth.
Anonymous (c. 13th century-14th century), *The Deity Called Erlang Plunders the Mountain Area* [Ink and color on silk]. Museum of Fine Arts, Boston.

East #9   Leonardo da Vinci (c. 1489-1491), *Lady With an Ermine* [Oil on walnut panel]. Czartoryski Museum, Kraków.
Cui Bai (11th century), *The Autumn Lotus Leaves, Hibiscus, and Birds* [Ink and color on silk]. National Palace Museum, Taipei.

East #10 Leonardo da Vinci (c. 1490), *Vitruvian Man* [Pen and ink with wash over metalpoint on paper]. Gallerie dell'Accademia, Venice.
Anonymous (c. 12th century-13th century), *Kings of Heaven*.

East #11 Leonardo da Vinci (1490s), *The Last Supper* [Fresco]. Santa Maria delle Grazie, Milan.
Qiu Zhu (1567), *Leisure Time* [Ink and color on silk].

East #12 Leonardo da Vinci (c.1490-1499), *An Angel in Green With a Vielle* [Oil on poplar wood]. National Gallery, London.
Lü Ji (c. 15th century-16th century), *Morning Mist on the River Bank* [Ink and color on silk]. British Museum, London.

East #13 Leonardo da Vinci (c.1499-1500 or c.1506-1508), *The Virgin and Child With Saint Anne and Saint John the Baptist* [Charcoal, black and white chalk on tinted paper mounted on canvas]. National Gallery, London.
Li Cheng (10th century), *Travelers in a Wintry Forest* [Ink and color on silk]. Metropolitan Museum of Art, New York City.

East #14 Leonardo da Vinci (c. 1503-1506, perhaps continuing until c.1517), *Mona Lisa* [Oil on poplar panel]. Louvre, Paris.
Anonymous (c. 14th century-17th century), *Flower and Two Yellow Birds.*

East #15 Raphael (c. 1504-1506), *Self-Portrait* [Tempera on panel]. Uffizi Gallery, Florence.
Chen Mei (1738), *Tour Under the Moon: Harvesting Lotus Roots in June* [Ink and color on silk]. Palace Museum, Beijing.

East #16 Raphael (1508), *Saint Catherine of Alexandria* [Oil on panel]. National Gallery, London.
Liu Songnian (c. 12th century-13th century), *Go to Yaochi, Where Queen Mother West Lives, To Wish Her Birthday* [Ink and color on silk]. National Palace Museum, Taipei.

East #17 Michelangelo (c. 1509), *The Delphic Sibyl* [Fresco]. Sistine Chapel, Vatican City.
Lu Zhi (1566), *Everlasting Peace and Luck* [Ink and color on silk]. National Palace Museum, Taipei.

East #18 Michelangelo (1509-1510), *The Fall and Expulsion From Garden of Eden* [Fresco]. Sistine Chapel, Vatican City.
Yin Hong (c. 15th century-16th century), *Birds Gather Under the Spring Willow* [Ink and color on silk]. Cleveland Museum of Art, Cleveland.

East #19 Raphael (1509-1511), *The School of Athens* [Fresco]. Vatican Museums, Vatican City.
Anonymous (c. 1100-1125), *Literary Gathering* [Ink and color on silk]. National Palace Museum, Taipei.

East #20 Michelangelo (1511), *The Creation of the Sun, Moon, and Plants* [Fresco]. Sistine Chapel, Vatican City.
Chen Rong (13th century), *Five Dragons* [Ink and color on paper]. Tokyo National Museum, Tokyo.

East #21 Michelangelo (c. 1511), *The Libyan Sibyl* [Fresco]. Sistine Chapel, Vatican City.
Chen Xing (1670), *Prosperity and Honor Belong to You* [Ink and color on silk]. Shan xi Fine Art Academy, Taiyuan.

East #22 Michelangelo (c.1512), *The Creation of Adam* [Fresco]. Sistine Chapel, Vatican City.
Yi Yuanji (11th century), *Autumn Landscape With Gibbons and Deer* [Ink and color on silk]. Freer Gallery of Art, Washington, D. C..

East #23 Raphael (c. 1513-1514), *Sistine Madonna* [Oil on canvas]. Gemäldegalerie Alte Meister, Dresden.
Li Rongjin (14th century), *Han Palace* [Ink and color on silk]. National Palace Museum, Taipei.

East #24 Titian (1548), *Portrait of Isabella of Portugal* [Oil on canvas]. Museo del Prado, Madrid.
Jiao Bingzhen (1644-1911), *Pictures of Tilling and Weaving* [Ink and color on paper]. Library of Congress, Washington, D. C..

East #25 Paolo Veronese (1563), *The Wedding Feast at Cana* [Oil on canvas]. Louvre Museum, Paris.
Qiu Ying (16th century), *The Hall of Precious Paintings* [Ink and color on silk]. Freer Gallery of Art, Washington, D. C..

East #26 El Greco (1600), *Portrait of Fernando Niño de Guevara* [Oil on canvas]. Metropolitan Museum of Art, New York City.
Li Anzhong (1126), *Birds of Prey* [Ink and color on paper]. Seattle Art Museum, Seattle.

East #27 Diego Velázquez (c. 1650), *Portrait of Innocent X* [Oil on canvas]. Galleria Doria Pamphilj, Rome.
Anonymous (c. 10th century-13th century), *Bamboo and Birds* [Ink and color on silk]. National Palace Museum, Taipei.

East #28 Johannes Vermeer (1662-1663), *A Woman Holding a Balance* [Oil on canvas]. National Gallery of Art, Washington, D.C..
Anonymous (c. 13th century-14th century), *Flower and Birds.* National Palace Museum, Taipei.

East #29 Johannes Vermeer (c. 1665), *Girl With a Pearl Earring* [Oil on canvas]. Mauritshuis, The Hague.
Xu Ze (c. 13th century-14th century), *Falcon on a Perch* [Ink and color on silk]. Museum of Fine Arts, Boston.

East #30 Johannes Vermeer (1666-1668), *The Art of Painting* [Oil on canvas]. Kunsthistorisches Museum, Vienna.
Qiu Ying (16th century), *Painting Album Imitates Artists in Song Dynasty: Portrait of Wang*

Xizhi [Ink and color on silk]. Shanghai Museum, Shanghai.

East #31 Jacques-Louis David (1793), *The Death of Marat* [Oil on canvas]. Royal Museums of Fine Arts of Belgium, Brussels.
Wang Qian (16th century), *Unsullied but Tenacious* [Ink and color on silk]. Tianjin Museum, Tianjin.

East #32 Jacques-Louis David (1801), *Napoleon Crossing the Alps* [Oil on canvas]. Château de Malmaison, Rueil-Malmaison.
Yuan Jiang (c. 17th century-18th century), *Epang Palace* [Ink and color on silk]. Palace Museum, Beijing.

East #33 Caspar David Friedrich (c.1818), *Wanderer Above the Sea of Fog* [Oil on canvas]. Hamburger Kunsthalle, Hamburg.
Ma Lin (c. 12th century-13th century), *Three Officials Out for an Inspection* [Ink and color on silk]. National Palace Museum, Taipei.

East #34 Gustave Courbet (1842-1844), *Self-Portrait With a Black Dog* [Oil on canvas]. Musée d'Orsay, Paris.
Lü Ji (15th century), *Flower and Birds of the Four Seasons: Autumn* [Ink and color on silk]. Tokyo National Museum, Tokyo.

East #35 John Everett Millais (1851-1852), *Ophelia* [Oil on canvas]. Tate Britain, London.
Zhou Wenju (10th century), *Ladies Fishing in the Lotus Pavilion* [Ink and color on silk]. National Palace Museum, Taipei.

East #36 John Everett Millais (1856), *The Blind Girl* [Oil on canvas]. Birmingham Museum & Art Gallery, Birmingham.
Anonymous (c. 14th century-17th century), *Joyful Tigers and Leopard* [Ink on paper].

East #37 Edgar Degas (1857-1858), *Self Portrait in a Soft Hat* [Oil on canvas]. Clark Art Institute, Williamstown.
Qiu Ying (16th century), *Painting Album Imitates Artists in Song Dynasty: Pavilion of Prince Teng* [Ink and color on silk]. Shanghai Museum, Shanghai.

East #38 Jean-François Millet (1857-1859), *The Angelus* [Oil on canvas]. Musée d'Orsay, Paris.
Zhou Yuan (1367), *A Stag, a Doe, and Red Camellias in Snow* [Ink and color on silk]. Freer Gallery of Art, Washington, D. C..

East #39 Edgar Degas (1858-1867), *The Bellelli Family* [Oil on canvas]. Musée d'Orsay, Paris.
Anonymous (c. 12th century-13th century), *Geisha of the Court* [Ink and color on silk]. Shanghai Museum, Shanghai.

East #40 Edgar Degas (1860-1862), *Young Woman With Ibis* [Oil on canvas]. Metropolitan Museum of Art, New York City.
Anonymous (c. 10th century-13th century), *Picture of the New Year* [Ink and color on silk]. National Palace Museum, Taipei.

East #41 Edgar Degas (1861), *Semiramis Building Babylon* [Oil on canvas], Musée d'Orsay, Paris.
Anonymous (c. 10th century-13th century), *Painting of Rhapsody on the Luo River Goddess* (Song dynasty copy) [Ink and color on silk]. Palace Museum, Beijing.

East #42 Édouard Manet (1866), *The Fifer* [Oil on canvas]. Musée d'Orsay, Paris.
Mu Xi (13th century), *Tiger* [Ink on silk]. Indianapolis Museum of Art, Indianapolis.

East #43 Ilya Repin (1870-1873), *Barge Haulers on the Volga* [Oil on canvas]. State Russian Museum, St. Petersburg.
Chen Rong (13th century), *Two Dragons Brawling the Sea* [Ink on silk]. Saint Louis Art Museum, St. Louis.

East #44 James McNeill Whistler (1871), *Arrangement in Grey and Black No. 1* [Oil on canvas]. Musée d'Orsay, Paris.
Zhao Mengfu (1471), *Tethered Horses Under a Tree* [Ink and color on silk]. British Museum, London.

East #45 Claude Monet (1872), *Impression, Sunrise* [Oil on canvas]. Musée Marmottan Monet, Paris.
Qiu Ying (1528), *Fishing by the Maple Creek* [Ink and color on paper]. Hunan Museum, Changsha.

East #46 Pierre-Auguste Renoir (1876), *Bal du moulin de la Galette* [Oil on canvas]. Musée d'Orsay, Paris.
Xiao Rong (11th century), *Flower and Birds* [Ink and color on silk]. National Palace Museum, Taipei.

East #47   Gustave Caillebotte (1877), *Paris Street in Rainy Weather* [Oil on canvas]. Art Institute of Chicago, Chicago.
Zhu Duan (c. 15th century-16th century), *Searching For Plum Blossoms* [Ink and color on silk]. National Palace Museum, Taipei.

East #48   Mary Cassatt (1878), *Little Girl in a Blue Armchair* [Oil on canvas]. National Gallery of Art, Washington D.C..
Lü Ji (15th century), *Apricot Blossoms and Peacocks* [Ink and color on silk]. National Palace Museum, Taipei.

East #49   Mary Cassatt (1880), *The Tea* [Oil on canvas]. Museum of Fine Arts, Boston.
Chen Mei (1738), *Tour Under the Moon: Sitting in the Pavilion and Admiring the Fish in the Pond* [Ink and color on silk]. Palace Museum, Beijing.

East #50   Pierre-Auguste Renoir (1881), *Two Sisters* [Oil on canvas]. Art Institute of Chicago, Chicago.
Anonymous (c. 13th century-14th century), *Flowers, Rooster, Hen, and Chicks* [Ink and color on paper]. National Palace Museum, Taipei.

East #51   Édouard Manet (1882), *A Bar at the Folies-Bergère* [Oil on canvas]. Courtauld Gallery, London.
Chen Lin (1254), *Golden Pheasants* [Ink and color on silk].

East #52   Georges Seurat (1884-1886), *A Sunday Afternoon on the Island of La Grande Jatte* [Oil on canvas]. Art Institute of Chicago, Chicago.
Zhou Fang (8th century), *Court Ladies Wearing Flowered Headdresses* [Ink and color on silk]. Liaoning Museum, Shenyang.

East #53   Edgar Degas (1885), *The Racecourse* [Pastel on paper]. Private Collection.
Wang Ximeng (1113), *A Panorama of Rivers and Mountains* [Ink and color on silk]. Palace Museum, Beijing.

East #54   Vincent van Gogh (1885), *The Potato Peeler* [Oil on canvas]. Metropolitan Museum of Art, New York City.
Bian Jingzhao (15th century), *Bamboo and Cranes* [Ink and color on silk]. Palace Museum, Beijing.

East #55   Vincent van Gogh (1887), *The Italian Woman* [Oil on canvas]. Musée d'Orsay, Paris.
Huang Jucai (10th century), *Pictures of Flower and plants* [Ink and color on silk].

East #56   Vincent van Gogh (1888), *Fishing Boats on the Beach at Saintes-Maries* [Oil on canvas]. Van Gogh Museum, Amsterdam.
Zhang Gui (c. 1156-1161), *Divine Turtle* [Ink and color on silk]. Palace Museum, Beijing.

East #57   Paul Gauguin (1888), *Self-Portrait With Portrait of Emile Bernard* [Oil on canvas]. Van Gogh Museum, Amsterdam.
Anonymous (c. 10th century-13th century), *The Sunshine of Spring Symbolizes Eternal Youth* [Kesi]. National Palace Museum, Taipei.

East #58   Vincent van Gogh (1888), *Vase With Twelve Sunflowers* [Oil on canvas]. Philadelphia Museum of Art, Philadelphia.
Sheng Shiyan (c. 10th century-13th century), *Young Woman Reading a Book of Poems* [Ink and color on silk]. Freer Gallery of Art, Washington, D. C..

East #59   Vincent van Gogh (1888), *Sunflowers* [Oil on canvas]. National Gallery, London.
Anonymous (c. 14th century-17th century), *Picture of Dressing Up* [Ink and color on silk].

East #60   Vincent van Gogh (1888), *The Night Café* [Oil on canvas]. Yale University Art Gallery, New Haven.
Tang Yin (1470-1524), *Court Ladies of the Former Shu* [Ink and color on silk]. Palace Museum, Beijing.

East #61   Vincent van Gogh (1888), *Café Terrace at Night* [Oil on canvas]. Kröller-Müller Museum, Otterlo.
Liu Songnian (c. 12th century-13th century), *Poets' Gathering in the Western Garden* [Ink and color on silk]. National Palace Museum, Taipei.

East #62   Paul Gauguin (1888), *Vision After the Sermon* [Oil on canvas]. Scottish National Gallery, Edinburgh.
Chen Mei (1738), *Tour Under the Moon: Admiring the Moon on the Terrace* [Ink and color on silk]. Palace Museum, Beijing.

East #63   Vincent van Gogh (1888), *Memory of the Garden at Etten* [Oil on canvas]. The State Hermitage Museum, St. Petersburg.
Chen Mei (1738), *Tour Under the Moon: Admiring the Chrysanthemums in Late Autumn* [Ink and color on silk]. Palace Museum, Beijing.

East #64   Vincent van Gogh (1888), *Portrait of Madame Ginoux* [Oil on canvas]. Musée d'Orsay, Paris.
Lü Ji (15th century), *Lion-Head Goose* [Ink and color on silk]. Liaoning Museum, Shenyang.

East #65   Vincent van Gogh (1888), *Bedroom in Arles* [Oil on canvas]. Van Gogh Museum, Amsterdam.
Leng Mei (c. 1723-1735), *Girl Tired From Reading* [Ink and color on silk]. Tianjin Museum, Tianjin.

East #66   Vincent van Gogh (1888), *Van Gogh's Chair* [Oil on canvas]. National Gallery, London.
Qian Yuan (1294), *Flower and Birds* [Ink and color on paper]. Tianjin Museum, Tianjin.

East #67   Vincent van Gogh (1888), *Gauguin's Chair* [Oil on canvas]. Van Gogh Museum, Amsterdam.
Wang Yuan (1344), *Bamboo and Golden Pheasants* [Ink and color on silk]. Palace Museum, Beijing.

East #68   Vincent van Gogh (1889), *Self-Portrait With Bandaged Ear* [Oil on canvas]. Courtauld Gallery, London.
Qiu Ying (16th century), *The Shanglin Park: Imperial Hunt* [Ink and color on silk]. Freer Gallery of Art, Washington, D. C..

East #69   Vincent van Gogh (1889), *Woman Rocking a Cradle* [Oil on canvas]. Metropolitan Museum of Art, New York City.
Qiu Ying (16th century), *Ten Scenes of Wangchuan* [Ink and color on silk]. Liaoning Museum, Shenyang.

East #70   Vincent van Gogh (1889), *Portrait of Joseph Roulin* [Oil on canvas]. Kröller-Müller Museum, Otterlo.
Qiu Ying (16th century), *Ten Scenes of Wangchuan* [Ink and color on silk]. Liaoning Museum, Shenyang.

East #71   Vincent van Gogh (1889), *The Starry Night* [Oil on canvas]. Museum of Modern Art, New York City.
Anonymous (c. 14th century-17th century), *Wanghai Tower* [Ink and color on silk]. National Palace Museum, Taipei.

East #72   Vincent van Gogh (1889), *Self-Portrait* [Oil on canvas]. Musée d'Orsay, Paris.
Xia Yong (14th century), *Storeyed Pavilion* [Ink and color on silk]. Tokyo National Museum, Tokyo.

East #73   Paul Gauguin (1889), *The Yellow Christ* [Oil on canvas]. Albright-Knox Art Gallery, Buffalo.
Qiu Ying (16th century), *Ten Scenes of Wangchuan* [Ink and color on silk]. Liaoning Museum, Shenyang.

East #74   Vincent van Gogh (1890), *Almond Blossom* [Oil on canvas]. Van Gogh Museum, Amsterdam.
Tang Yin (c. 15th century-16th century), *A Standing Figure of a Woman* [Ink and color on paper]. Freer Gallery of Art, Washington, D. C..

East #75   Vincent van Gogh (1890), *Irises* [Oil on canvas]. Van Gogh Museum, Amsterdam.
Ignatius Sichelbart (1773), *White Hawk* [Ink and color on silk]. Palace Museum, Beijing.

East #76   Vincent van Gogh (1890), *Sorrowing Old Man* [Oil on canvas]. Kröller-Müller Museum, Otterlo.
Zhao Mengfu (c. 13th century-14th century), *Three Horses* [Ink and color on silk]. Princeton University Art Museum, Princeton.

East #77   Vincent van Gogh (1890), *Thatched Cottages at Cordeville* [Oil on canvas]. Musée d'Orsay, Paris.
Yuan Yao (18th century), *The Palace of Nine Perfections* [Ink and color on silk]. Palace Museum, Beijing.

East #78   Paul Gauguin (1891), *Portrait of the Artist With the Yellow Christ* [Oil on canvas]. Musée d'Orsay, Paris.
Liang Kai (c. 12th century-13th century), *Owl Perched on a Branch* [Ink on paper]. Private Collection.

East #79   Edvard Munch (1893), *The Scream of Nature* [Oil on canvas]. National Museum of Art, Architecture and Design, Oslo.

Zhang Xian (1072), *Ten Odes* [Ink and color on silk]. Palace Museum, Beijing.

East #80 Paul Cézanne (1893-1894), *Drapery, Pitcher, and Fruit Bowl* [Oil on canvas]. Whitney Museum of American Art, New York City.
Anonymous (c. 13th century-14th century), *Four Magpies as Harbingers of Spring* [Silk embroidery]. National Palace Museum, Taipei.

East #81 Paul Cézanne (1894-1895), *The Card Players* [Oil on canvas]. Musée d'Orsay, Paris.
Yi Yuanji (11th century), *Three Gibbons Raiding an Egret* [Ink and color on silk]. National Palace Museum, Taipei.

East #82 Paul Gauguin (1891), *Tahitian Women on the Beach* [Oil on canvas]. Musée d'Orsay, Paris.
Paul Gauguin (c. 1892-1894), *The Midday Nap* [Oil on canvas]. Metropolitan Museum of Art, New York City.
Paul Gauguin (1894), *Reclining Tahitian Women* [Oil on canvas]. Ny Carlsberg Glyptotek, Copenhagen.
Tang Yin (c. 15th century-16th century), *The Night Revels of Han Xizai* [Ink and color on silk]. Three Gorges Museum, ChongQing.

East #83 Paul Cézanne (1895), *Ginger Jar and Fruit* [Oil on canvas]. The Barnes Foundation, Philadelphia.
Mi Fu (c. 11th century-12th century), *Crane* [Ink and color on silk]. British Museum, London.

East #84 Paul Cézanne (1895), *Portrait of Gustave Geffroy* [Oil on canvas]. Musée d'Orsay, Paris.
Huang Jucai (10th century), *Birds and Flowers* [Ink and color on silk]. Freer Gallery of Art, Washington, D. C..

East #85 Frederic Leighton (1895), *Flaming June* [Oil on canvas]. Museo de Arte de Ponce, Ponce.
You Cui (18th century), *Apricot Blossom and Pheasants* [Ink and color on silk]. Anhui Museum, Hefei.

East #86 Henri Rousseau (1897), *The Sleeping Gypsy* [Oil on canvas]. Museum of Modern Art, New York City.
Zhao Yong (1352), *Horses* [Ink and color on silk]. National Palace Museum, Taipei.

East #87 Edgar Degas (c. 1899), *Four Dancers* [Oil on canvas]. Chester Dale Collection.
Anonymous (c. 14th century-17th century), *Lotus and Birds* [Ink and color on silk].

East #88 Henri Matisse (1905), *Open Window* [Oil on canvas]. Collection of Mr. and Mrs. John Hay Whitney.
Zhang Ruoai (1746), *Illustrating Gaozong's Poem on Autumn Flowers* [Ink and color on paper]. National Palace Museum, Taipei.

East #89 Henri Matisse (1905), *Woman With a Hat* [Oil on canvas]. San Francisco Museum of Modern Art, San Francisco.
Huang Jucai (10th century), *Pictures of Flower and Plants* [Ink and color on silk].

East #90 Gustav Klimt (1907), *Portrait of Adele Bloch-Bauer I* [Oil on canvas]. Neue Galerie, New York City.
Anonymous (c. 10th century-13th century), *Phoenix* [Ink and color on silk].

East #91 Gustav Klimt (c. 1905-1909), *Fulfillment* [Oil on cardboard]. Museum of Applied Arts, Vienna.
Gustav Klimt (1907-1908), *The Kiss* [Oil on canvas]. Österreichische Galerie Belvedere, Vienna.
Anonymous (c. 13th century-14th century), *The Deity Called Erlang Plunders the Mountain Area* [Ink and color on silk]. Museum of Fine Arts, Boston.

East #92 Henri Matisse (1908), *The Dessert: Harmony in Red* [Oil on canvas]. Hermitage Museum, St. Petersburg.
Anonymous (c. 10th century-13th century), *Magpie Announces the Birth of a New Life* [Kesi]. National Palace Museum, Taipei.

East #93 Frederick Carl Frieseke (1910), *Afternoon-Yellow Room* [Oil on canvas]. Indianapolis Museum of Art, Indianapolis.
Wen Shu (1631), *The Leaves of Jade Fabricate the Feathers* [Ink and color on silk]. Shanghai Museum, Shanghai.

East #94 Gustav Klimt (1912), *Mäda Primavesi* [Oil on canvas]. Metropolitan Museum of Art, New York City.
Zhu Bang (c. 1481-1487), *Portrait of an official in front of the Beijing Forbidden City* [Ink and color on silk]. British Museum, London.

East #95 Gustav Klimt (1913), *The Virgin* [Oil on canvas]. National Gallery Prague, Prague.
Li Di (c. 12th century–13th century), *Flower and Birds* [Ink and color on silk]. National Palace Museum, Taipei.

East #96 Marc Chagall (1913), *Paris Through the Window* [Oil on canvas]. Solomon R. Guggenheim Museum, New York City.
Qiu Zhu (16th century), *Painting of Women Playing Musical Instruments* [Ink and color on silk]. Palace Museum, Beijing.

East #97 Egon Schiele (1915), *Edith Schiele in Gestreiftem Kleid Sitzend* [Oil on canvas]. Leopold Museum, Wien.
Lü Ji (15th century), *Flower and Birds of the Four Seasons: Summer* [Ink and color on silk]. Tokyo National Museum, Tokyo.

East #98 Marc Chagall (1917–1918), *The Promenade* [Oil on canvas]. State Russian Museum, St. Petersburg.
Hua Yan (1739), *Three Lions* [Ink on paper]. Lüshun Museum, Dalian.

East #99 Amedeo Modigliani (1918), *Portrait of the Artist's Wife* [Oil on canvas]. Norton Simon Museum, Pasadena.
Anonymous (c. 14th century–17th century), *Tiger Under Snowy Pines* [Ink and color on silk]. Freer Gallery of Art, Washington, D. C..

East #100 Anonymous (c. 55–79), *Woman With Wax Tablets and Stylus* [Fresco on gesso]. National Archaeological Museum, Naples.
Bian Lu (mid-14th century), *Peacock and Hollyhocks* [Ink and color on silk]. Metropolitan Museum of Art, New York City.

Protrait of Mark Harris Lin Chaoyang (2015), *Portrait of Mark Harris* [photography].
Anonymous (c. 13th century–14th century), *Ten Tigers and Three Savage Cubs*.

Mark Harris

MARK HARRIS

Artist
Writer
Chinese Homophones Writer
Chinese Full-Rhymes Writer
Chinese Alliterations Writer

He is from China and now lives in Los Angeles.
His Chinese name is transliterated as Yemen Chen. However, his pen name is Mark Harris, which is taken from the name of the protagonist of the first beloved Chinese American TV series, *Man From Atlantis*.

PUBLICATIONS
Mark Harris: East 100 (2022) Los Angeles: Losget Press.
A Different Vision: Mark Harris's Arts of Illusion (2021) Los Angeles: Losget Press.
Michelangelo DiCaprio: The Best Actor (2021) Los Angeles: Losget Press.
Book of Chinese Homophones (2019) Los Angeles: Losget Press.
Book of Chinese Full-Rhymes (2019) Los Angeles: Losget Press.
Book of Chinese Alliterations (2019) Los Angeles: Losget Press.
The Words of Yemen Chen (2018) Los Angeles: Losget Press.
Ballads of China (2002) Haikou: Hainan Publishing House.
Paper Tiger (2002) Haikou: Hainan Publishing House.

ACHIEVEMENTS
Originator of "full-rhyme article".
Originator of "alliteration article".
Originator of "same-root homophone article".
Originator of "same-tone same-root homophone article".
Writer of the most homophone articles in the world.
Writer of the most full-rhyme articles in the world.
Writer of the most alliteration articles in the world.
Discoverer of the close contact between a three-eyed alien and a pregnant female hidden in Michelangelo's painting of the Sistine Chapel ceiling.
Discoverer of a natural friar relief in Moro Beach, Newport Beach, California, USA.

RECORDS
The first "full-rhyme article" in the world.
The first "alliteration article" in the world The first "same-root homophone article" in the world.
The first "same-tone same-root homophone article" in the world.
The first homophones collection in the world.
The first full-rhymes collection in the world.
The first alliterations collection in the world.
The most homophones in the world up to now.
The most full-rhymes in the world up to now.
The most alliterations in the world up to now.
The most tongue twisters in the world up to now.

BOOKSELLING

UNITED STATES
www.amazon.com/dp/1951364112

UNITED KINGDOM
www.amazon.co.uk/dp/1951364112

GERMANY
www.amazon.de/dp/1951364112

FRANCE
www.amazon.fr/dp/1951364112

SPAIN
www.amazon.es/dp/1951364112

ITALY
www.amazon.it/dp/1951364112

JAPAN
www.amazon.co.jp/dp/1951364112

CANADA
www.amazon.ca/dp/1951364112

AUSTRALIA
www.amazon.com.au/dp/1951364112

NETHERLANDS
www.amazon.nl/dp/1951364112

FOR MORE

VIDEO
youtube.com/channel/UCdysRNQWLO15TcuRdjlMSkQ

PRINTS
artmajeur.commark-harris-us

SHOP
redbubble.com/people/LosgetAcademy/shop

NFT
opensea.io/collection/east100

HOME PAGE
imarkharris.com/mark-harris-east-100

BEHANCE
behance.net/mark-harris

FACEBOOK

INSTAGRAM

PINTEREST

TWITTER

Artist: Mark Harris
Editor-in-Chief: Mark Harris
Editors: Kehui Li, Elaine V. Kuang
Cover design/Book design: Mark Harris

LOSGET Copyright © 2021-2022 by Mark Harris
All rights reserved.
Published in the United States by Losget Press, Los Angeles.
Originally published in paperback in the United States by Losget Press, in 2022.
Library of Congress Cataloging-in-Publication Data
Names: Harris, Mark, author.
Title: Mark Harris: East 100/ Mark Harris.
Description: First edition. | Los Angeles: Losget Press, 2022.
Identifiers: LCCN: 2022904733/ ISBN: 978-1-951364-11-3
Cover design/Book design by Mark Harris
www.imarkharris.com
E-mail: contact@losget.com
First printing. 2022.